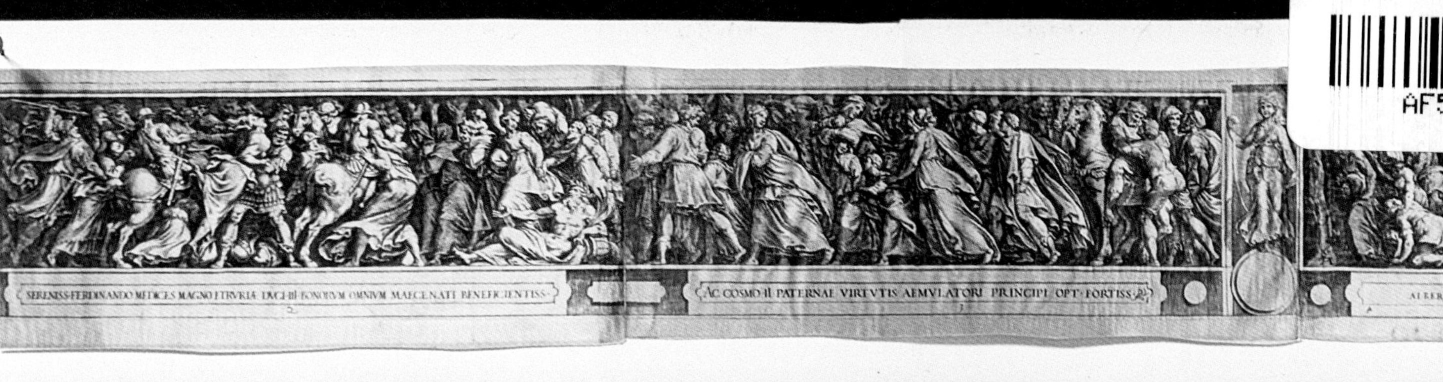
SERENISS·FERDINANDO MEDICES MAGNO ETRVRIÆ DVCI III BONORVM OMNIVM MAECENATI BENEFICIENTISS
AC COSMO II PATERNAE VIRTVTIS AEMVLATORI PRINCIPI OPT·FORTISS
ALBERTVS ALBERTI OBSERVANTIAE ERGO D

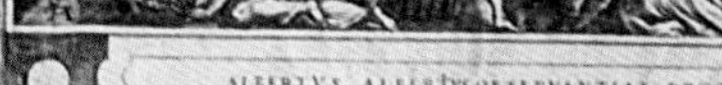
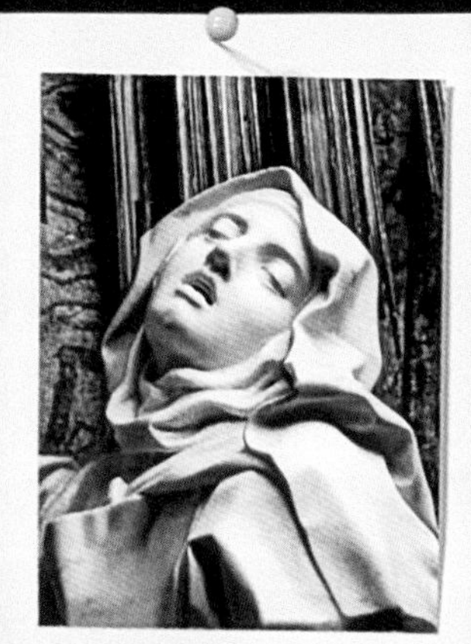
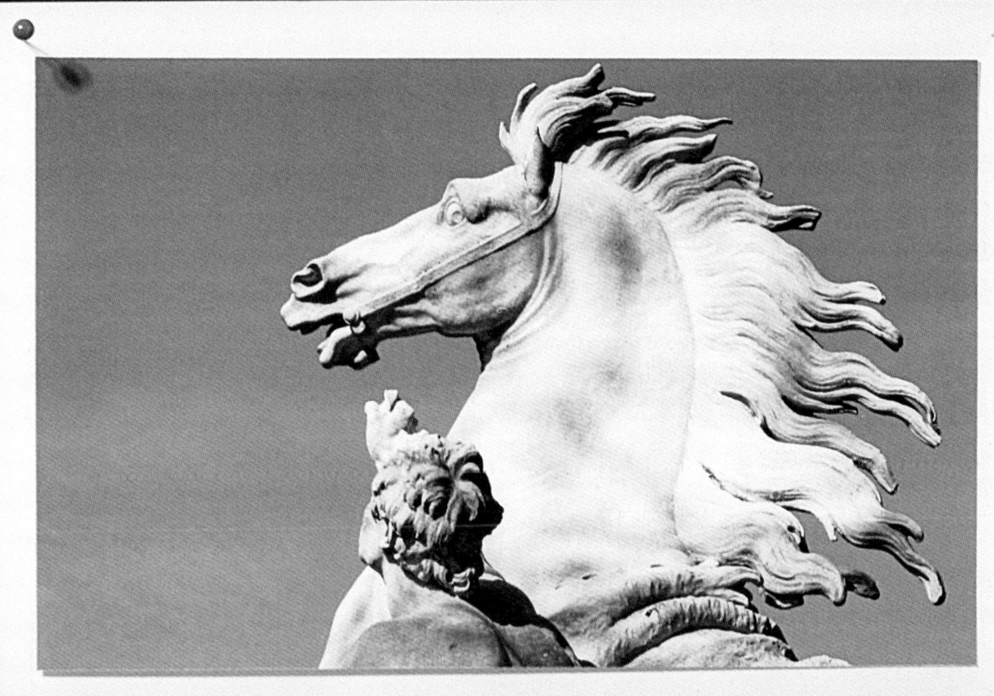
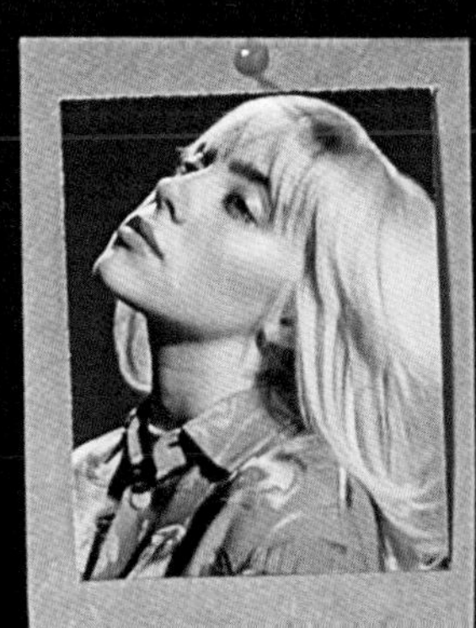
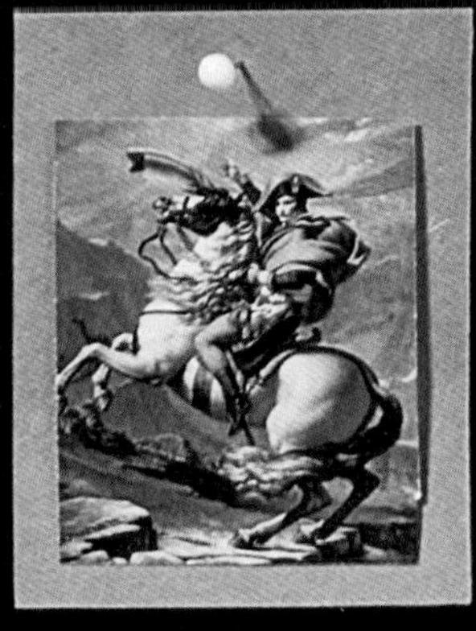
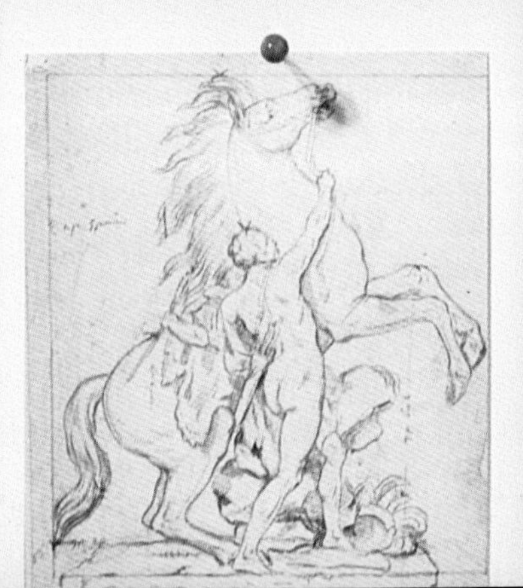
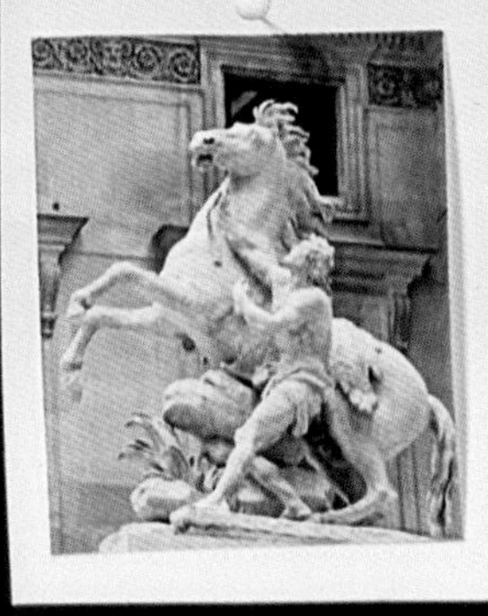
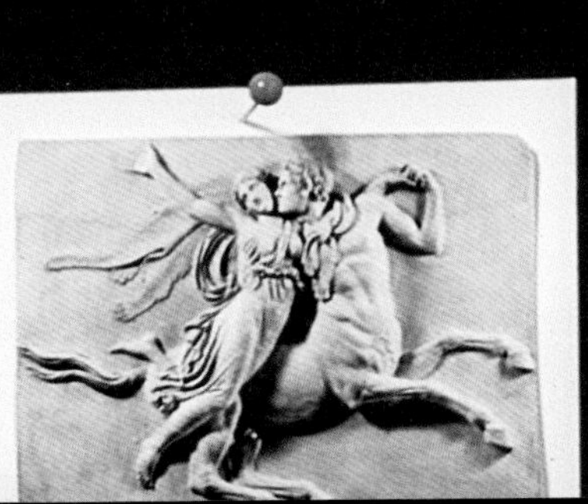

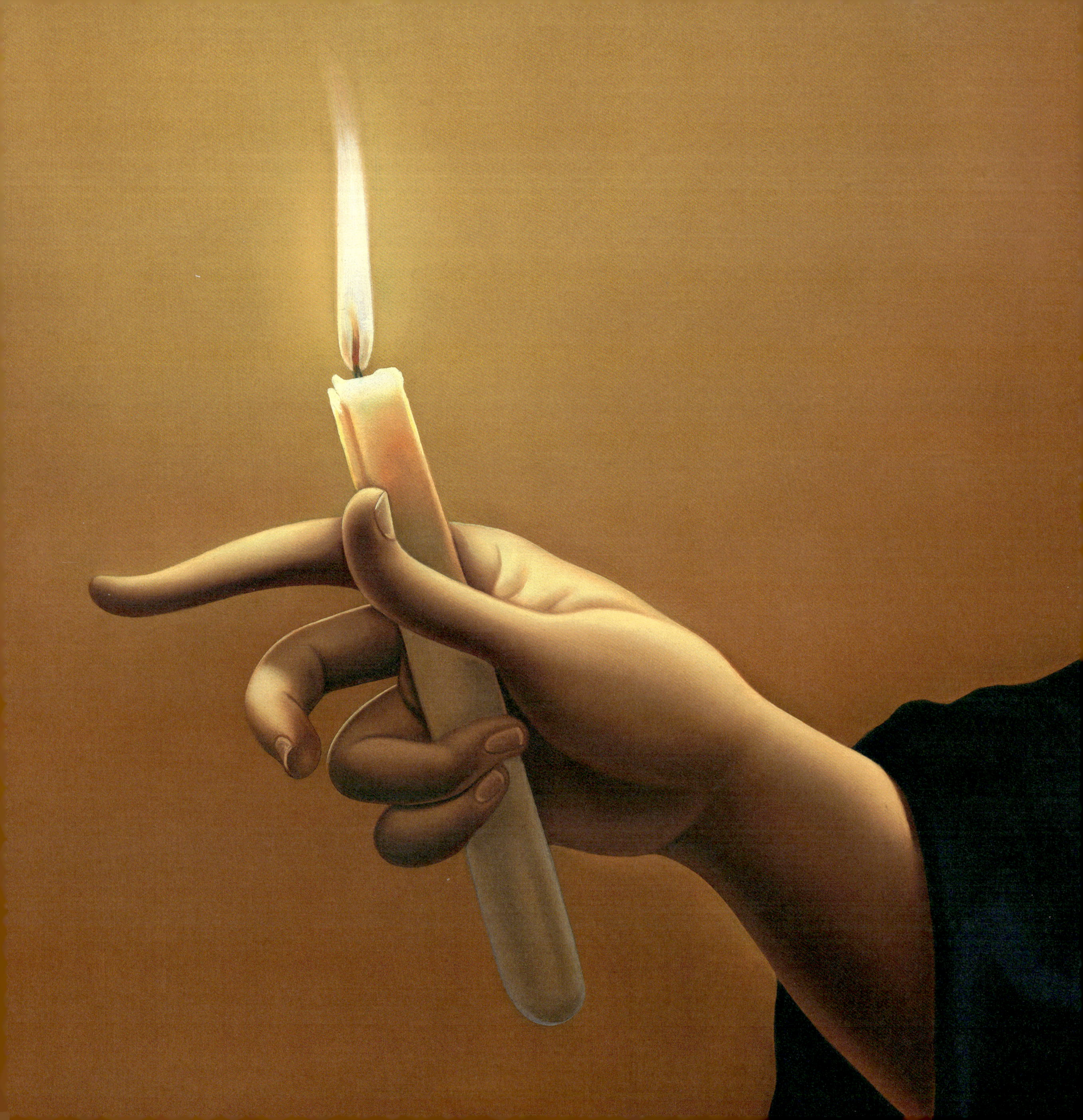

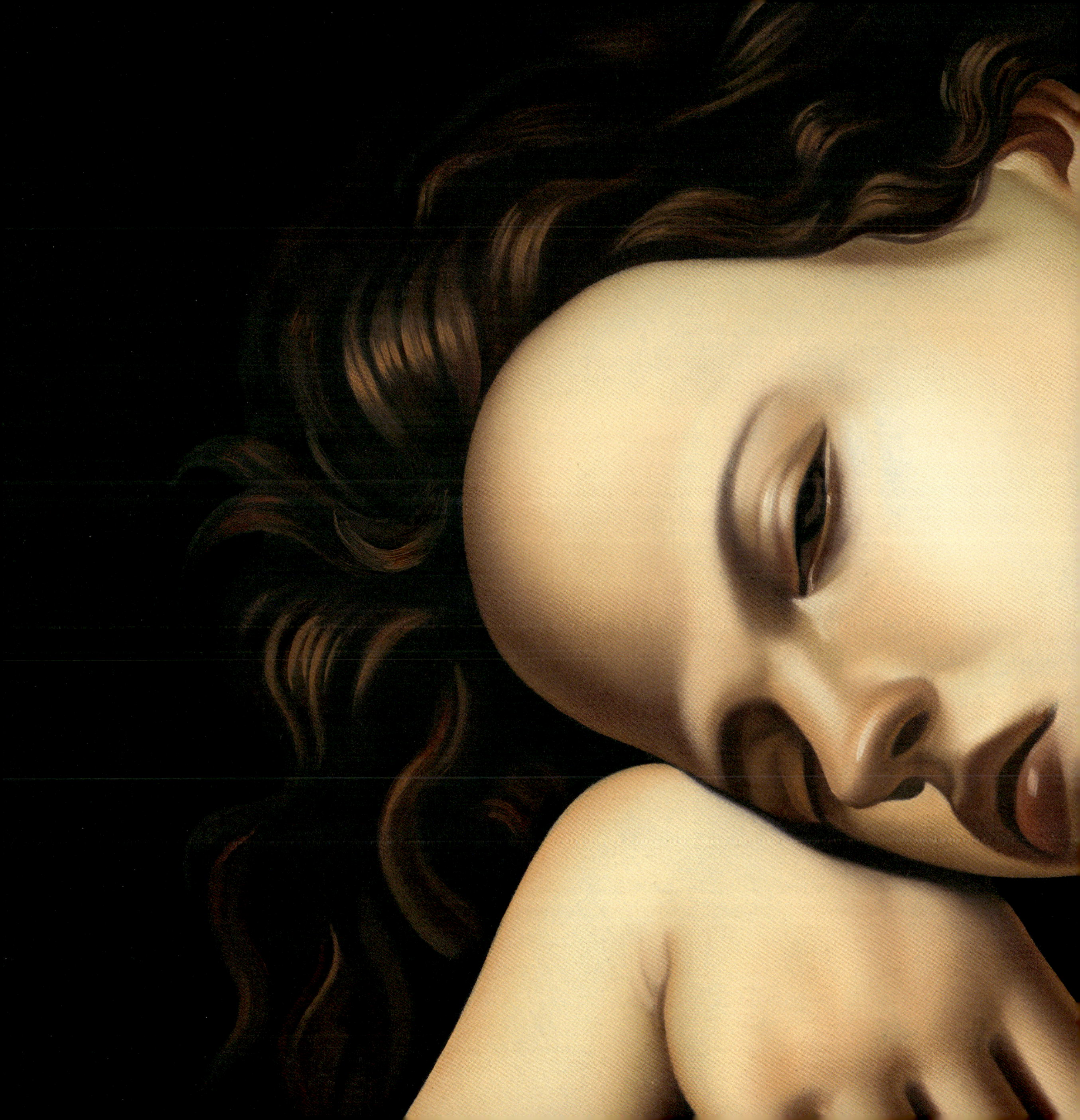

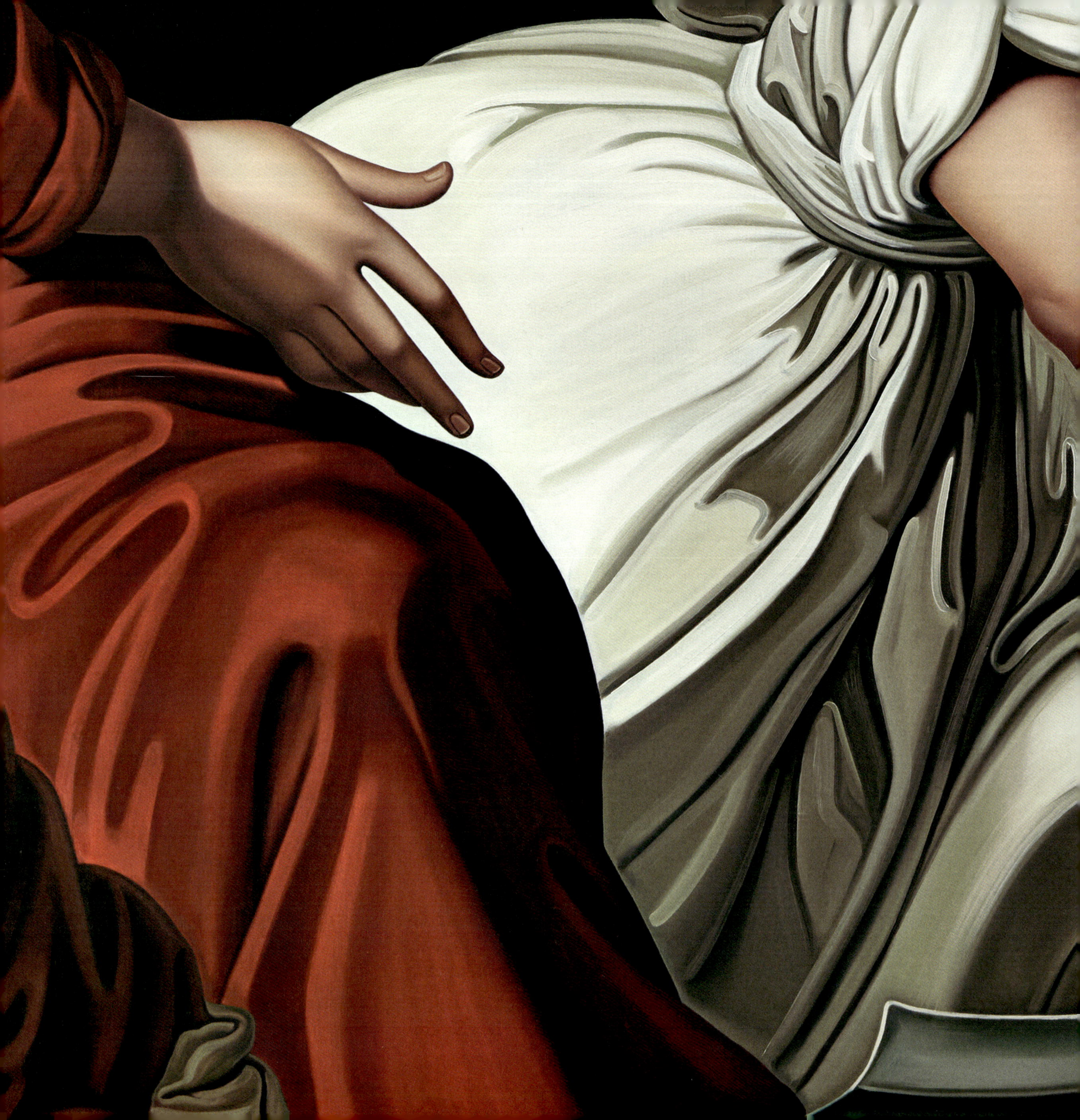

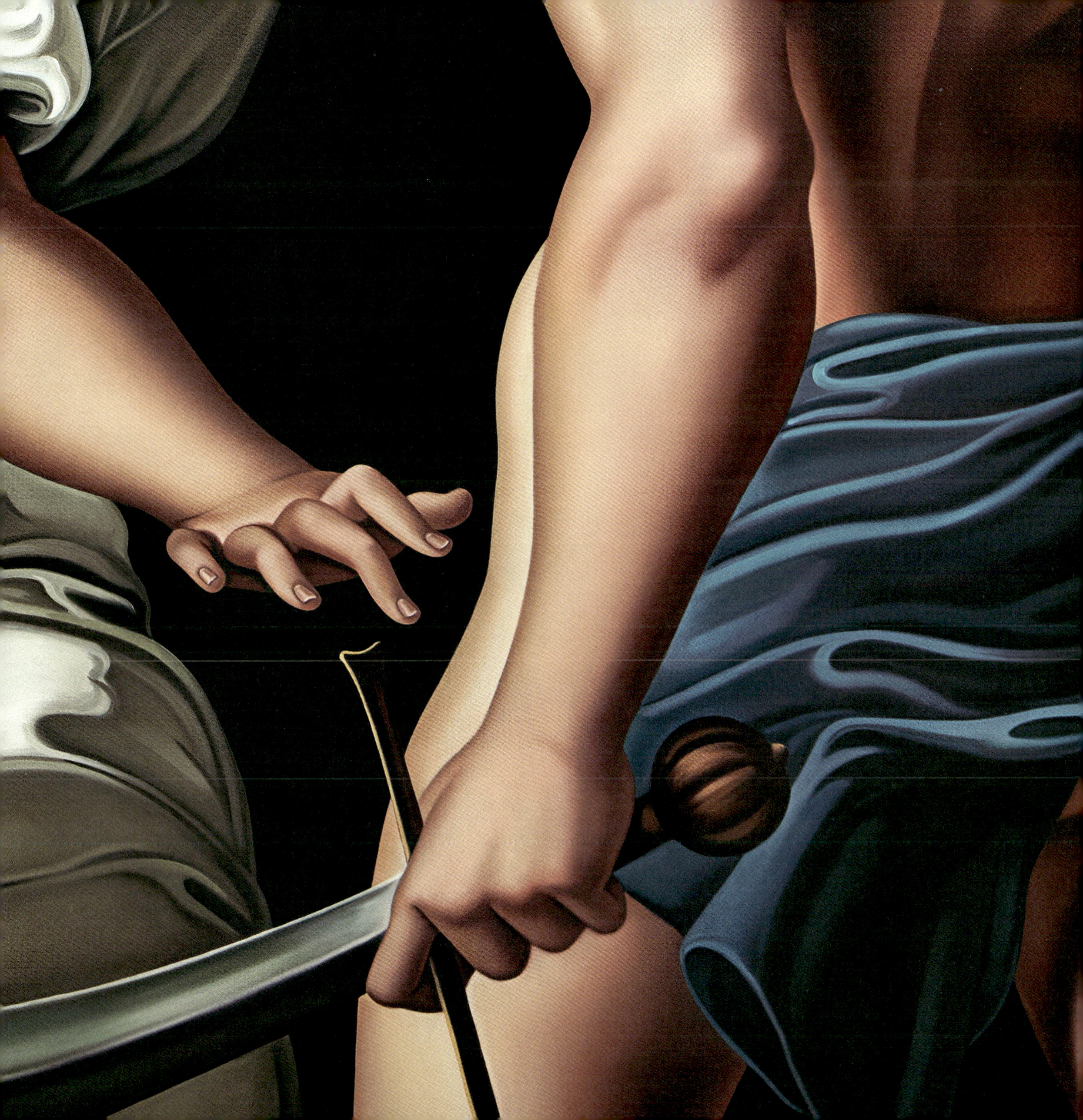

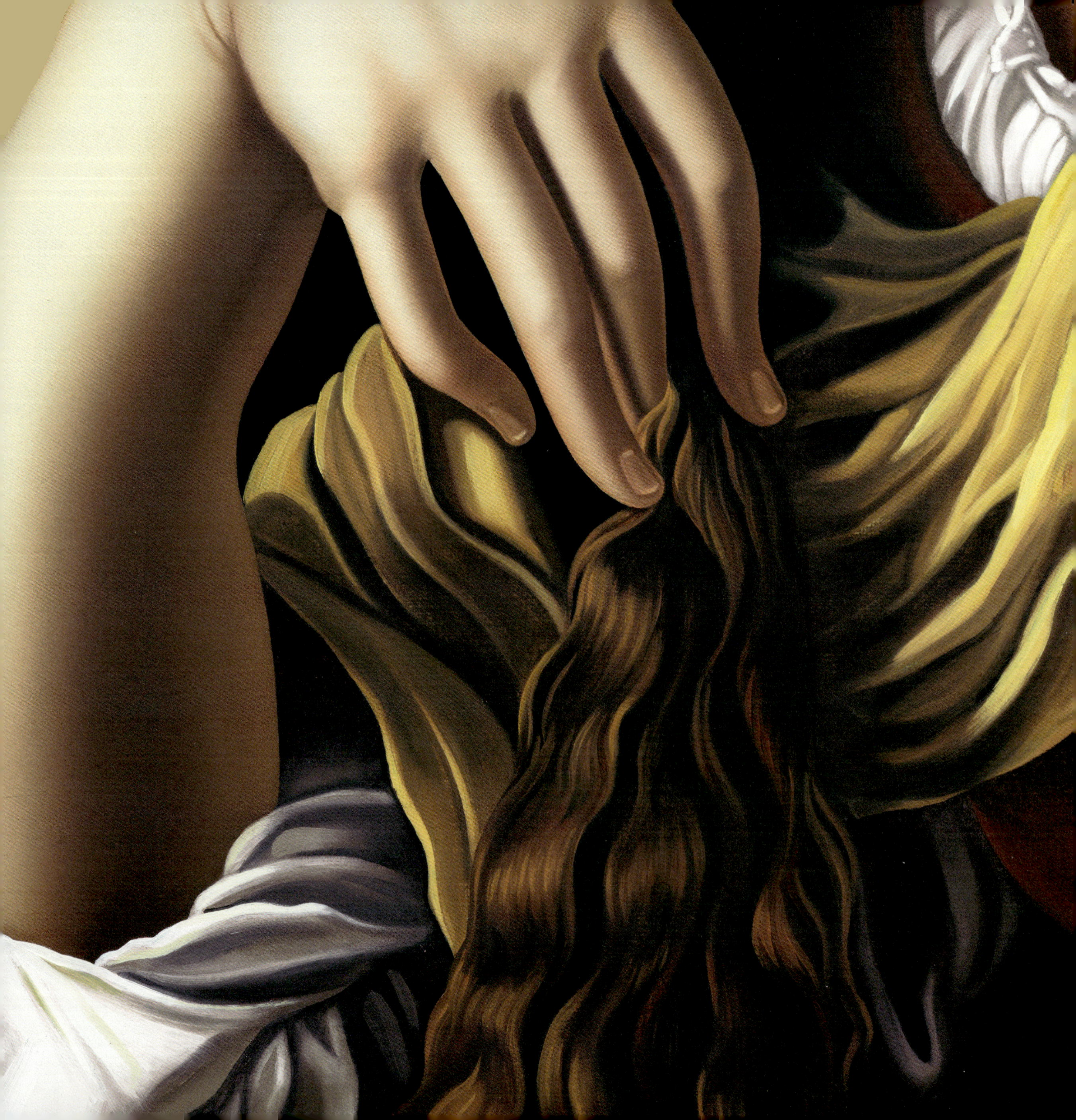

Edited by Adam Harris Levine

Jesse Mockrin
Echo

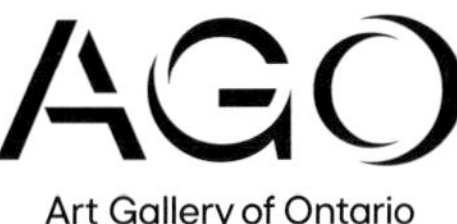

DelMonico Books • D.A.P.
New York

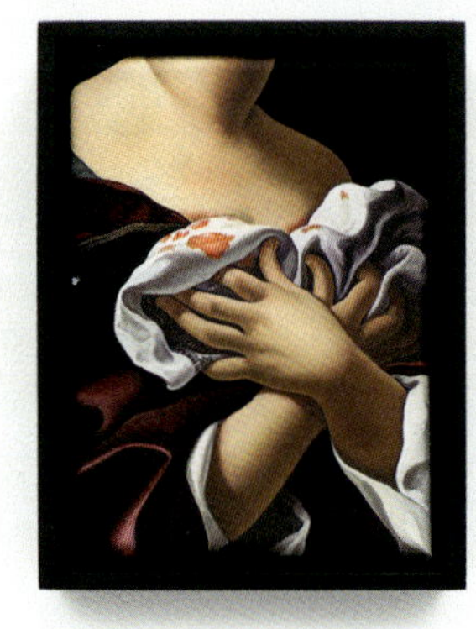

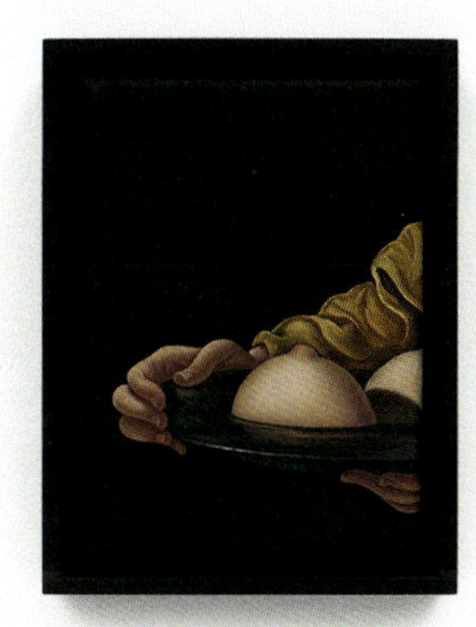

Stephan Jost

Director's Foreword

Echo is the fruit of Jesse Mockrin's close study, over several years, of the historic European art collection at the Art Gallery of Ontario. Her latest body of work is a testament to the wealth and depth of knowledge we continue to find in art made in the centuries before our time. I express my deep appreciation to Mockrin for collaborating with us on this, her first solo museum exhibition. It was a true honour for the AGO. We are grateful to Mockrin's team, including Sascha Feldman and David Norr at James Cohan Gallery in New York, and Davida Nemeroff and her team at Night Gallery in Los Angeles, for their thoughtful consultation and support.

This exhibition and publication would not have been possible without dedication of Mockrin's collectors, who have been foundational to its development. We thank those who lent their artworks to the exhibition, including: Ellen and Jamie Copaken; Glenn and Amanda Fuhrman, courtesy The FLAG Art Foundation; David Hoberman; Mark and Louise Nelson; Robert Simon; and three private collections, including one courtesy Kristy Bryce Art Advisory. Many of Mockrin's collectors shared their artworks for the exhibition and provided financial support to make this publication possible. Our special thanks to Circa 1881; Hooman and Tiffany Dayani; Robin and Vanessa Delmer; Nish and Ali de Gruiter; Lydia Melamed Johnson and Paul Shufro; Amy and Drew McKnight; Julie Montague; Sally and Ralph Tawil; and Bobby and Kylie Whitman. We thank Steven Cohen, and Shawn Kimel and Kate Schatzky, for their support for this publication. Thank you all for coming together to make this wonderful celebration of Mockrin's work possible.

I commend the countless colleagues for their passionate efforts in bringing the *Echo* exhibition and publication to life. In particular, I want to thank the exhibition curator, Adam Harris Levine, Associate Curator of European Art at the AGO; Project Manager Melissa Ramage; Curatorial Coordinator Wendy Hebditch; Designers Evelina Petrauskas and Marco Cheuk; and Interpretive Planner Nadia Abraham. This stunning and dynamic book is the work of AGO Publishing Director Jim Shedden, Coordinator Kathryn Yuen, and Editor Kieran Grant, alongside Toronto-based designer Alina Skyson; thank you to Carmen Maria Machado and Jacoba Urist, whose written contributions reveal deep ways to appreciate Mockrin's practice.

Special thanks to our fundraising team, led by Chief Development Officer Kate Halpenny, in helping to cultivate a community committed to this artist and project. Finally, I want to express my gratitude to our Presenting Partner, Max Mara, and to Robert & Cecily Bradshaw, David Cottingham & Kathryn Wyatt Cottingham, and the Gennaro and Rosalia Family Charitable Foundation for their generous support.

We are proud to have acquired one of Mockrin's paintings for the AGO's permanent collection. We purchased *Fracture* (2024) with funds from the F.P. Wood Fund. During the run of the exhibition, *Fracture* will hang alongside its companion painting, Nicolas Tournier's *Judgement of Solomon*, made in the 1620s.

Jesse Mockrin has built a whole world of her own. Her paintings are populated with characters from ancient myth and faces from our everyday. Her command of oil paint speaks to her deep curiosity in and attention to art history, but her composition and finished work is as visually alluring as it is intellectually rich—contemporary, vibrant, and new.

Stephan Jost
Michael and Sonja Koerner Director, and CEO
Art Gallery of Ontario

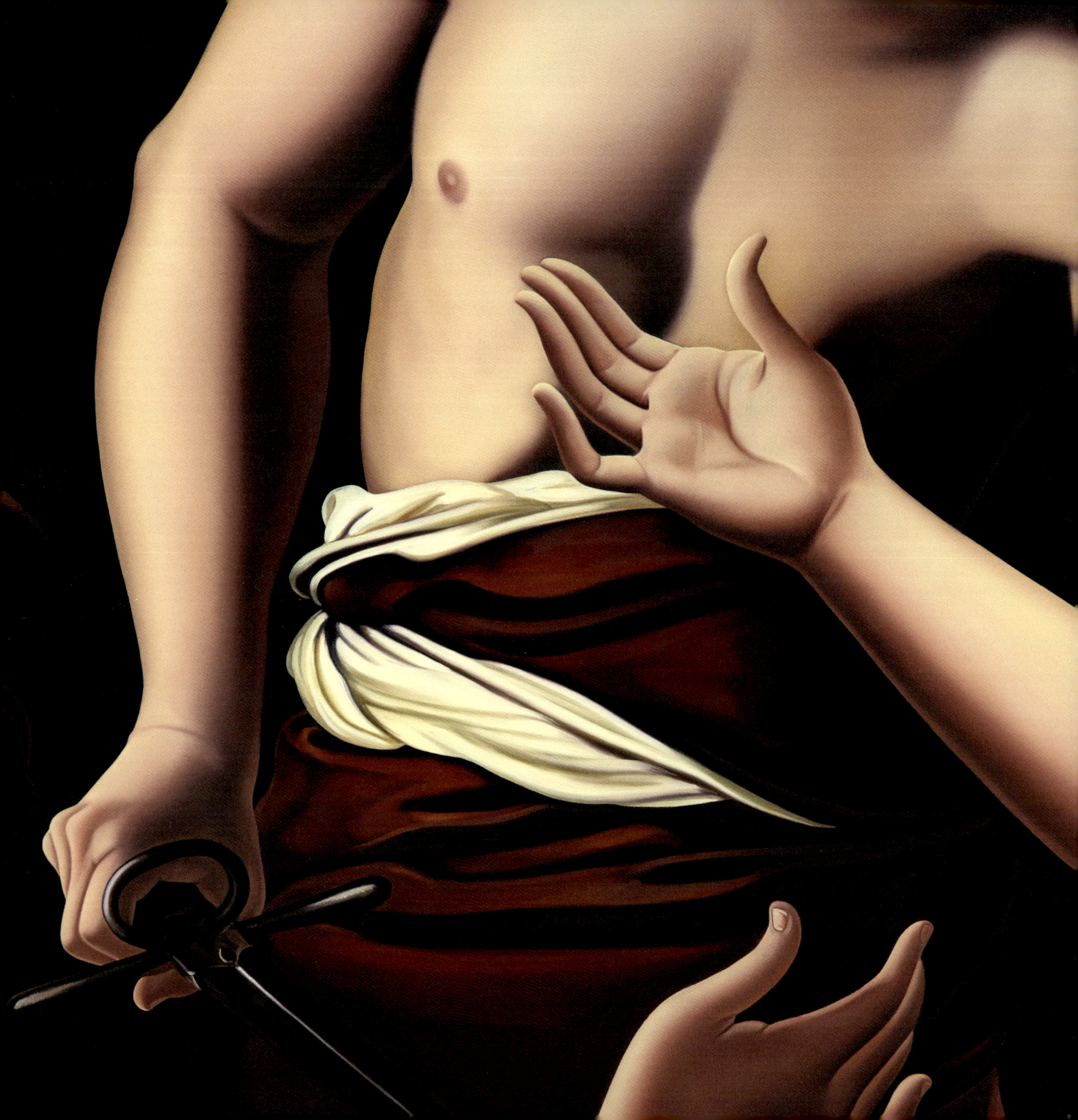

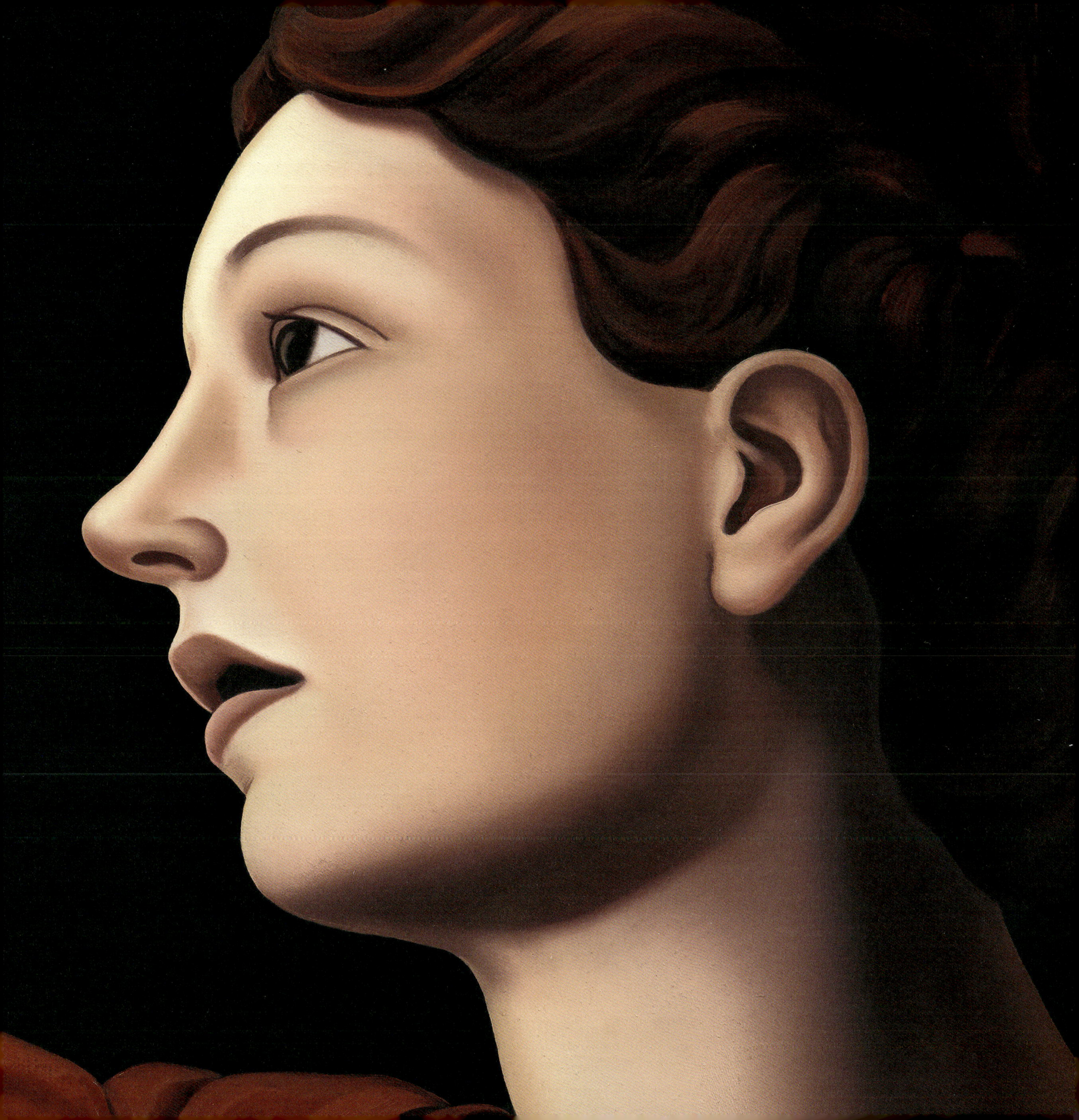

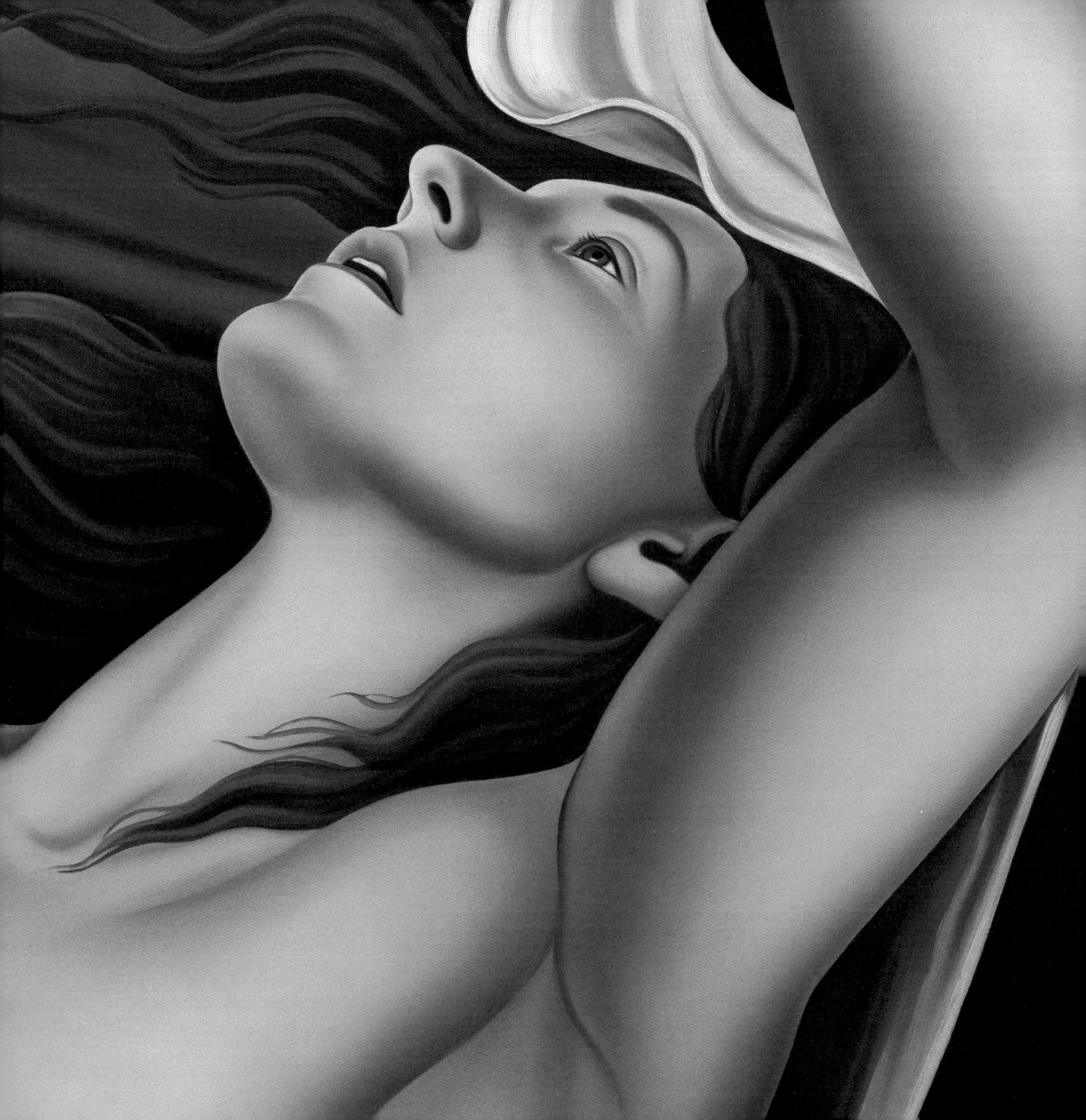

Adam Harris Levine

Echo's Fate

In ancient Roman myth, Jupiter, king of the gods, entrusted the wood nymph Echo with an important task: she should distract Jupiter's wife Juno with conversation while Jupiter carried on affairs with other nymphs. Juno came to think of Echo as a friend and enjoyed their talks, until she realized that this was all a ruse. In her rage, Juno cursed Echo so that she could not form sentences of her own but instead only repeat the last word spoken to her.

Echo loved the handsome young mortal Narcissus, and she watched helplessly as he wasted away, enraptured by his own reflection in the surface of a pond. She could not save him, and with his last breath he bid himself, his beloved, goodbye. Echo was left to repeat her love's goodbye. In her sadness, Echo faded, vanishing slowly until all that was left was her haunting voice. Thus, echoes were born into the world.

Jesse Mockrin is an anthropologist of echoes. Her practice explores ancient stories that are told again and again, in text and in image, and reverberate into our present day. In the body of work she presents in this exhibition, Jesse explores the fates of women narrated in Ovid's *Metamorphoses* and the Jewish and Christian bibles. Echo's story is like many in mythology: an elaborate origin tale for a natural phenomenon, a tale that concludes with a punishment that does not fit the crime. Figures like Echo, Syrinx, Daphne, Rachel, Eve, and so many others suffered cruel and strange fates. Over centuries, we have retold their stories to explain why the world is the way it is. Echo and Syrinx and Daphne, punished for things that are not their fault, are transformed into everything from plants to audiological phenomena. Rachel wants a child all her life, God grants her two and then kills her (in childbirth) before she can experience a life of motherhood. Eve experienced an unquenchable thirst for knowledge and has been a scapegoat for essentially everything bad on Earth ever since.

It is easy to dismiss mythology as trivia or proof of how naive humans were thousands of years ago. And yet the echoes of these stories still reach our ears. They were repeated throughout the Middle Ages, during the Renaissance, and beyond. Jesse is drawn to these stories, and draws our attention to them, because they offer insight into how and why society still expects women to be treated with cruelty and seems to delight in their suffering.

Jesse's process begins with extensive research. She studies the breadth and variety of iconographies that artists employed over centuries to represent a particular narrative. I am so grateful that she has chosen to base much of her research for this project on artworks at the Art Gallery of Ontario. We have a robust and exciting collection of seventeenth-century paintings, sculpture, decorative arts, and works on paper here in Toronto. Jesse zeroed in quickly on the *most Baroque* of the Baroque, such as deeply incised virtuosic ivories carved at the German princely courts, paintings by northerners working in Caravaggio's wake, like Hendrick ter Brugghen, Georges de La Tour, and Nicolas Tournier, and, of course, Peter Paul Rubens.

Working from her assembled web of references, Jesse creates baroque paintings for twenty-first-century audiences. Her compositions combine her observations of many different source images. This cutting and sewing together is made clear for viewers by abrupt and disorienting cropping and reframing. Jesse's choices make her paintings both familiar and uncanny: one lets their guard down thinking they are in familiar territory, only to realize that things are not quite as they seem. Jesse's cuts and excisions add rather than take away. They draw our attention to overlooked corners or make us examine familiar characters with new empathy and curiosity.

Jesse's study of art history goes beyond iconography down to brushstrokes: she prepares her canvases with a dark blue wash that resembles the middle-tone blue paper that Venetian Renaissance artists favoured. (In recent years, Jesse has also produced intimate drawings on blue paper. They are potent and devastating.) After building up her figures, she completes the composition with a series of thin glazes, an oil-painting technique that artists have been practising for hundreds of years. When the painting is finished, however, Jesse diverges from the historical path. She does not varnish her paintings like painters before her. This restraint provides her paintings with a perfectly flat, matte surface. Jesse's unvarnished surface lays everything bare: it makes the viewer hyper-aware that the image they are looking at, a fiction of light and shadow and volume, is a contemporary painter's invention.

On a personal note, I would like to thank Jesse for entrusting me, and the AGO, with her first solo museum exhibition. She has affirmed my belief that the art of the past continues to inform critical understandings of our world today. The edited conversation that follows offers a glimpse of what it's like to work with Jesse: she is an energetic polymath and omnivorous learner, and approaches heavy, dark work with curiosity and openness. Jesse works with a wonderful team of gallerists, and Sascha Feldman at James Cohan Gallery deserves special credit for her remarkable support of our project. I am very grateful to the teams at James Cohan Gallery and Night Gallery for the enormous help they have been in making this exhibition come to be. At the AGO, Melissa Ramage, Wendy Hebditch, Marco Cheuk, Evelina Petrauskas, and many others have brought the project to fruition.

This catalogue has been an absolute delight to work on. Many thanks to Jim Shedden, Kathryn Yuen, and Kieran Grant at the AGO, and to our designer, Alina Skyson, for making the book beautiful. Thanks to Jacoba Urist for her insightful short essay, "Forbidden Fruit," which provides a contemporary art historian's perspective, and to Carmen Maria Machado for her text "It Seemed to Him." This work emerged from a very cool program run by The FLAG Art Foundation, which stages dialogues between contemporary artists and writers, offering the viewer/reader time and space to explore a theme in depth. Black-and-white photographs throughout the book draw upon Jesse's fascinating visual archive. As part of her making process, she compiles many different reference images before constructing her compositions. Her files resemble the research project that art historian Aby Warburg (born and died Hamburg, 1866–1929) undertook, called "The Afterlife of Antiquity." Warburg charted thousands of images made in the Middle Ages and Renaissance that demonstrated artists' commitment to maintaining and nurturing tropes established in the ancient world. Our black-and-white photographs, shot by Torontonian photographer Paul Weeks, serve as an homage to the delightful and surprising ways that Mockrin and Warburg's projects intersect and intertwine.

Adam Harris Levine is Associate Curator of European Art at the Art Gallery of Ontario. His research typically focuses on medieval and renaissance sculpture.

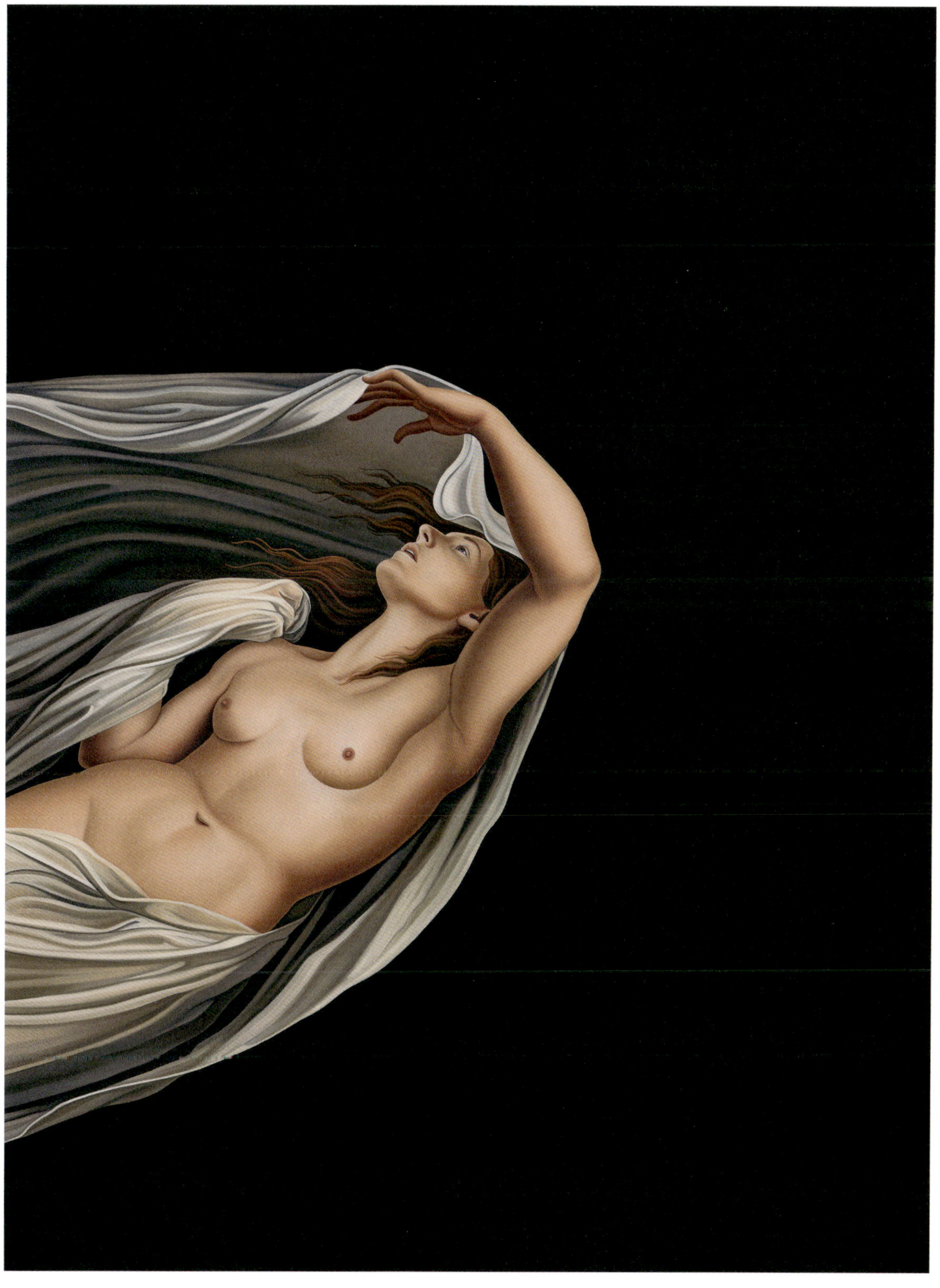

Only Sound Remains 2025

Forbidden Fruit

In the last gasps of winter 2023, I sat down with Jesse Mockrin to discuss a new body of work for her solo debut at James Cohan Gallery in Lower Manhattan's Tribeca neighbourhood. At the time, she informally referred to it as her "ladies with mirrors show." Pulling from historical masters like Giovanni Bellini and Gustave Courbet, as well as makeup artists she follows online, *The Venus Effect* reinvented the luscious boudoir scene, mythologies of toilette and allegories of vanity. The overlap between the painting *of* the face and the painting of *faces* fascinated Mockrin. Obsessively blending each stratum of paint for the skin, she achieves hyper-flawless artificiality, where the pursuit of idealized beauty skews grotesque. That bloodless skin as well as the deliberate stroke-free finish of her oil painting is signature Mockrin. So too the artist's clever use of gender fluidity. I had first discovered Mockrin's work in 2020, when *Vogue* commissioned her to make a portrait of Billie Eilish, the groundbreaking Grammy-winning singer known for her non-binary self-expression. The result: Eilish reimagined as Caravaggio's s 1593 *Boy with a Basket of Fruit*, transgressing the proverbial male gaze by rooting a contemporary icon in the past and adding insects to the classic cornucopia—the decay of youth and the dangers of fame. Mockrin places a girl-goth alternative for Caravaggio's boy; where the original is bare-shouldered, Eilish is buttoned up in a turtleneck *and* a jacket; his sexy, yielding "come hither" vibe becomes her "try me" look. Unveiling her take, Mockrin told *Vogue* that she wished she'd had a celebrity like Eilish, who challenged gender as a construct, to look up to as a teenager. Instead, she came of age in the Britney Spears era of traditional notions of pink-panty sex appeal and a kind of soft-peddled misogyny lurking beneath the inherent contradictions of third-wave feminism.

Mockrin is a standout feminist artist of her generation alongside Cecily Brown and Nicole Eisenman, who mine art history, the literary canon, and world events with similar irreverence. Mockrin's source materials are almost always paintings originally made by men. By appropriating familiar female biblical and mythological characters—"redeemed prostitute" Mary Magdalene, Jewish matriarch Rachel, who dies in childbirth—Mockrin radically recentres our perspective. Her version of legendary European art crops and zooms in on the details that elevate women to protagonists in their own stories. Keenly aware of her politics of location, Mockrin reads—and paints—ancient stories and myths through the lens of an artist, and now of a mother, in the 2020s. She directs our attention to the gender disparities and violence inherent in each of these narratives, the crucial part of the story rarely depicted or exhibited on museum walls before now.

But for all the ancient material Mockrin ingests—stories about women written by men for men's consumption—she is an unapologetic product of '80s and '90s pop culture. It's impossible to miss the influence of artists like Barbara Kruger or the Guerrilla Girls in Mockrin's subversive art-making. Formed in mid-1980s New York, the Guerrilla Girls—an anonymous, all-women group of feminist artists—challenged the hegemony of white men in the art world. Wearing gorilla-mask disguises, the collective highlighted the lack of work *by* women in museums and galleries, even though there were plenty of women *painted* by men. Their iconic poster, originally placed on New York City buses, *Do Women Have to Be Naked to Get into the Met. Museum?*, featured a reclining nude from Jean Auguste Dominique Ingres's *Grand Odalisque* (1814), in a gorilla mask, alongside the statistic that less than five percent of the artists in the Modern Art Sections are women, but eighty-five percent of the nudes are female. In a similar vein, Kruger's photographic silkscreen *Untitled (Your body is a battleground)*, produced for the 1989 Women's March in Washington, has remained a call-to-arms for thirty-five years. While Kruger borrows from tabloid media and commercial advertising, Mockrin renders oil paint to rip at the art-historical canon of European painting, revealing that this reality stretches back for millennia.

And yet, several years after that initial studio visit, for many of us the promise of late-twentieth-century feminism and the hope of a safer future for women—the one we pondered as Mockrin finished canvases for *The Venus Effect*—recede farther into the rearview. As *The Atlantic* critic Sophie Gilbert writes in her recent book *Girl on Girl*, the overturning of *Roe v. Wade* in 2022 "marked the most tangible rollback of women's rights in half a century." Against this moribund backdrop, *Echo*, Mockrin's first major institutional exhibition, feels more urgent, more prescient, than ever.

Echo is a soulful conversation across a vast ocean of artistic production and countless lifetimes. Mockrin has created seventeen new large-scale paintings, four of which are a direct response to pieces in the Art Gallery of Ontario's expansive Baroque collection. Thematically, the show traverses gender violence in European art history, from the judgement of Solomon to the eponymous Echo, filtering Greek and Roman mythological drama and Judeo-Christian tradition through Mockrin's uniquely post-contemporary viewpoint. Three tondos retell the Old Testament story of Rachel, for example, a character seldom depicted in art history. Jacob's favourite wife (he's tricked into first marrying her older sister), Rachel struggles desperately with infertility, eventually dying while giving birth to her second son, Benjamin. Complex female relationships, infertility-heartbreak, and maternal mortality resonate deeply in the modern global landscape.

In another painting, Mockrin reinterprets the abduction of Daphne, a nymph pursued by Apollo, who begs for help from her river-god father, Peneus, to avoid rape. Indeed, Peneus does save her, transforming Daphne into a laurel tree, jailed for her own protection. But in Mockrin's rendition—unlike Gian Lorenzo Bernini's life-sized marble sculpture—Apollo never appears; the narrative is all Daphne's. Meanwhile, the polyptych *Bitter Seeds* (PAGE 55) encapsulates Mockrin's continued drive to experiment in the interplay of past and present. Referencing seventeenth-century iconography of the Penitent Magdalene and grisaille stills from mid-twentieth-century footage of women and girls from the Magdalene laundries of Ireland, the artwork unfurls over twenty panels. It is a breathtaking expansion of Mockrin's terrain, cinematic and empowering. Until as late as 1996, "promiscuous" unwed mothers—or "Magdalenes"—could be confined for life by Catholic orders in workhouse institutions, washing, ironing, and sewing without pay.[1] The late Irish singer and activist Sinead O'Connor, for example, shared openly about her tragic time in one as a thirteen-year-old girl. In 2015, New York sculptor Patricia Cronin erected *Shrine for Girls* at the Venice Biennale. A pile of hijabs signified the 276 Nigerian Chibok schoolgirls kidnapped by the terrorist group Boko Haram the previous year, while pale aprons symbolized those worn by "fallen women" in the Magdalene asylums. *Bitter Seeds* places Mockrin among the very few feminist artists who have engaged with the Magdalene laundries, a legacy historians are still unravelling.

OPPOSITE
Bitter Seeds (detail) 2024

1 Magdalene workhouses operated in Britain and Ireland between the 1700s and 1900s, as well as in North America, Australia, and Sweden for a period during the 1800s. The earliest were Protestant penitentiaries for sex workers and unwed mothers. The notorious Irish laundries dated back to Dublin's Magdalen Asylum for Penitent Females, opened by the (Anglican) Church of Ireland in 1767. Later, most Magdalene laundries were run by Roman Catholic religious orders (with state support after 1922). Inmates, or "clients," included sex workers, unwed mothers of multiple children, sexual abuse survivors, so-called problem adolescents, and intellectually disabled women and girls. The Irish government issued a formal apology in 2014, paying out €33 million in restitutions to over 800 survivors by 2022.

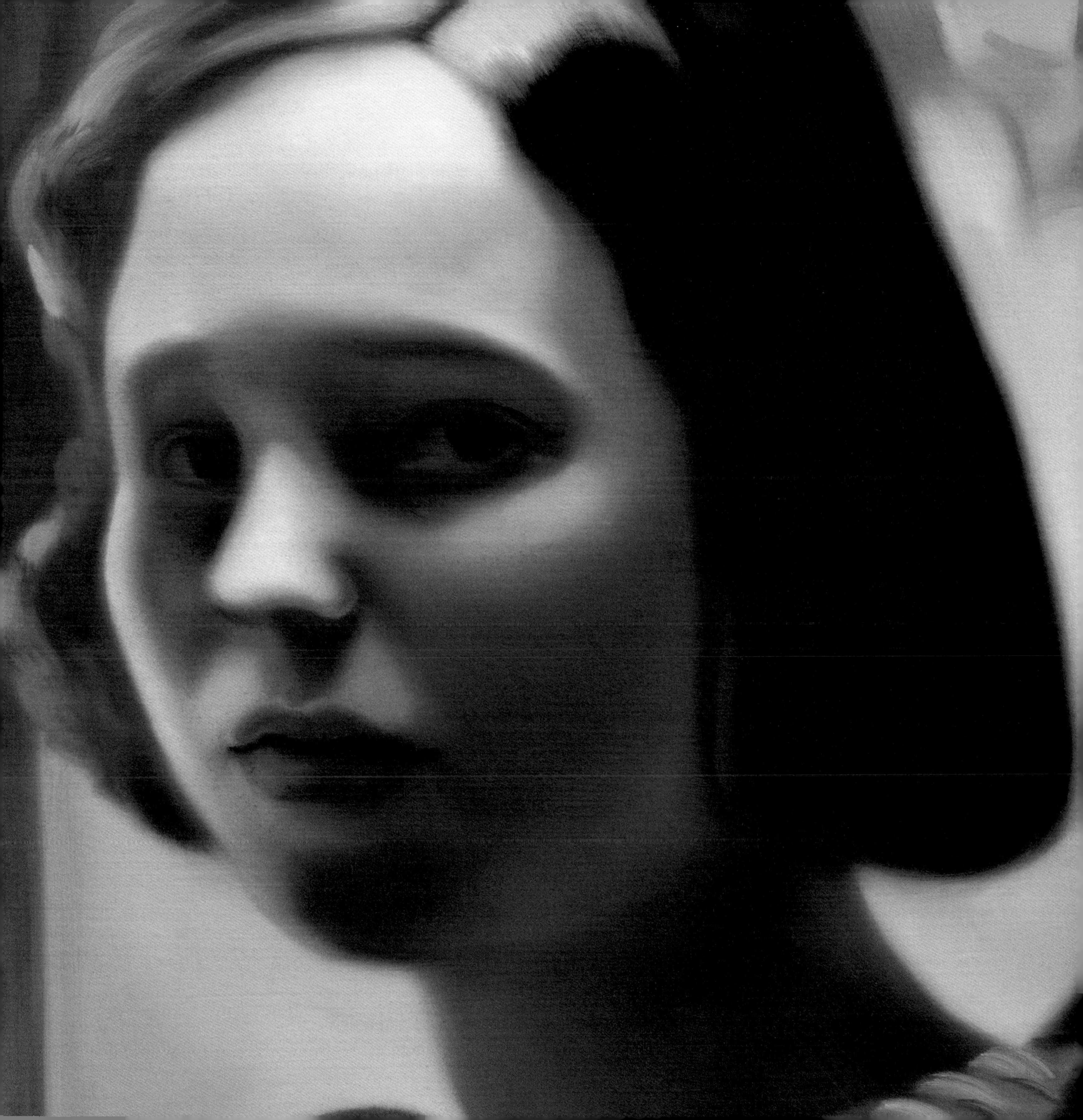

A woman's agency, or lack thereof, over her own body—and thus her destiny—is the current that runs through this body of work. In *Forbidden Fruit* (PAGE 89), Eve holds a spray of pennyroyal leaves in place of the usual fig leaf. Pennyroyal appeared frequently in medieval texts on women's medicine; for centuries, women used the flowering plant as an abortifacient. Mockrin draws a connection between Eve's original sin—the desire for knowledge—with women's ancient, collective, and furtive understanding of their own bodies. Midwifery was often nefariously misconstrued as witchcraft. *Old Magic* (PAGE 92) references a 1500s Dutch painting made during the heights of the witch hunts in Europe. Mandrake and dittany plants grow near the protagonist's feet, both used throughout Ancient Rome and the Middle Ages for a wide array of treatments, including abortion.

Stunningly executed, Mockrin's methods relate to sixteenth- and seventeenth-century technique, but the finished paintings drastically diverge from those revered for centuries. While Baroque painters were intently didactic, Mockrin's cropping makes her work a thoroughly contemporary invention, whether she's pushing male characters out of the frame, implying the fragmented knowledge about these stories from the past, or obstructing the very narrative itself. At the same time, Mockrin's framing and light quality borrows from the language of photography, her original medium at Barnard College, before graduate school. I am reminded of some of her greatest contemporaries: Cindy Sherman's full-length self-portrait as Judith and the head of Holofernes, or Mickalene Thomas's *Le déjeuner sur l'herbe: Les trois femmes noires* (2010), a critique of Édouard Manet's original wherein three regal Black, Afro-styled women fix their gaze upon the viewer. Mockrin's muses hold the same sway. Indeed, she is the heir to Baroque painting. You don't need to know any of the biblical or art references to viscerally experience the power of her brush or the brilliance of her composition. The enduring beauty of *Echo* is that nobody could ever confuse Mockrin's work with the museum's European holdings. Hers will remain forever, distinctly now.

Jacoba Urist is an art writer for *The Financial Times, W* Magazine, *Artforum*, *The Art Newspaper*, *ARTNews*, *Galerie*, and *Smithsonian Magazine*, as well as the New York Arts Editor for *Cultured Magazine*. This is her sixth monograph essay for an artist exhibition.

OPPOSITE
Forbidden Fruit (detail) 2025

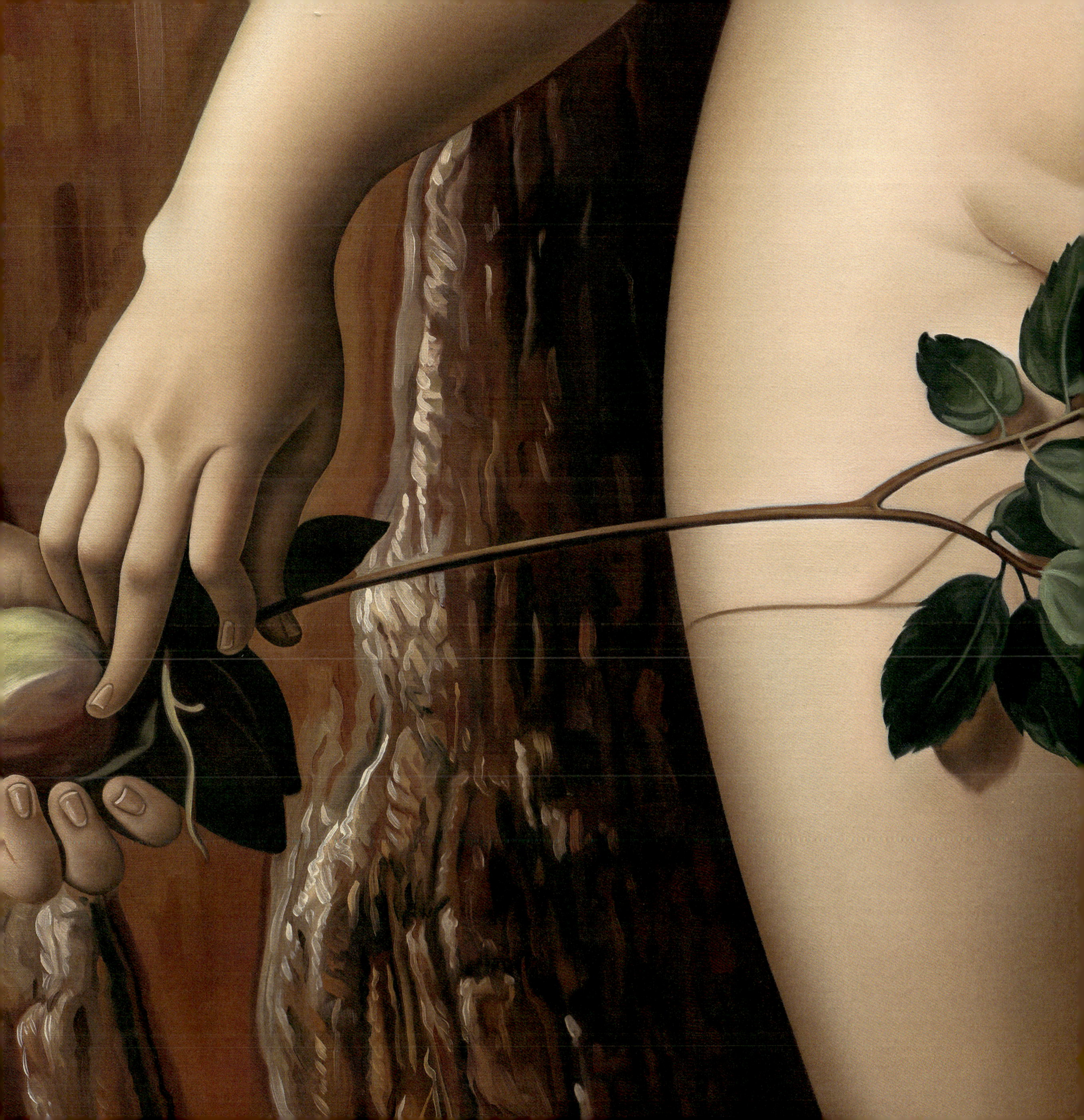

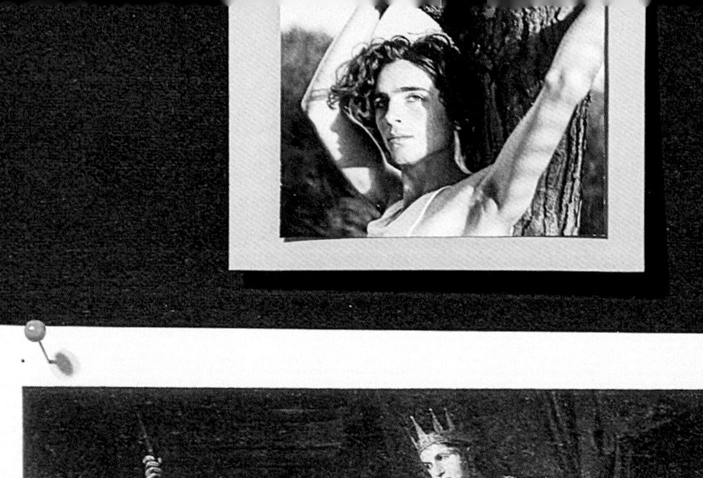
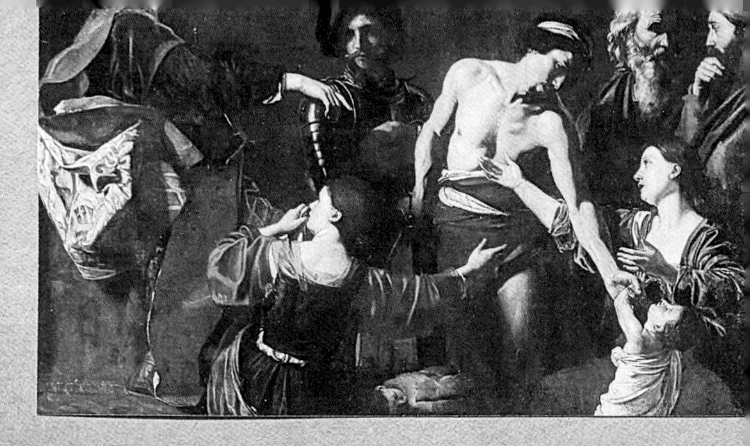
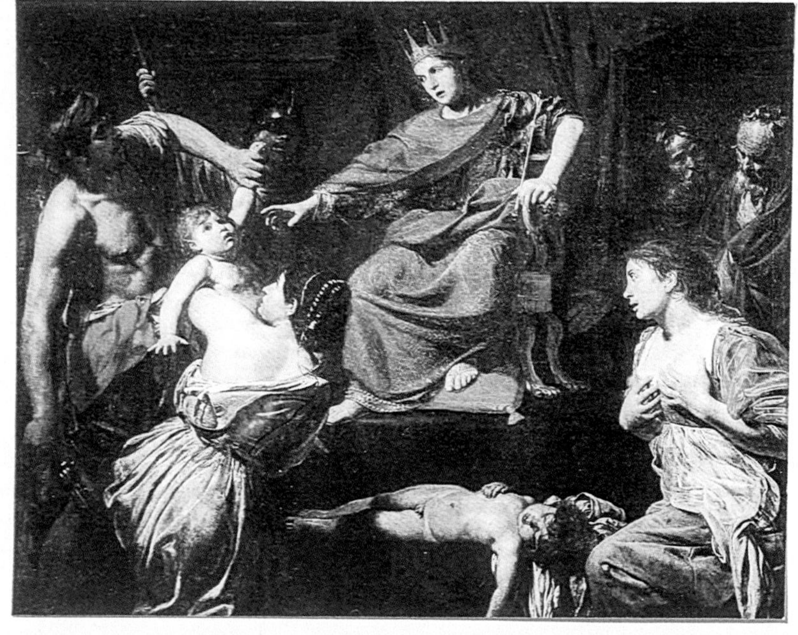
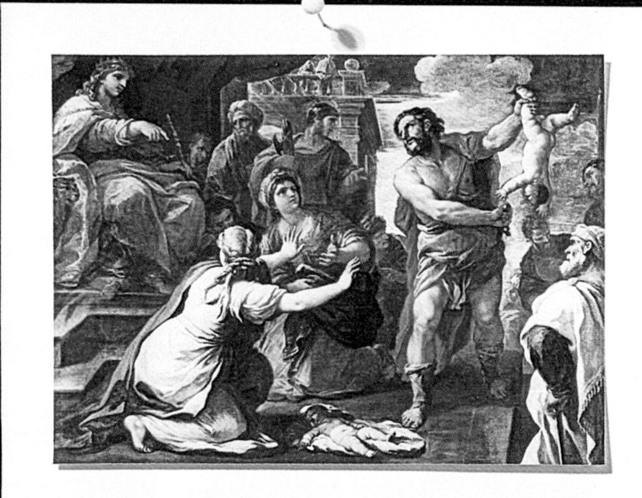
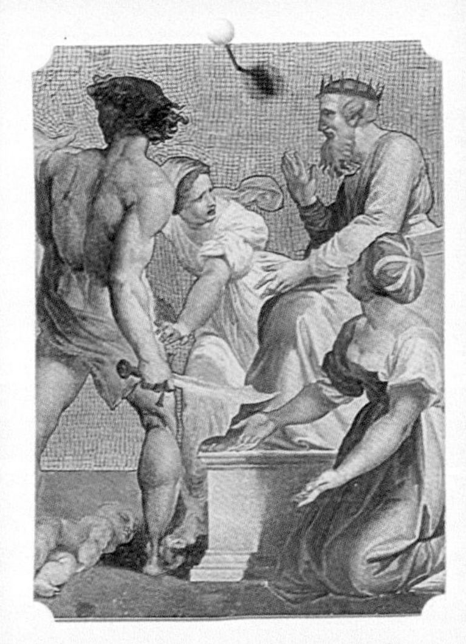
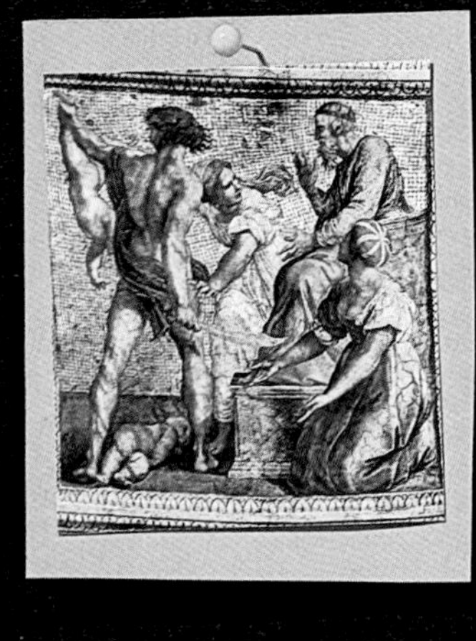
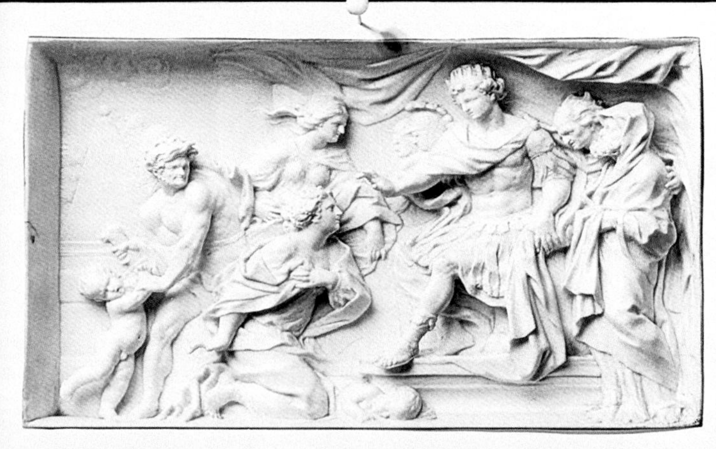
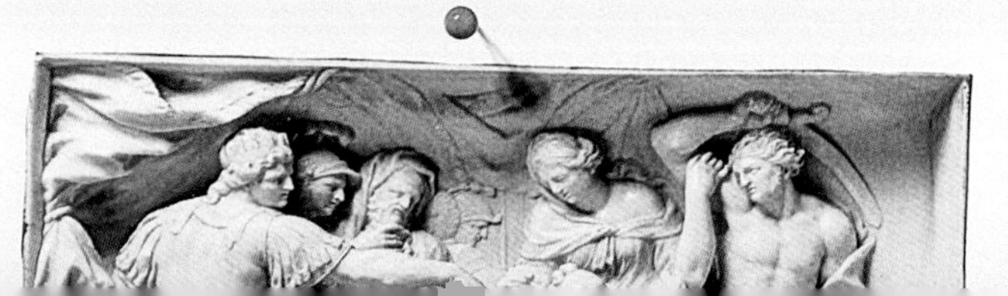

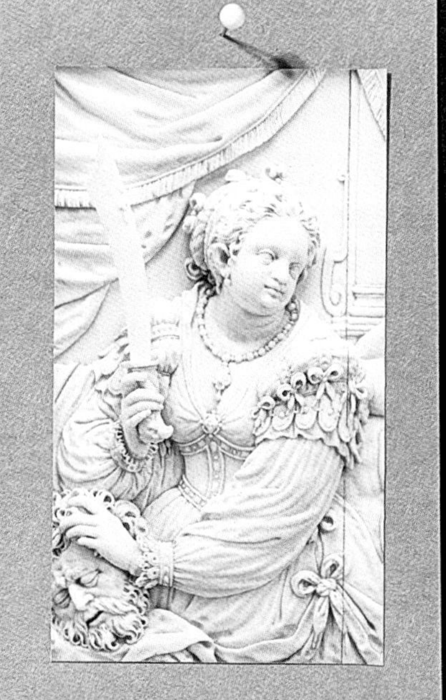
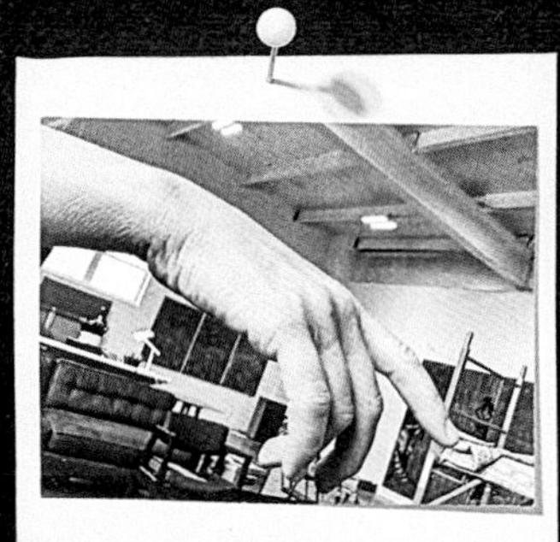
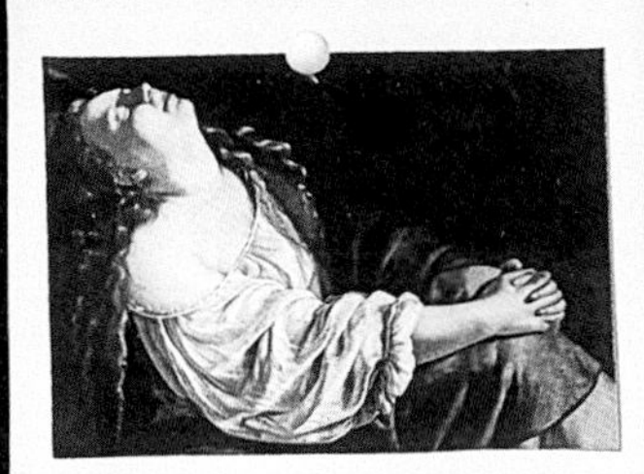
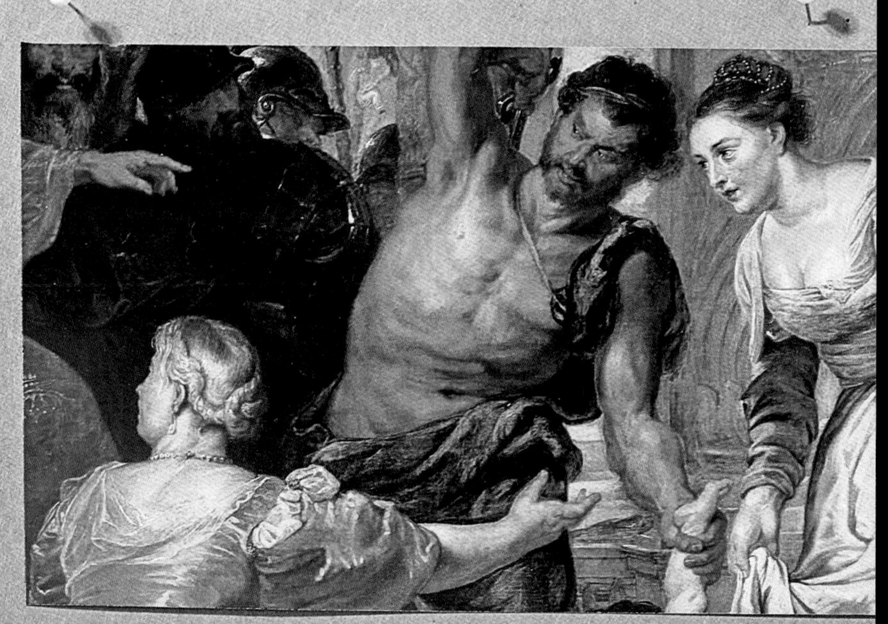
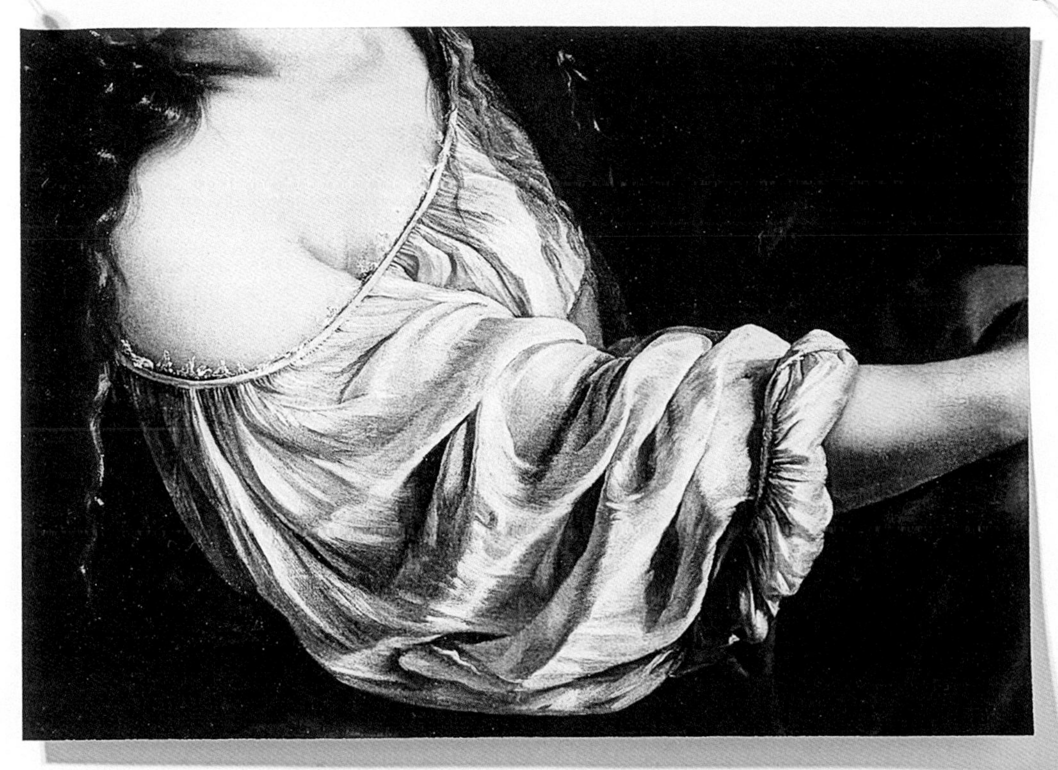
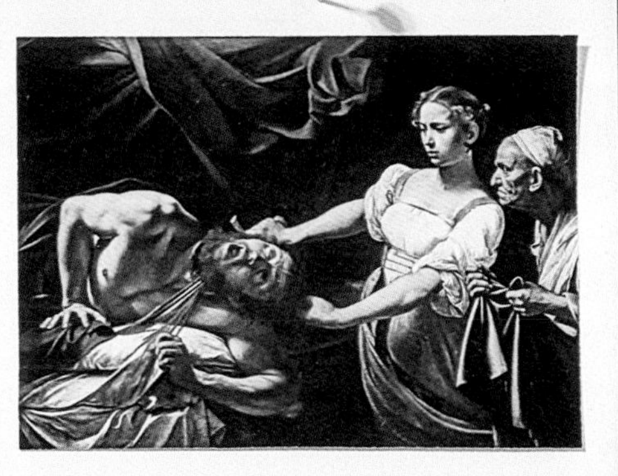
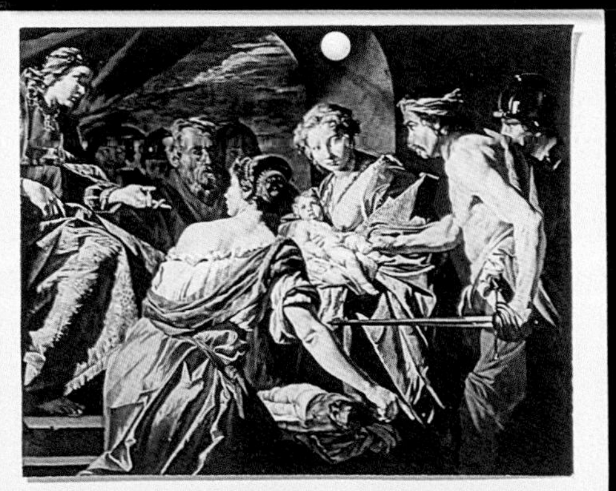
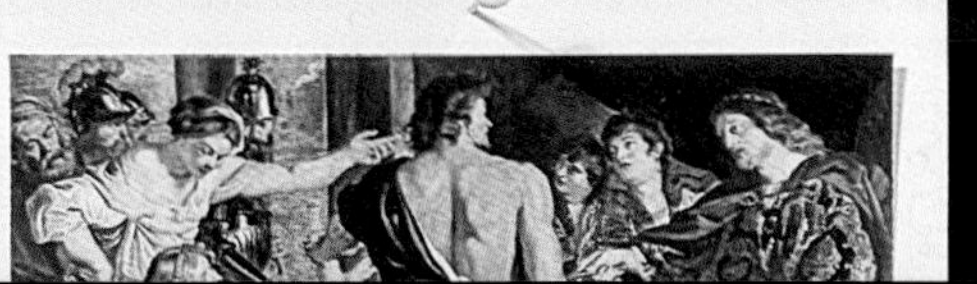

The following interview was conducted over two days in February 2025. It has been condensed and edited for clarity.

Jesse Mockrin in conversation with Adam Harris Levine

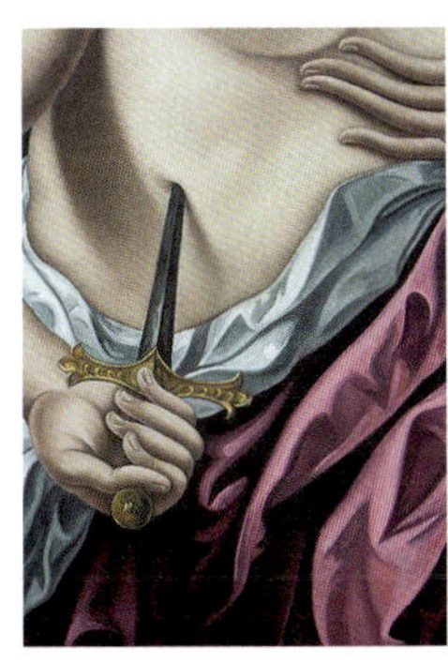

FIG. 1
Jesse Mockrin
A stranger came last night
2019

AHL: My first question is about how you conceive of your paintings in relation to the historical artworks you examine in your research. It seems very rare for one of your works to be singularly *about* another artwork, right? I've inferred that you're often referencing multiple artworks at once or thinking about a range of representations of a particular scene. Is that true?

JFM: There is usually one core historical reference for each painting I create, but I might pull in additional ones to build out the fragment of the scene I'm reimagining. I tend to think about things in series. I'm interested in the repetition of iconographies over time in European art history. Take the Lucretias (FIG. 1), for example. I wasn't so much interested in just one Lucretia, but in all of the Lucretias[1]—or the ones that appealed to me. The proliferation is what interests me—image after image of Lucretia that I found in books or online. They are not all paintings that would have existed together in a historical context. Maybe these paintings are spread throughout museums and continents, so they never get shown together. I want to see them all together and to highlight the repetition of certain imagery. For example, with the Daphne triptych[2] I'm working on now, the figure on the left is from a 1677 painting by René-Antoine Houasse (FIG. 2), the one in the middle comes from a 1518 engraving by Baccio Bandinelli (FIG. 3), and the one on the right is Bernini (FIG. 4). The pose of the figure from the original is almost always what I'm citing. I might find a different face or change the lighting....

AHL: And you make those changes to bring them into a series?

JFM: Exactly, to make them coexist well. I also need to solve each painting as its own work—since I'm often expanding a section of a larger existing composition, it may have unresolved areas I need to reinvent. Or I change the light to use it as a character in the work.

AHL: I think ter Brugghen, de La Tour and Caravaggio[3] use light as a character too, where it's just a single figure, like a woman saint, it does feel like she's not necessarily alone, if you start to think that light is there with her (FIG. 5).

JFM: That seems spot on: the lighting in a de La Tour is probably representing a religious presence in communion with the saint. Certainly, working with representational painting, lighting is really *the* thing. That's something I think about a lot in the works, because while I want them to be illusory and convincing, I also want them to always be alerting you to their falseness. That's part

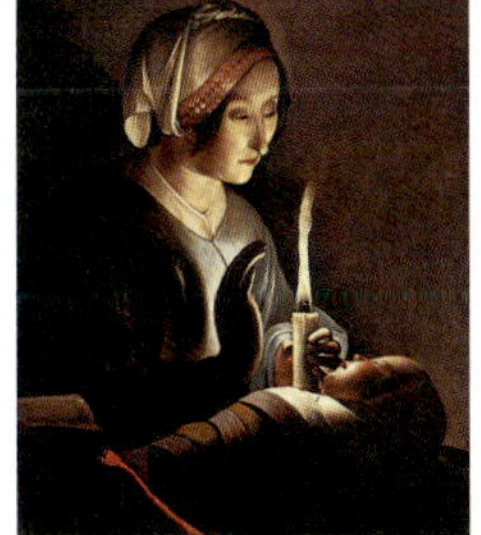

FIG. 5
Georges de La Tour
Saint Anne with the Infant Jesus
c. 1645–1650

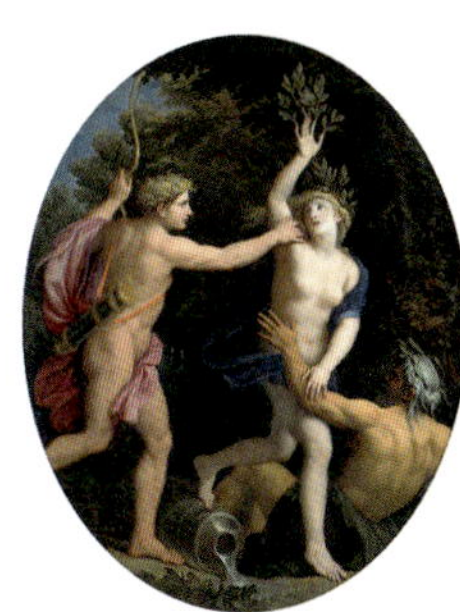

FIG. 2
René-Antoine Houasse
Apollon et Daphné
1677

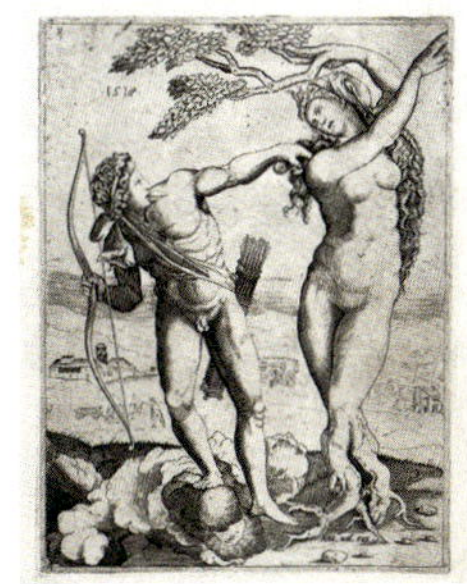

FIG. 3
Baccio Bandinelli
Apollo and Daphne
1518

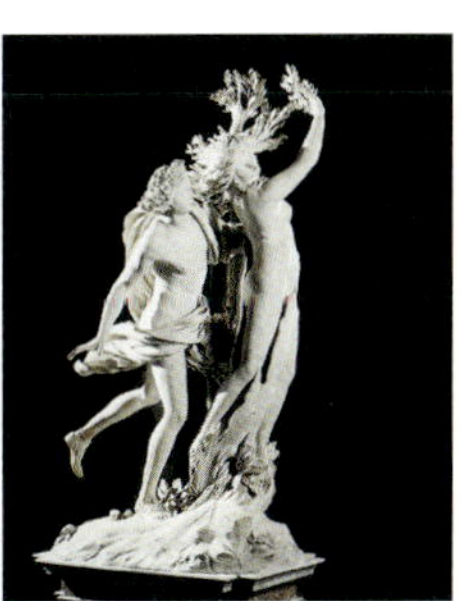

FIG. 4
Gian Lorenzo Bernini
Apollo and Daphne
1622–1625

1 Lucretia was a Roman noblewoman whose rape by Tarquin, the son of the king, and subsequent suicide served as a symbol of the monarchy's excesses and cruelty. Following her death in 510 BCE, the Romans overthrew the king and established the republic. Lucretia's suicide was a popular subject for Renaissance painters.

2 Daphne's story mirrors Lucretia's in key aspects. Roman mythology tells us that the laurel tree comes into existence when Jupiter's son Apollo tries to rape the nymph Daphne and she runs from him. She calls out to her father, a river god, for help, and he turns her into a laurel tree, in which form Apollo cannot rape her.

3 The painters Hendrick ter Brugghen (The Hague, 1588–Utrecht, 1629), Georges de La Tour (Vic-sur-Seille, 1593–Lunéville, 1652), and Michelangelo Merisi da Caravaggio (Milan, 1571–Porto Ercole, 1610) are each celebrated for their dramatic use of light to create dynamic compositions.

of the reason I like the black backgrounds and the cropping—they contribute to a sense of flatness, because you're not seeing the full scene, you're seeing a fragment, and that alerts you to, hopefully, the whole construction of it as a conceit.

AHL: That's super interesting, because I think in the sixteenth century there's this preoccupation with naturalism to the point that the painter sees themselves as a competitor of nature.

JFM: Artists thought they could create nature better than the natural world itself?

AHL: Exactly. I think that the black backgrounds and the flatness in your work are so otherworldly—just like your queer, hyper-extended fingers that I so love. Yours is an extremely self-aware painting.

JFM: I think that comes out of a modern condition of approaching things from a critical perspective. This idea that completely photorealistic painting will *save us* or that there could be any pursuit that would be really, truly pure...? I don't know, it feels like I'm working with these complicated subjects, which are about the violation of women or the abuse of power, and to act as if they're flawless representations of the real world doesn't feel right to me. They feel like they have to let you know that they are aware of all their problematic issues. *The Judgement of Solomon* is a great example.

AHL: You recently made two paintings exploring that story (PAGES 52–53 & 72–73), and it's so interesting because it's more about the threat of violence than enacted violence, but that threat is so real and so scary and so cruel. Can you talk through the story?

JFM: Solomon was a biblical Jewish king who was famed for his wisdom and for coming up with creative solutions to problems.[4] And two women, who some biblical scholars say are sex workers, come to court to ask for his help.[5] Both are mothers of babies, one of the babies has died, and both claim that the living baby is theirs and the dead baby is the other woman's. Solomon proposes to cut the baby in half and give each of them half, and one woman immediately yields her claim to the baby, so Solomon concludes that she must be the true mother because she's willing to sacrifice her happiness for the life of the baby. I like revisiting these stories and the way they've been depicted because I think a lot of narrative details are lost on the general public today. And when I was making these paintings, I was really interested in the experience of the two women. So, I cropped parts of the composition and removed the men's faces. The woman who lost her baby and is claiming another woman's baby is suffering this horrific loss. Why doesn't this story—that is about celebrating male wisdom—acknowledge that it's at the expense of women's suffering?

AHL: I was so pleased when you first arrived at the AGO and focused in on Nicolas Tournier's *The Judgement of Solomon* first (FIG. 6). I have always loved that painting because it illustrates such a dramatic—frankly, melodramatic—moment in painting in the 1600s. Let's zoom

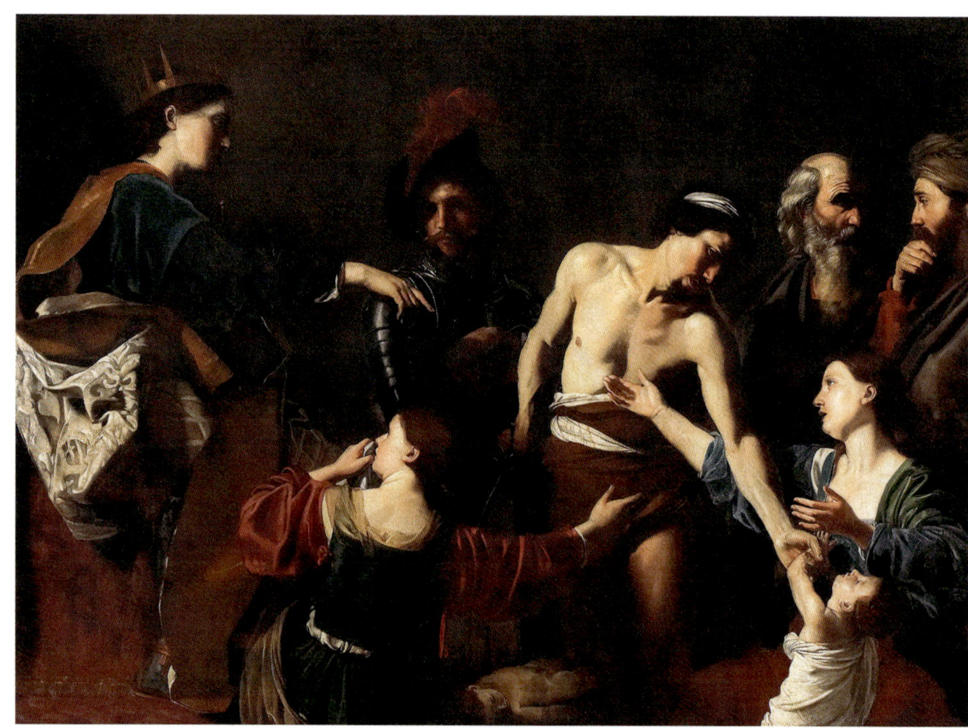

FIG. 6
Nicolas Tournier
The Judgement of Solomon
c. 1625

4 This story comes from 1 Kings 3:16–28.

5 The women are named in the books of Kings. The text mentions that they live together and are not married, so many scholars have interpreted this to mean that they are sex workers and occupy a particularly marginalized place in Solomon's kingdom.

in on your process. Do you work with life models, for instance, and do you know these men and women? How do you take a "'real" image to this place that is self-aware, surreal or not real? How does that work for you?

JFM: I don't work from life models. I didn't go to art school, so I didn't really get that training, which I think in some ways is helpful because I didn't have to unlearn anything. Had I gotten a serious traditional art education, I wouldn't be able to make my fingers curly because I would know anatomy too well. I work from photographs. I start from the original source material. Then things get Frankensteined together. If I don't like the face, I'll find another face. If the lighting is not working for me, I will take my own reference picture for lighting. So I have a lot of pictures, probably dozens of pictures for each painting—images of different kinds of plants and leaves and trees, of hair, of faces. And I use my own body a lot. To get the angle of lighting on an arm, I use my own body (FIG. 7), and I also use pictures of my husband. Along the way, I have taken pictures from time to time of friends for various reasons. My friend Mariquita Davis (FIG. 8), whom I went to grad school with, has a great face, and I've used her face in several paintings. I'm going to take pictures of my friend Jennifer Archie next week as a reference. I also look at models and celebrities who have interesting faces. Timothée Chalamet gets a lot of representation in the practice, and I look up Hunter Schaefer a lot.[6] She's one of the references for one of the two witches (PAGE 91)—the pregnant witch, actually, which is maybe complicated by her gender identity. But it's not a portrait of her pregnant. It's just looking at her beautiful face and the lighting on it and making it fit the painting.

AHL: Tilda Swinton once said that she has a face that makes more sense in paintings than it does in photographs. And there are certain faces that just feel painterly or like they want to be painted. Can you narrate a bit how you learned to paint?

JFM: I drew a lot as a kid but I didn't do any painting until high school. I went to a public high school in Montgomery County, Maryland, and we had a great art teacher who introduced oil painting in class. I was maybe a sophomore in high school, and it was just a very brief introduction, but I got to make a big painting. I painted my best friend, Lily, nude, sitting in front of the open door of a washing machine. It was weird, but I was captivated by the process.

The art teacher recommended that I take classes with Walter Bartman, who taught at another high school and at the Yellow Barn Gallery in the summer. Mr. Bartman taught us to work from life. He would have us pose for each other. He once lay down on the ground in the parking lot for hours for us to draw him—he staged a whole scene of a car accident with his jeep and a discarded bicycle. He took us to do plein air painting all around Bethesda, Maryland, and DC. We painted the National Cathedral. What I learned about myself very quickly was that wherever we were, I was painting the people. I didn't feel such a connection to the architecture or the landscape, but I always found a way to put figures into the works. That was probably the most technical painting education I ever got. From then on my arts education was more theoretical.

I went to Barnard College, a women's liberal arts college and part of Columbia University, and then did my MFA at University of California San Diego. At the time, in the late aughts, and probably still today, the American fashion was to focus on the conceptual underpinnings for artwork and not spend much time on technique, unless you attended a real art school, like RISD [Rhode Island School of Design] or MICA [Maryland Institute College of Art] or something. At Barnard, I tried lots of different subjects before deciding on visual arts and art history as my major. My first-year undergrad painting class was taught by Elizabeth Peyton,[7] of all people, who was teaching adjunct at Columbia, even though she was already very successful. She would have her handsome male TAs pose for us. She taught us to paint like her—to use transparent paints so the white of the canvas would show through. I also got really into photography there and that's what I ended up focusing on for my senior thesis show.

After college, I lived in Honduras for two years. I didn't have a space to paint, so I did photography there. I got into grad school at UCSD with a photography portfolio. My wonderful advisor, Amy Adler,[8]

6 Hunter Schaefer (b. 1998) is an American trans supermodel and actor.

7 Elizabeth Peyton (b. 1965) is an American portraitist known for painting beautiful men.

8 Amy Adler (b. 1966) is an American artist.

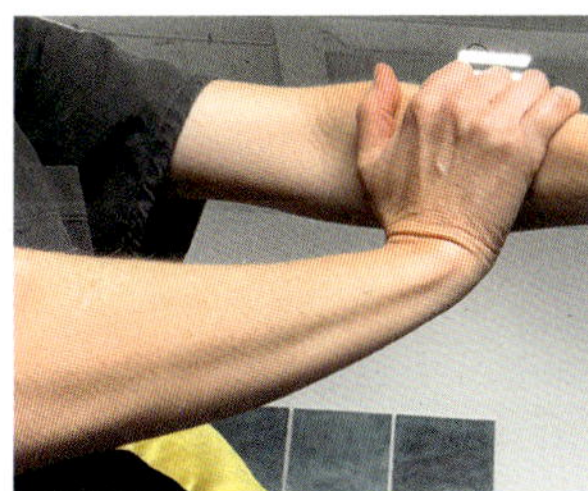

FIG. 7
Studio reference photo of the artist's arm for *A story told this many times becomes the forest*

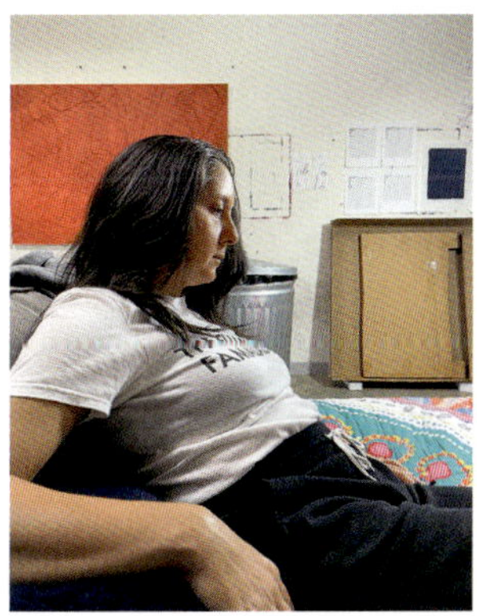

FIG. 8
Studio reference photo of Mariquita Davis

told us to start making work immediately. I had been making social documentary photography, but I didn't know anyone in San Diego to photograph. I had a studio again, so I started painting from my own photographs. From that point on, I became obsessed with oil painting.

AHL: Anytime one makes an image, they are cropping, but photography seems especially brutal in its cropping. In painting, insofar as it is invention by default, you might create a composition around a whole figure, whereas a photograph constantly uses these four rigid lines to cut and to bisect and to include and exclude. Your photographic training appears very clearly in your paintings.

JFM: It's the foundation for the way I think about composition: each composition as a rectangle, within which the space is divided by the figures, so those four walls are always present.[9] And then it's about the relationship of the body to those boundaries. I think all that background in photography made me feel like I had this little viewfinder I could apply to these historical works that I was so interested in—focus in on, say, that little snippet of it that could be its own painting. And what would happen if that piece of this painting was reproduced by me in this moment?

AHL: I'm wondering about how you approach negative space in your work.

JFM: I hope that the void of the negative space in the work creates an anxiety about what's not presented—what lies outside the frame, or what the black is covering up. There's a movie called *The Descent*,[10] which shares the name of the largest painting in the show (PAGES 66–69). It's a horror movie about women who go caving and get trapped. The film's darkness was described in one review as both terrifyingly close and terrifyingly vast.[11] Maybe that's what the darkness in my paintings does. Do you think it creates anxiety?

AHL: Your works reveal and conceal. That cropping is an omission that inspires curiosity because we want to know what is beyond the crop you were just hinting at. And that is, for me, both liberatory and anxiety-inducing.

9 This echoes a canonical idea of Renaissance art theorist Leon Battista Alberti, disseminated in his 1435 treatise *De Pictura.* Alberti began conceiving of a painting this way: "First of all, on the surface which I am going to paint, I draw a rectangle of whatever size I want, which I regard as an open window through which the subject to be painted is seen."

10 Directed by Neil Marshall (2005).

11 Ebert, Roger. "Into the Maelstrom," rogerebert.com, August 3, 2006.

12 Gian Lorenzo Bernini's *Apollo and Daphne* is dated between 1622 and 1625 and is housed in the Galleria Borghese in Rome.

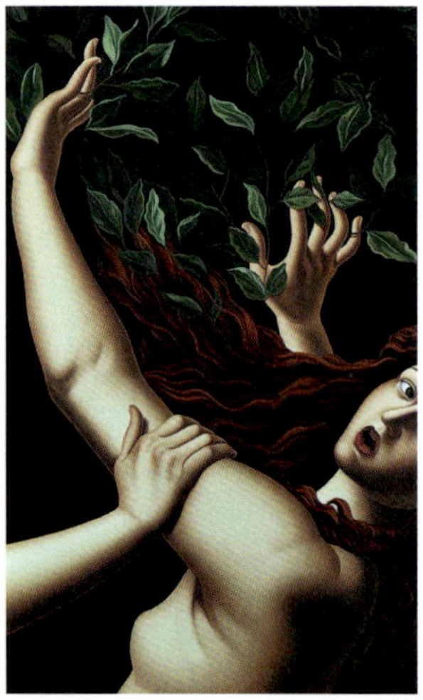

FIG. 9
Jesse Mockrin
A story told this many times becomes the forest (detail)
2025

I am an anxious person who craves freedom, and maybe that's why I like your work. There is this freedom in being able to imagine the rest of the image on your own. Yet there is the ominous recognition that you, Jesse, are the author, and that I, as the viewer, don't know what lies beyond the crop.

JFM: So you have a sense that there is an authority who knows something?

AHL: Well, for instance, a disembodied arm that reaches out from beyond, for me, certainly means unanswered questions in a painting. When I look at, say, Apollo's arm grabbing Daphne [when the rest of his body is out of frame] (FIG. 9; PAGES 84–85). If you do not know the story, then that arm could be a benevolent gesture or a threatening one. Looking at it, we have enough clues from the rest of the painting that it's one or the other, and if you are familiar with the myth, then you know it's very, very threatening.

JFM: Maybe there is room for optimism in the work, because, as you said, you could imagine that this is a helping hand. In the left panel and centre panel, those are the reaching arms of Apollo, but on the right panel, which is referencing the Daphne by Bernini (FIG. 4),[12] Apollo is standing behind her. That arm is not his arm. That's an arm I added (FIG. 7) because I also think of this painting as relating to images of the Three Graces—you have three female figures together, and they're woven together by these reaching hands, connecting across the three panels (PAGES 84–85). I've been questioning that myself: this hand that I've added, could it be trying to hold her as she's falling backward? I like this possibility that maybe someone is trying to help.

AHL: I think that also goes to talking about the authorship, and then re-authorship, of these stories by men and by women. Ovid's stories[13] are unfailingly cruel to women, in a way that if a woman were tasked with retelling the stories they surely would undergo transformation—even if she were instructed, "Tell the same story." There would be some way to make it more bearable for the women protagonists. And maybe if someone were with Daphne in this moment of brutal

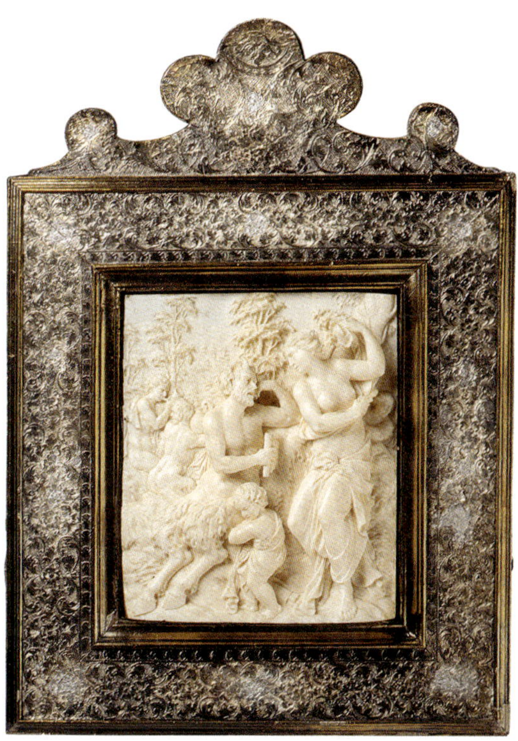

FIG. 10
Ignaz Elhafen
Pan and Syrinx
1690–1695

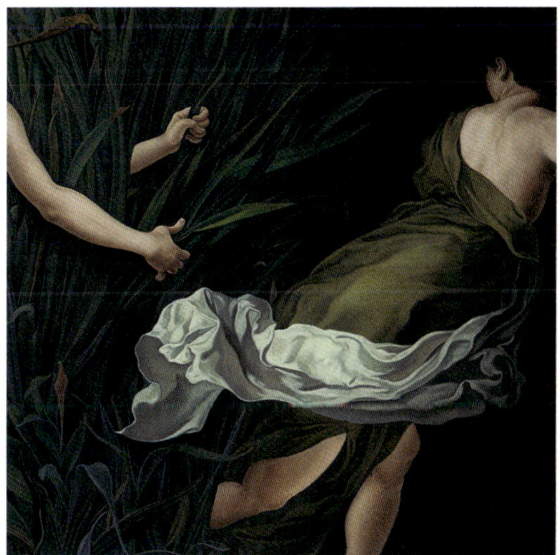

FIG. 11
Jesse Mockrin
Syrinx (detail)
2018

transformation, somehow that would make it feel more bearable that she's not alone.

JFM: Syrinx, too! She is transformed by the nymphs of the river.[14] So she runs into the arms of her sisters and I think that's a moment that speaks to the importance of not being alone.

AHL: Ovid's rape narratives all seem to justify violence because they always result in the gods creating something that humans enjoy, like Daphne's laurel leaves, which Romans used to make crowns celebrating ictory, or Syrinx turning into reeds that Romans used to make flutes out of (FIGS. 10 & 11; PAGE 81). This makes me think about one of the ultimate examples of this trope of sexual violence, the Rape of the Sabine Women.

JFM: It's an important example, and [the legend is] much older than Ovid.

AHL: Right! The story comes from Livy,[15] who tells us that when the city of Rome was founded, men needed wives in order to grow the city.

JFM: Exactly. And these early Roman men go around to neighbouring towns asking men for their daughters' hands in marriage. When they are rejected, they kidnap the virgin daughters of the Sabine people and carry them back to Rome.

AHL: And these women are made to be the mothers of the first generation of Roman-born citizens. What a violent way to start a city. I remember your first visit to the AGO, when we looked at the ivory tankard by Ignaz Elhafen (FIG. 12) that is carved with this scene.[16]

JFM: It struck me as so cruel that this vessel used for social drinking is decorated with this elaborate and beautifully carved imagery of rape.

AHL: And the painting that you made in response, *The Descent* (PAGES 66–69), is one of your largest and most ambitious paintings. It's five panels across and it takes up an entire wall. I love that you chose to render the figures in grisaille,[17] because it at once references the

13 Ovid (43 BCE–17/18 CE) is one of the best-known poets of ancient Rome. His greatest work, a "continuous poem" called *Metamorphoses*, was completed in the year 8 CE. It comprises fifteen books and narrates the history of the world from creation to Ovid's present day. The text is a compilation of over 250 stories explaining the origin of things that came to be through dramatic transformation.

14 In Book 1 of the *Metamorphoses*, Ovid recounts the story of Syrinx, a wood nymph who has taken a vow of virginity in honour of the goddess Artemis. The god Pan tries to rape her, and Syrinx begs a group of river nymphs for help. The nymphs transform her into the reeds that grow on riverbanks; Pan cuts her down and fashions her into a pan flute.

15 Livy, or Titus Livius (59 BCE–17 CE), wrote a monumental history of Rome called *Ab Urbe Condita*. This is the earliest known account of the Rape of the Sabine Women.

16 Ignaz Elhafen (Innsbruck, 1658–Dusseldorf, 1715) was a sculptor who worked for princes in Vienna and Dusseldorf.

17 Art historical term for greyscale.

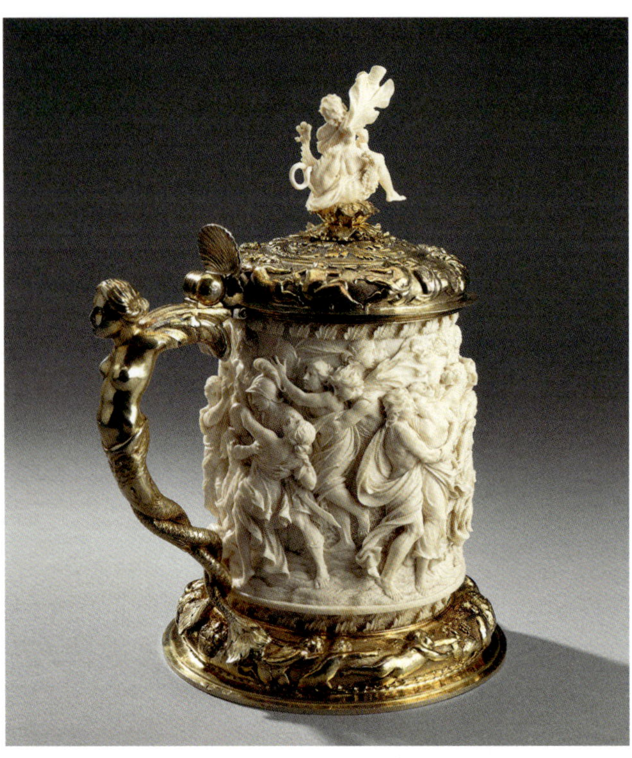

FIG. 12
Ignaz Elhafen (ivory); Octavian Cocssel (silver)
Tankard: The Abduction of the Sabine Women, and Samson and the Lion
1697

ivory of the tankard and also the marble that was used to carve earlier scenes of the same story in the ancient world.

JFM: When I made that composition, I looked at the ivory tankard but I also looked at paintings, friezes, prints, drawings, and sculptures. I rearranged the figures, moving the men to the side so the focus centres on the women and what is happening to them. And I used grisaille to bring all those disparate sources together and make the figures feel monumental, like the sculptures and friezes themselves. The divisions between panels create a third space from which the figures disappear, emerge, or merge into new bodies. The historical works about the rape of the Sabine women seem to celebrate the strength and action of the men. I hope my version tells the story of the women as the main characters.

AHL: Your invitation to empathize with the Sabines reminds me of what you do with Bathsheba and her attendant. Bathsheba is a married woman and a great beauty. Her husband [Uriah] is a general in the army, and King David sees her bathing and sends one of his attendants to summon her. Apparently, after she is summoned, they have sex.[18] I've always interpreted this as rape, even though that's not explicitly stated in the biblical sources. David, to cover up his transgression, sends her husband into battle so that he will die. It sort of makes David's problem go away [when he marries the widowed Bathsheba]. In seventeenth-century paintings, the attendant that David sends is so often a woman, and often a Black woman, even though everyone else in the painting is white, and even though the biblical story, the original source, was created before these racial categories were invented.

JFM: I was struck by that when I saw the Giordano painting in your collection (FIG. 13) on display at the AGO.[19] It doesn't feel that common to see a person of colour represented in historical European painting. We talked about what that choice meant, because you very deliberately considered that in hanging the work, right?

AHL: Yeah. In seventeenth-century Europe, a lot of Black people who are depicted in paintings are enslaved. So, rather than sending a servant, King David is, in this

18 These events are recounted in 2 Samuel 11–12.

19 This is the AGO's painting of Bathsheba bathing, by Luca Giordano, dated c. 1663 (91/88). Giordano (born and died Naples, 1634–1705) was a painter and printmaker who worked in Italy and Spain.

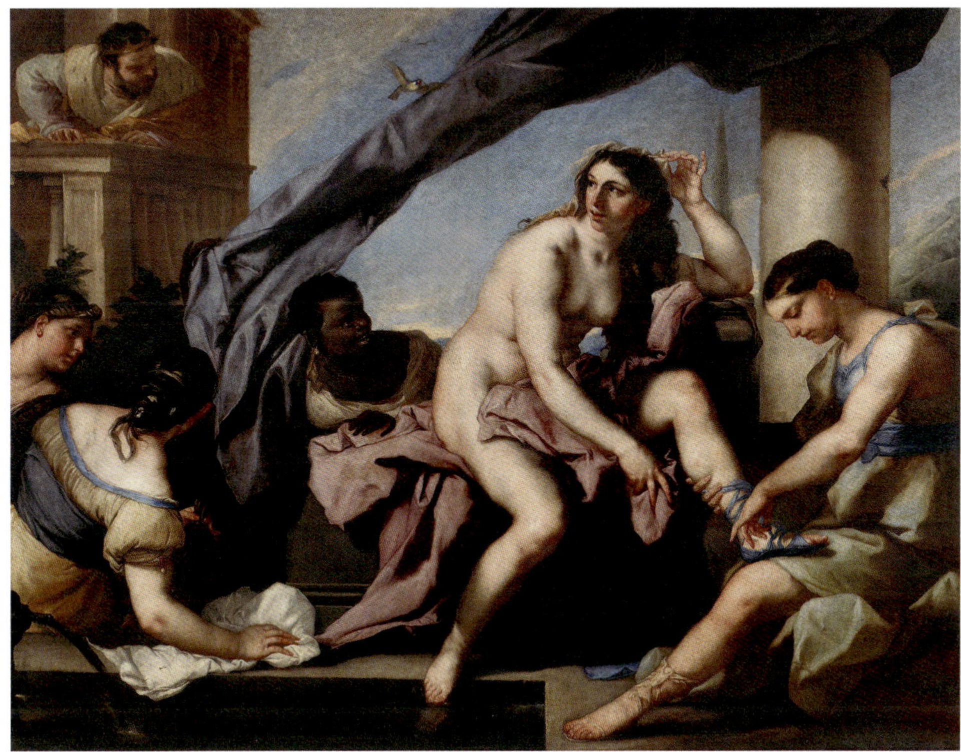

FIG. 13
Luca Giordano
Bathsheba Bathing
c. 1663

context, sending an enslaved woman. Already at that moment, a lot of the anti-Black and misogynist ideas about Black womanhood are constructed to justify European and transatlantic slavery. I think this servant becomes this kind of avatar of lasciviousness and duplicitousness. Giordano includes this woman as a servant being told to perform a task, but she also kicks off this whole story of Bathsheba being raped and her husband being murdered. It's interesting to look at her and ask, What is her life like, and what is it like for her to perform this task? Is she aware of everything that she's setting into motion? And to go back to this idea of women not being alone at these moments: Is she company for Bathsheba?

JFM: I think, too, there are multiple levels of powerlessness depicted in the work. I think you're right to call it rape, because I don't think Bathsheba has the power to refuse, physically or legally—or, frankly, in any way. The servant is in a similar position, but even less empowered, right? But she's also serving this very important role of witnessing.

AHL: What's exciting to me about your practice is that it allows us to look at so many characters in these historical or mythological narratives with newfound empathy and curiosity about what their interior lives are like.

JFM: That's the goal, really! To think about this from their perspective. I thought about that with Syrinx: What kind of desperation would you experience where you would rather be turned into a plant than be raped? And that this woman's terror was subjugated in the narrative, so that the story became all about Pan and how lust is transformed into creative expression. His frustrated desire for Syrinx becomes the impetus for him to cut the reeds and create music—and, how much better is the world now that we have artistic expression, and this is what frustrated lust can lead to: amazing human potential. But what if we just centre the woman in this story and ask, What does that feel like?

AHL: In this painting, where the biblical story is all about Bathsheba but Giordano adds this other woman, it's interesting to ask about both of them: What is it like to be in this painting, or to be in this story, and what is it like to be added by Giordano to, in some ways, be made a villain, for your race and for your gender? David is clearly the actual villain here.

JFM: When we were standing in front of the painting, you said that being in community is hindered by patriarchy, which is totally what we're talking about here: about dividing women against each other.

AHL: You're painting them as a diptych (PAGE 61). The distance between the two paintings, I think, is a nice metaphor for that distance between these two women.

JFM: I agree. Even though they are both victims of this story, they are divided from each other rather than united together.

AHL: I'm interested in how you pick your protagonists. You're making a new body of work that examines the stories of women like Judith, Rachel, Daphne, Echo, and Eve. What draws you to these women?

JFM: Have you ever read Susan Smith's *The Power of Women* (FIG. 14)?[20] She charts this medieval and Renaissance tradition called the Weibermacht, or the "Power of Women," which is considered an inversion of the male-dominated sexual hierarchy. So: works of art illustrate the stories of Judith, Phyllis riding Aristotle,[21] Samson and Delilah, Salome, Yael, and then the witches as well.

AHL: Let's start with Judith. What drew you to her?

JFM: There's such a large set of iconography of Judith.[22] Judith with the head of Holofernes; Judith with the sword. It's interesting to me because it's a representation of a strong woman. She's courageous and heroic. I was looking in the original text, because I often pull titles from the original textual references; from the *Metamorphoses* if it's a mythological story, or from the Bible if it's a biblical story. I also sometimes pull titles from later literary retellings of those stories—from poetry or from, say, a Shakespeare rewrite of a story from Ovid. Looking at those retellings unfolding over time, and their rippling effect, is interesting because it feels like it parallels the repetitions of iconographies in visual arts, too. Anyway, in the biblical text, Judith is not specifically described as having actually seduced Holofernes! She gets him drunk. When he's inebriated, she takes his head off. The text is all about her beauty—that is how she gains entrance to the camp, the way she gets him on his knees. This woman is strong and brave—she has the strength to hack a man's head off with a sword, and the text just keeps talking about how attractive she is! When I was looking at a Judith painting by Jan Massys (FIG. 15),[23] I was interested to see that she's naked, her dress is pulled down around her waist. She's holding the head. It implies that she achieved what she did through the seductive capacities of her body, as opposed to her brain, her brawn, and her cunning.

AHL: Another thing that's interesting to me about that composition of her, bare-chested and holding the decapitated head of Holofernes, is that a lot of ancient sources and Renaissance sources are obsessed with women's capacity to create life. And so breasts especially become a symbol of life-giving and nurturing. This way, Judith is understood as being remarkable because she has this power to give life and to take it.

JFM: I recently saw a Super Bowl ad that was all about boobs. I was watching it with women friends, and at first we couldn't tell what direction it was going. Is this objectifying? At the end a woman orders a coffee, you see a man is staring at her chest, and she's like, "Seriously?" Then the text reads, "So much attention. Yet so ignored." It's all about the boob-obsessed culture we live in, and then inverting that message to say: people are obsessed with boobs and yet not concerned about breast-cancer awareness or women's health.

AHL: Anthropologically speaking, breasts are markers of sexual difference; they're understood as one of the main distinguishing factors between men and women.

JFM: For that reason, it's the area of the body that I feel the least comfortable painting. Probably because breasts are traditionally the focus of the nude paintings that objectify the female body. But if I show somebody's naked butt or back, it's androgynous. It's not necessarily a female body. When there are breasts, it gets to me. It enters into questionable territory: How do you know if this is objectifying or not?

AHL: This reminds me of a line from *Erin Brockovich*.[24] It's one of my favourite movies of all time. Julia Roberts, playing Erin Brockovich, is asked by her older, male boss how had she convinced a government employee to hand over classified documents. She says, "They're called boobs, Ed." It's one of the greatest lines in American cinema, I think. And it also speaks to this idea behind "Judith, how on earth did you disarm this incredible army general?" The male biblical writers are thinking about a task that feels impossible, right? And the biblical answer is: "They're called boobs, Ed."

JFM: I love that. I think that with this artistic convention of Judith undressed, we see this societal need, whether it's to titillate, or to show Holofernes's lust, to explain how Holofernes met his end at the hands of a woman...these are all interesting questions to ask when you see her naked, as opposed to, say, seeing her booking it out of the

20 Susan L. Smith (1947–2021) was a professor at University of California San Diego. Her 1995 book, *The Power of Women: A Topos in Medieval Art and Literature*, expanded on her PhD research at the University of Pennsylvania.

21 The apocryphal Phyllis was a beautiful woman who seduced the philosopher Aristotle, who lost his wits and crawled around like a horse with Phyllis riding him; this was presented as a cautionary tale against lust's capacity to override intellect.

22 Judith's narrative survives in the biblical text named after her. The book of Judith recounts that she was a wise and brave Jewish widow. When her people are besieged by the Assyrian army, she becomes frustrated with the feckless leadership of the men in her community. Taking matters into her own hands, she gains the trust of their general, Holofernes. One night, she gets him drunk, and when he passes out, she cuts his head off. The Assyrian army panics and deserts the siege, and Judith saves her people.

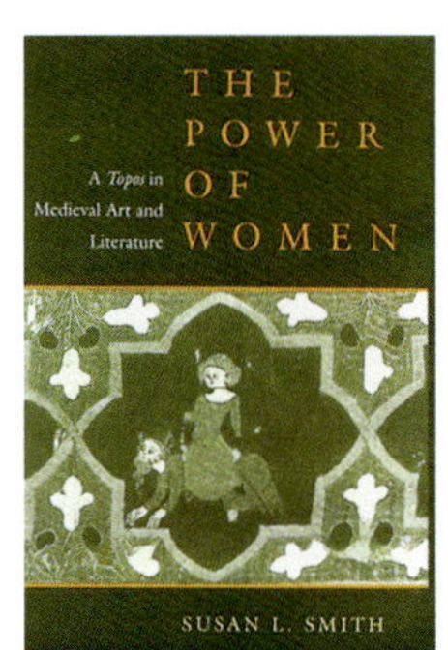

FIG. 14
Book cover of
The Power of Women
by Susan L. Smith

army camp fully clothed. But I learn a lot by returning to the original text from which these stories come. I didn't grow up with a religious tradition. I didn't go to Sunday school or Jewish school, so I didn't learn these stories in that way. I've experienced them more just through art history, through images. I have this understanding of them, which I think is similar to what most people have, right? You just see this in the museum, and you're like, "She cut his head off?!" Looking them up is really illuminating about the gender beliefs at the time these stories were created. That's what's interesting to me, [that and] hopefully trying to elucidate that to the audience as well. So, through my little education process, I get to share that information with others. For instance, with Rachel, I only came across her story because of an amazing painting.

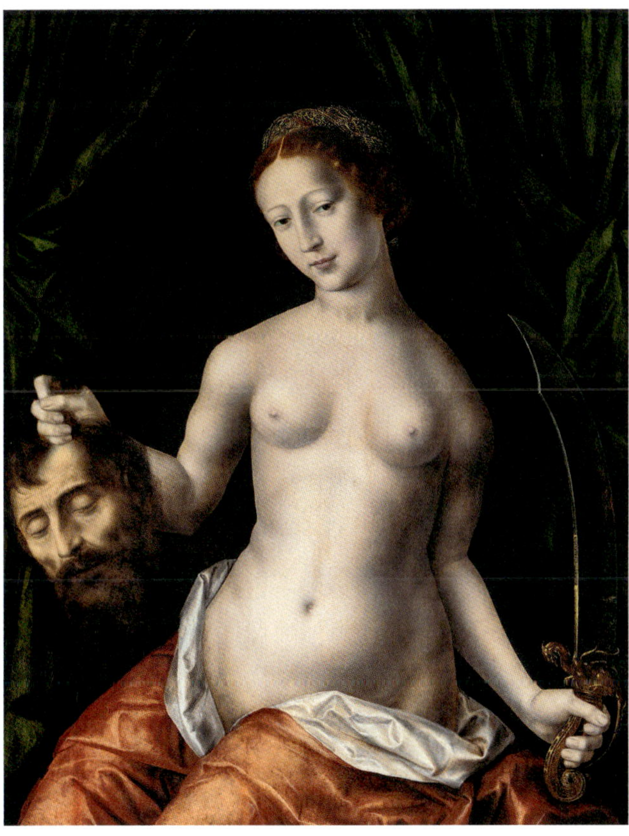

FIG. 15
Jan Massys
Judith with the Head of Holofernes
1543

23 Jan Massys (born and died Antwerp, c. 1510–1575).

24 *Erin Brockovich* (2000), directed by Steven Soderbergh, tells the story of an American legal researcher who mounts an unprecedented class-action lawsuit against an electric company that poisoned a community's drinking water.

25 Rachel's narrative appears in Genesis 29–35.

26 Francesco Furini (born and died Florence, c. 1600–1646). Several versions of this composition survive, but the best is in the Alte Pinakothek, Munich.

27 While caesarean-section births had been common earlier, it was only in the 1500s that medical practitioners understood the procedure well enough to preserve the lives of both mother and child.

AHL: Can you tell me the story?

JFM: Rachel is one of Jacob's wives.[25] Leah, Rachel's sister, is also married to Jacob. Leah is the fertile one, and she's having baby after baby. Rachel is jealous and bereft and praying to God for a baby. And she finally becomes a mother. She has Joseph, then she conceives again and dies in childbirth, and that son, Benjamin, is Jacob's favourite son. There is this amazing painting by the Italian painter Furini called *The Birth of Benjamin and the Death of Rachel* (FIG. 16).[26] The maid in that painting is actually this figure. [Points to a nearby painting in the studio.] But what's happening here, where her dress is being stitched up? I read an article that was saying they think this is a reference to caesarean section, which was a brand-new procedure at the time.[27] I asked my friend Clarissa Esguerra, who's a curator of costume at LACMA, if it made any sense that there would be a seam in this part of her dress? She said, "No, that makes no sense." This is not appropriate to that garment. So you have this biblical story that's being retold at this particular moment in the seventeenth century, talking, in a way, about medical treatments now available to women, or the risks and dangers of those treatments. Can you imagine the pain of a caesarean section at that time? I do think in the beginning that procedure was really about saving the baby. The mother was going to die, but this was a way of saving the child, at least.

When I came across this painting, I wanted to know more about it and then read up on Rachel and thought it was a poignant story, because I think that's what's lost in a lot of this discussion around abortion rights and pregnancy. I spent a year trying to conceive and had a miscarriage before I had my first child. It's very emotional and very real, her longing for a child and then her tragic death as a result of it. It's just a moving, heartbreaking story that I think we can relate to now. We think we're not that similar to these people, but they were just people, same as us.

AHL: The other thing that hasn't changed is that women have always been accessing abortion, which is a thing that we've talked about before and is fascinating to think about. For probably all the history encompassed in your body of work that we're talking about, which is over

2,000 years with these ancient stories, women have been accessing abortion and contraception. Before 1588, abortion was widely accepted early on in pregnancy, before forty days of pregnancy.[28] And that's really fascinating because that number, forty days, comes up in current anti-abortion legislation in the United States. Which is scary! People are using ancient ideas to make laws about whether a fetus has been granted a soul.

JFM: Six weeks is now a common limit, after which women can't get an abortion in certain states. That's forty-two days, and just four weeks after a missed period.[29]

AHL: You've been studying plants used for women's health. Can you say a little about that?

JFM: To learn more of the history, I read this book, *Eve's Herbs*, by John M. Riddle (FIG. 17).[30] His argument is that in medieval times, women possessed incredible medicinal plant knowledge. They knew what plants to use for contraception, what they could use for abortion, and what they could use for lactation support, to help after the birth. All stages of women's health. There's this woman called Trota (FIG. 19) who authored a gynecological, women's health text.[31] There's a lot in her text about regulating the menstrual cycle, it's a lot of different things that women did to take care of their own health using plant medicine. Riddle's argument in *Eve's Herbs* is that around the Renaissance, this knowledge sort of falls away, with the rise of the medical profession and male doctors taking over from female healers and casting

28 This idea comes originally from ancient Greek philosophy and is the belief that when an expectant mother first felt a fetus moving in her uterus, this signalled the arrival of the soul.

29 At the time of writing, twelve states in the US had such laws in effect.

30 John M. Riddle, *Eve's Herbs: A History of Contraception and Abortion in the West*, first published by Harvard University Press in 1997.

31 Trota of Salerno was a healer and medical writer in the 1100s. She is the probable author of three texts on women's medicine that are collectively called *The Trotula*.

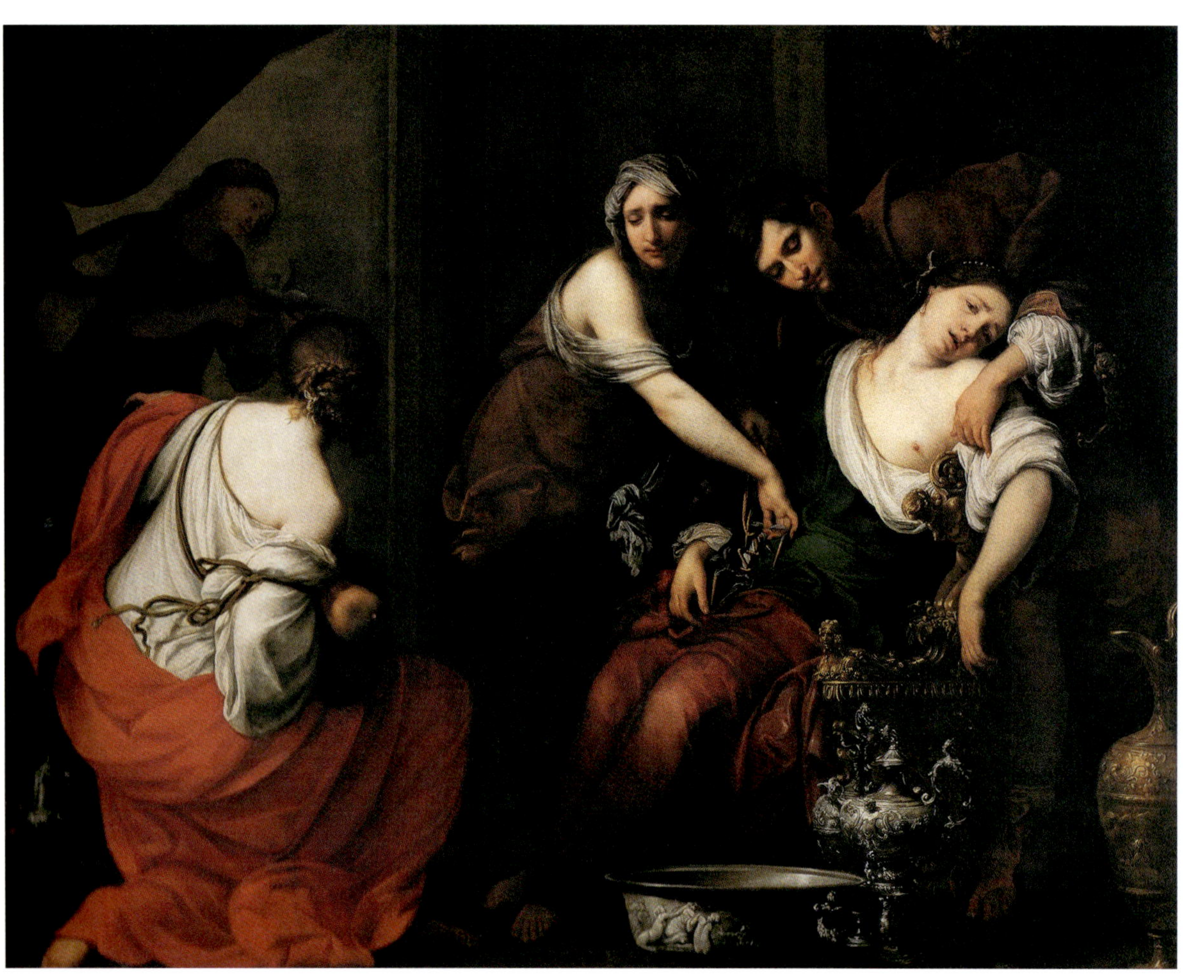

FIG. 16
Francesco Furini
The Birth of Benjamin and the Death of Rachel
first half of 17th century

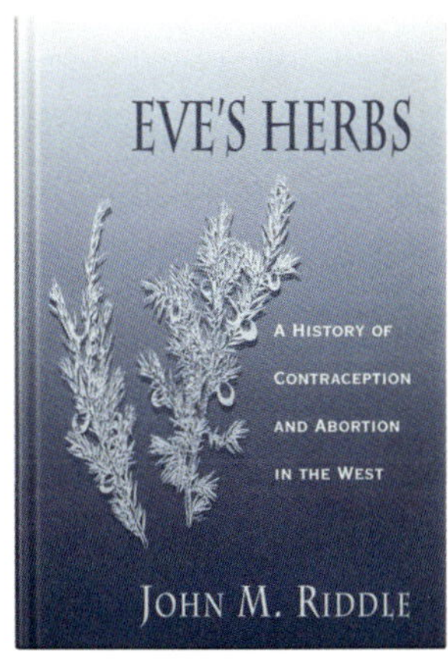

FIG. 17
Book cover of
Eve's Herbs
by John M. Riddle

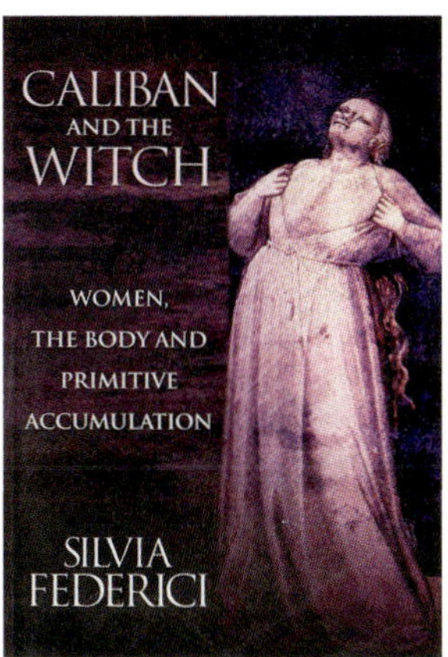

FIG. 18
Book cover of
Caliban and the Witch
by Silvia Federici

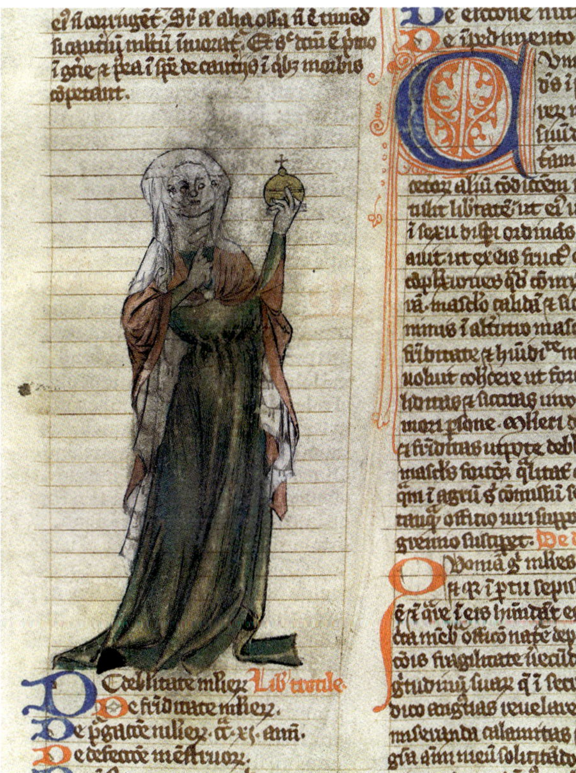

FIG. 19
Detail of an illuminated manuscript featuring a female healer (Trota), holding urine flask, 14th century

doubt on them. And I've also been reading *Caliban and the Witch* by Silvia Federici (FIG. 18), which really ties it all to capitalism... and she's arguing that with the rise of capitalism there was a need to build a labour force, which requires reproduction.[32] So it's all tied together: "Be fruitful and multiply" suddenly becomes: make more capitalistic subjects to work so the people on top get richer. It's relevant to the moment we're living through now, in terms of this huge wealth disparity in the US, and the rise of this oligarchy and Donald Trump... this big backlash against the kind of cultural progress that has been made up to this point. We think of rights as gradually increasing, hopefully, especially in this era where we're so "contemporary" and "civilized," but now that we have access to safe and reliable medical treatment, they're stripping away rights women had for millennia.

Riddle also talks about how the Supreme Court made its *Roe v. Wade* decision, and I thought that was fascinating. The judges took a historical view, and they concluded that in the nineteenth century, women had more access to abortion than they did in the twentieth. They looked at historical precedent, and it seems like it wasn't even really considered a crime unless the baby had already quickened, which would happen around fifteen or sixteen weeks, when you start to feel the baby moving. If a woman did take a potion after that point, they weren't going to be really penalized. It wasn't what we have now where they're saying, "You'll be arrested, your doctor will be arrested"—all this nonsense, depending on what state you're in.

AHL: And even treating women who miscarry with suspicion of crime, which feels so cruel.

JFM: It is so cruel. The reality is there's very little difference, physically. One of the herbs growing on the forest floor in *Natural Order* (PAGE 91) is Artemisia, also known as mugwort (FIG. 21). And then one of the witches is holding fennel (FIG. 20). Fennel was something they used as an aphrodisiac; there was this idea that it would help with conception. Artemisia was used as a woman's health plant, generally. I think it was an emmenagogue, like a menstruation-producing herb, and it's named after the Greek goddess of war, Artemis. And then there's Artemisia Gentileschi, of course, such a wonderful

32 Silvia Federici's *Caliban and the Witch: Women, the Body and Primitive Accumulation* (Autonomedia, 2004).

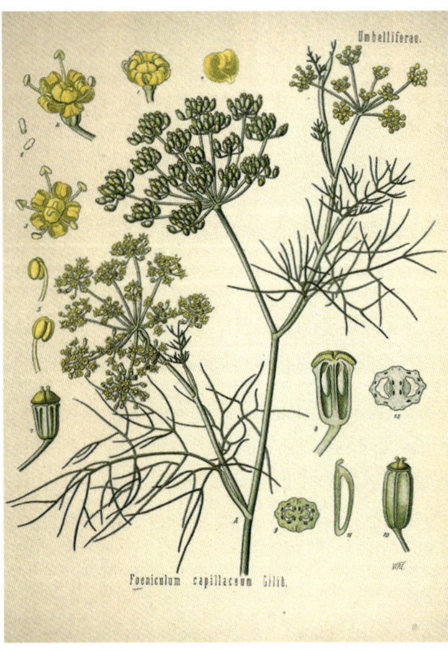

FIG. 20
Fennel (Foeniculum vulgare)
in *Köhler's Medizinal-Pflanzen*, vol. 2
1890

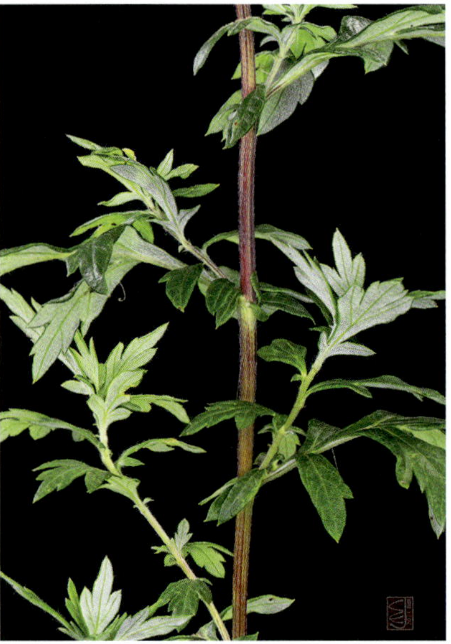

FIG. 21
Mugwort (Artemisia vulgaris)

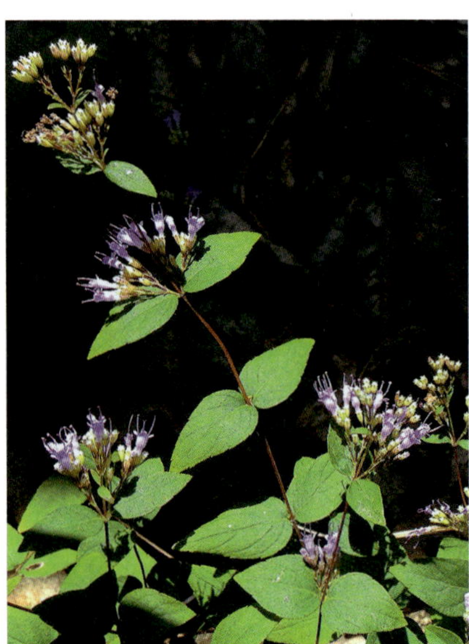

FIG. 22
Dittany (Cunila origanoides)

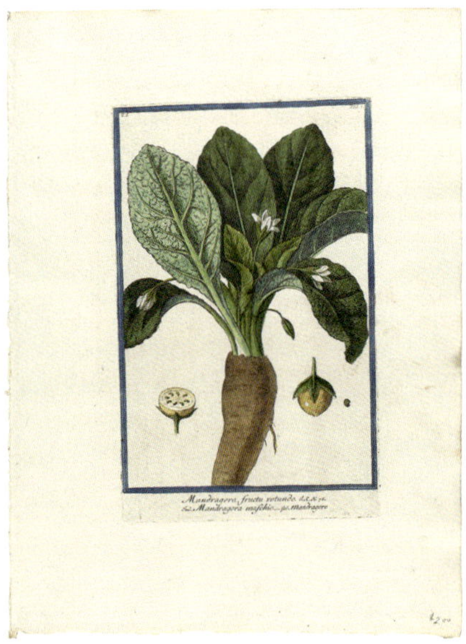

FIG. 23
Magdalena Bouchard (after Cesare Ubertini)
Mandrake (Mandragora Fructu Rotundo)
from Giorgio Bonelli's *Hortus Romanus*, vol. 1
1772

painter who painted all the powerful women from the Power of Women series.[33]

In the second painting I did with these plants, *Old Magic* (PAGE 92), I drew from a painting that shows this witch seated outside, drinking from a flask. In the original she's got her hand pointing down, but it's not really pointing at anything. I added some plants on the ground: dittany (FIG. 22), which is a powerful abortifacient, and mandrake (FIG. 23), which was used as a talisman. It was believed that if you slept with it under your pillow, it would have magical effects. The root is shaped like a human body. If you ingest the plant, you'll feel its hallucinogenic and sedating properties. It was used as an abortifacient, but when people accused women of being witches, they accused them of using mandrake in their concoctions. Also, there was a religious belief that women should suffer pain and childbirth because of Original Sin. Sometimes these herbalists would try to help women, like midwives. The *Trotula*, a treatise, argued that healers should give women something for the pain—that it's not a religious sin to help women in pain.

AHL: It's said that the Virgin Mary did not experience pain during childbirth. But one of the most profound cruelties I've ever read about was this belief in the Middle Ages that Mary experienced all the pain of childbirth at the moment of Christ's death. Often when we see her at the foot of the Crucifixion, she's doubled over. It's a pose that almost looks like her water is breaking, or like she's having a contraction (FIG. 24).[34] It's not just anguish. She's often grabbing at her stomach; sometimes it looks like she's in labour. Which seems so profoundly, well, cruel to me. To imagine that her kind of psychic loss would be coupled with pain at the same time.

JFM: We're talking actual physical pain?

AHL: Yes. Isn't that horrific? Men can only end life. Women can create it, and I think that is just profoundly threatening to men and embarrassing to men—embarrassing to them that they are reliant on women, even though they actively and frantically perpetuate this myth that women are weak and need to be governed. Women are capable of a thing that men can't even dream of. It's interesting that the sixteenth century, as you say, sees this new regulation against abortion and this is kind of the same moment that your source imagery starts to appear. Depictions of men and women interacting with each other, especially in myth and in biblical narrative, really start to proliferate in ways that inspire you and your work.

One thing that's especially interesting to me is the male gaze in both art-making and, specifically, in patronage. For whom are these paintings made? Who's doing the looking? Why are these women, who are often fearsome in the story, exposing their breasts and posed to tantalize or titillate? I don't know—how do you wade through these paintings that in many ways weren't made for you?

JFM: I feel a real connection to oil painting. This is the practice that called to me; physically it is what I can manipulate the best of all the media I've tried. Oil painting comes from this period in Europe, and you see its transformation in the Renaissance: "Oh, now we can depict things realistically." We have this incredible ability to create the illusion of space and to model flesh so convincingly and beautifully, because that is something that oil paint can do. There are a lot of oil painters who don't feel the same kind of obsession that I feel with the roots of the medium and what it's been used for. I'm interested in what we can learn about our culture from looking at the historical images we inherited from this European painting tradition. What does it teach us about how women were viewed then, or what the gender dynamics were like? What does it teach us about these narratives that kind of sculpt our history and are retold so many different times and ways? These are like cultural touchstones, so that's what I'm interested in. Some people are interested in writing. I'm just very interested in images. I think they have this way of making the past feel alive and relevant and still resonant, because you can see what people were wearing, you can see how they did their hair, how they presented themselves, how they fashioned themselves. Very few women were able to paint at that time. The ones who did were usually the children of other painters and had access to training. There are no such restrictions now, and the viewership has changed. It's no longer only the privileged who can see paintings. This is something we can access at every museum in the country, all around the world. My hope is that I can comment on gender dynamics from that era by appropriating poses and pieces from these old compositions and making something new out of them. By doing so, it can help us look at how far we've come—and how far we haven't—in this moment.

AHL: This feels like a good time to talk about Magdalene and the Magdalene workhouses. *Bitter Seeds* (PAGE 55) draws on seventeenth-century painting in colour and then has these grisaille paintings mixed together. Can you tell me about that piece and what you were studying while you were working on it? First, what is a Magdalene laundry?

JFM: They were run by the Catholic Church in Ireland into the twentieth century, and they were places where women pregnant outside of wedlock could be incarcerated to work as punishment for their sins.[35] It was also a place where women who were old and unmarried might be sent.

AHL: That's a crime, too?

JFM: Then, yeah, basically. And sex workers as well. There were often orphanages alongside. So, if a pregnant woman was held at a laundry, she would be forced to do labour, and when she gave birth, the baby would be taken away from her and raised by nuns in the orphanage. The children and the mothers were not allowed to interact, which just feels extremely cruel, and the women couldn't leave if they wanted to. They were held against their will, and they were treated terribly. And they were called the Magdalenes, a reference to Mary Magdalene, who was the closest female follower of Jesus and who was mistakenly associated with a former sex worker in the Bible. That confusion came through some sermon around the year 500 or something,[36] where Mary of Bethany is conflated with Mary Magdalene and all of a sudden her reputation has completely changed. You had told me that maybe she was just a wealthy widow who was close to Jesus?

AHL: Yes! A bunch of Marys get collapsed.

33 Artemisia Gentileschi (Rome, 1593–Naples, 1653) is widely regarded as one of the greatest Italian Baroque painters. She was the first woman to gain admission to Florence's Accademia delle Arti del Disegno.

34 An excellent essay on this subject is Amy Neff's "The Pain of *Compassio*: Mary's Labor at the Foot of the Cross," published in *The Art Bulletin* in 1998.

35 The first Magdalene laundry in Ireland opened in Dublin in 1767.

36 Eliza Griswold recently wrote a thorough history of this confusion. "Mistaking Mary Magdalene" was published in *The New Yorker* on April 19, 2025.

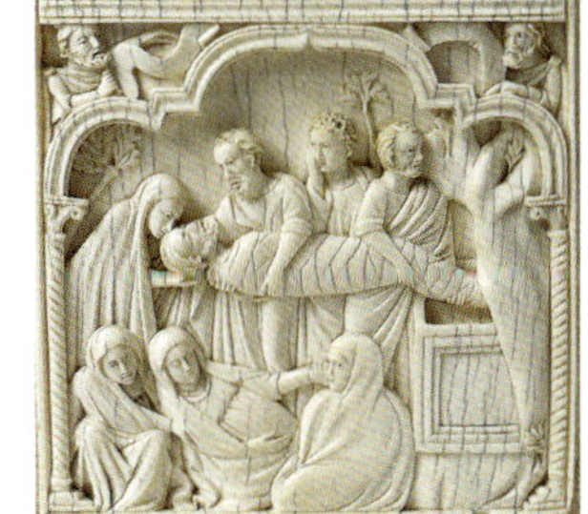

FIG. 24
Italian (Venice or Padua)
The Betrayal and Arrest of Christ, and The Entombment
late 14th century

JFM: It seems like a really effective takedown of this woman who was the closest follower of Jesus, to recast her as a sex worker and to diminish her, and what you wind up with is a lot of paintings in the seventeenth century depicting the penitent Mary Magdalene, where she's punishing herself or she is praying for forgiveness.

AHL: Yes! Wearing a hair shirt (FIG. 25) to torture herself. Can you say a little about the grisaille paintings in *Bitter Seeds*?

JFM: When I first started exhibiting my work, I was working from more contemporary pop cultural imagery. For the past eight years or so, it's been all references from 1500 to 1850. These grisaille images of the Magdalenes were the first images more recent than the nineteenth century that I have felt drawn to paint in almost a decade. But these felt different because they were real people, private people, not famous. The images that I painted are mostly extracted from a ten-minute film that was made inside one of these laundries (FIG. 26).[37] They are very grainy images from the original black-and-white film. I hoped that the lack of focus helped preserve the anonymity of these women.

AHL: Another kind of trope of womanhood in Christian history is the martyr saint. Saint Agatha features prominently in the show.[38] My academic research is on martyr saints, so I'm always thinking about them. It seems like Christianity has two ideals for women: one is a virgin mother, which is impossible, and the other is, well, dead. Those are the kinds of women that were heroine-ized in Christianity. And so, yeah, there are tons of these martyr saints and virgin martyrs, especially young women who have horrible things happen to them—and who happen to have never had sex. Agatha is one of these early Christians who lives in a dominant pagan society and refuses to practise the pagan religion. As punishment for her faith and her commitment to her faith, she has her breasts cut off. Agatha's trauma stands out as being particularly horrifying, but there's also the strange way she is lionized for this. What are these women like for you? What do you make of them?

37 A parish priest named Jack Delany (1906–1980) owned a film camera with which he documented life in working-class Dublin. His footage from the Magdalene laundry at the Our Lady of Charity Convent during the 1940s is thought to be the only footage of life in a Magdalene laundry and is today owned by the Irish Film Institute.

38 Saint Agatha was an early convert to Christianity at a time when the religion was banned. She committed her life to her faith and took a vow of virginity. A man tried to convince her to break her vow, betray her faith, and marry him. Eventually he turned her over to the authorities, who subjected her to a series of tortures, including having her breasts cut off, in the hopes that she would eventually abandon her religion and marry a non-Christian. She is the patron saint of breast cancer patients and rape survivors.

39 Ludovico Carracci's *Saint Sebastian Thrown into the Cloaca Maxima* (1612). The Cloaca Maxima was the sewer system of ancient Rome. Roman soldiers dumped Sebastian's body in the sewer so that he could not be afforded a Christian burial.

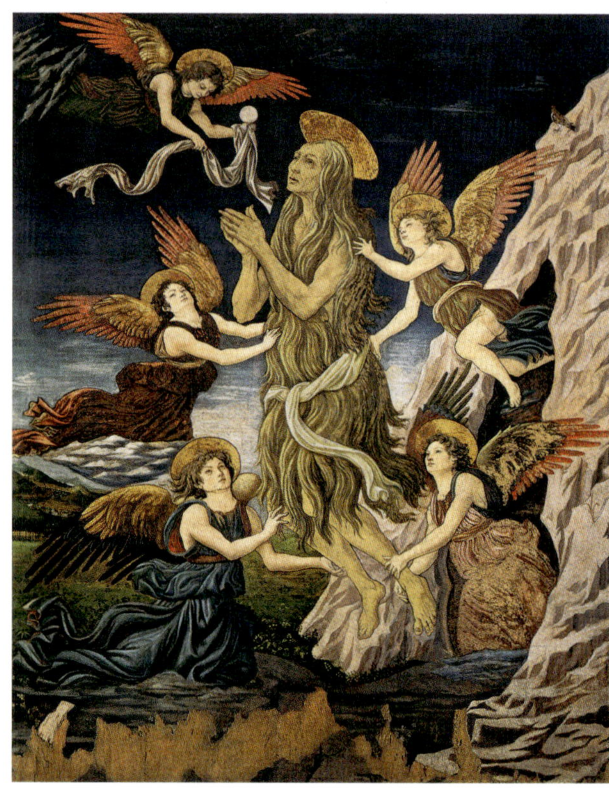

FIG. 25
Antonio del Pollaiuolo
Mary Magdalene communicated by Angels
c. 1460

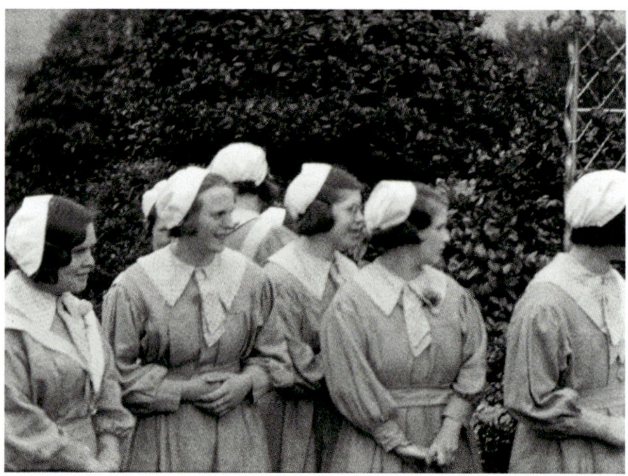

FIG. 26
Father Jack Delany
Magdalene Laundry
1940s

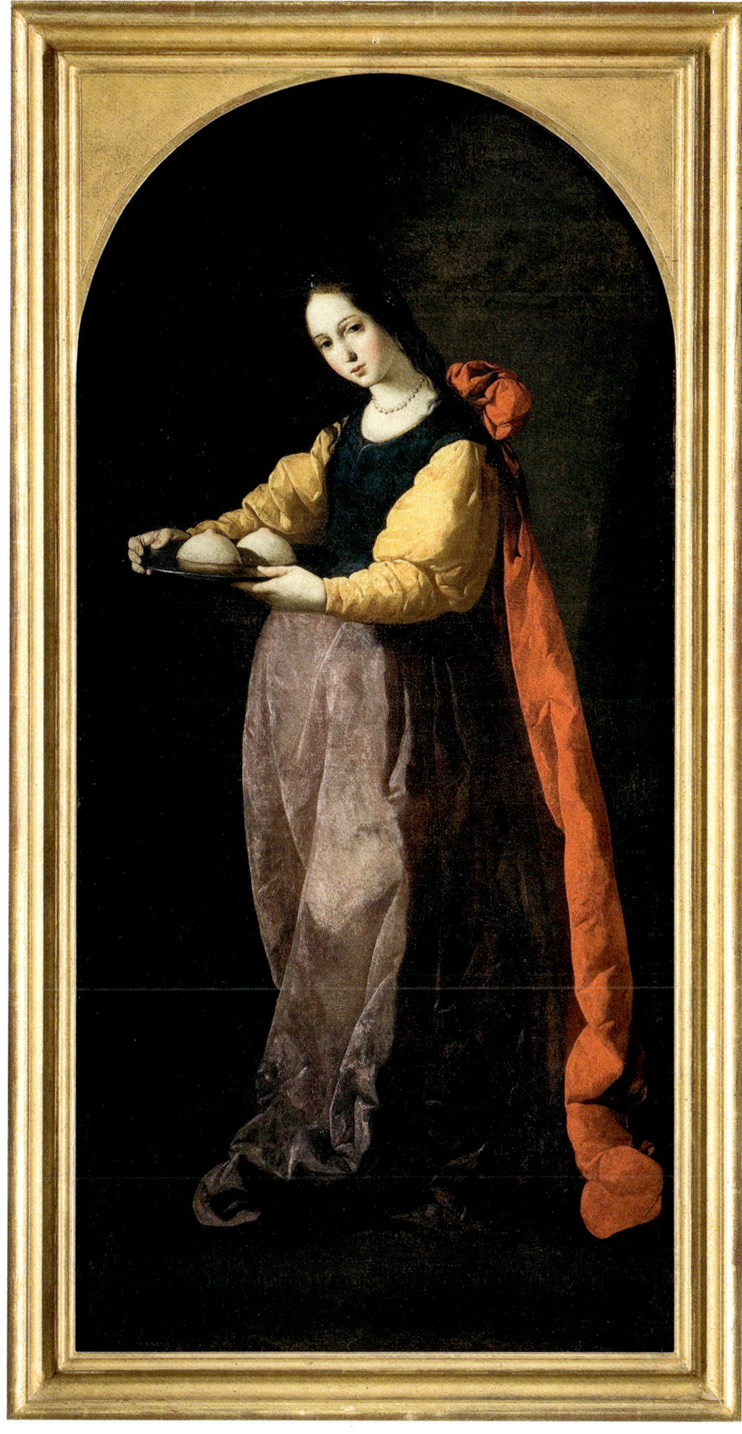

FIG. 27
Francisco de Zurbarán
Saint Agatha [*Sainte Agathe*]
c. 1635–1640

JFM: One of the most interesting things is the way they're painted in art history (FIG. 27). A portrait of Saint Agatha might show her as serene, with her breasts exposed, holding the pinchers that are going to be used against her. It's this celebration of the woman that doesn't acknowledge her suffering, right? Sometimes there is a lot of blood and gore, but often she is calmly holding her severed breasts on a platter. What caught my interest was that contradiction between the peaceful serenity and the torture and pain she was subjected to, and also the misogynist ways in which they are harmed. To cut off her breasts—it's just such a gendered form of violence.

AHL: Yeah, there are no male saints who have their penises cut off. What happens to Agatha after she has her breasts cut off?

JFM: She goes to jail and Saint Peter comes and heals her, and then the day before she's supposed to be executed, an earthquake hits or something. She survives! Then she dies in prison after a long time. It's not a happy ending, but the thing she's known for is not the thing that kills her in the end.

AHL: That is an interesting thing about storytelling and the parts we remember. You paint these moments that I think are the titular moments, or the archetypical moment that draws our collective memory back to these famous women, but you also then read these stories that often contain far more nuance when you go back to the original source. Recently, I was reminded by my friend Aoife Brady, a curator at the National Gallery of Ireland, that Saint Sebastian wasn't killed by arrows, he survives after they try to execute him with a bow and arrow! That's his big miracle, and then he ends up getting clubbed to death.

JFM: And thrown in a sewer!

AHL: The Cloaca Maxima! Do you know that Getty painting of Sebastian getting dumped in the Cloaca Maxima (FIG. 28)?[39]

JFM: I made a painting that referenced it! Mine is called *Outcast* (FIG. 29). I was interested in it because it's the only

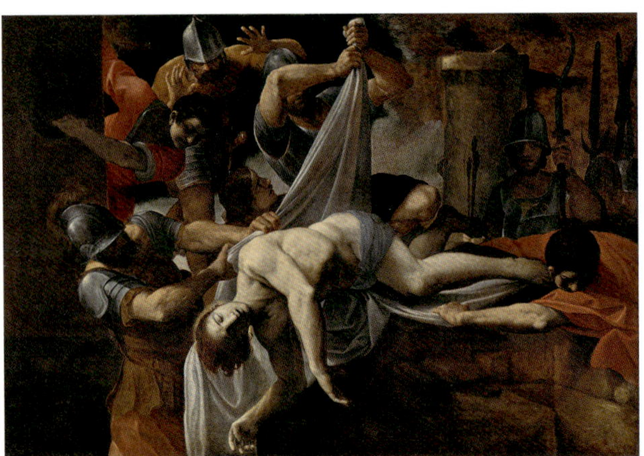

FIG. 28
Ludovico Carracci
Saint Sebastian Thrown into the Cloaca Maxima
1612

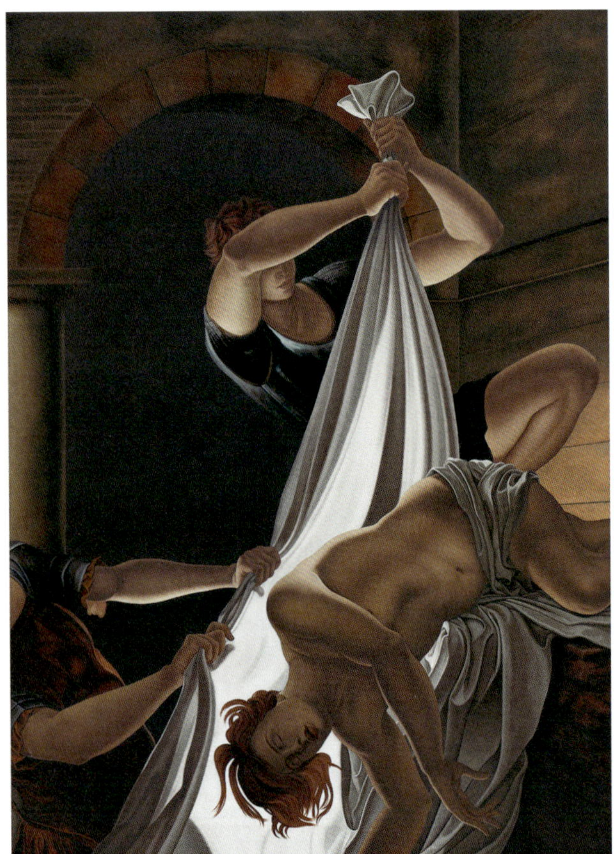

FIG. 29
Jesse Mockrin
Outcast
2021–2022

40 The story of Lilith does not come from the Bible but instead appears in later medieval sources. Lilith is believed to have been Adam's first wife, who refused to serve her husband and fled the Garden of Eden and eventually becomes a child-snatching witch.

painting I found that depicts his true death. And yeah, how degrading to be thrown into the sewer!

AHL: Tell me about Echo.

JFM: She's a figure from Greco-Roman mythology. When Zeus [Jupiter in Roman mythology] comes down from the mountaintop to have affairs, he has her intervene for him and go talk to Hera [Juno], his wife, and keep her distracted. When Hera learns this, she cuts out Echo's tongue, I think—maybe it's not so physical. Maybe she just does magic on her, but they liked their physical violence, so maybe she did cut her tongue out. Anyway, she makes it so that Echo can only repeat the last word that she hears. Echo falls in love with Narcissus, but she can only repeat him, and then he tragically falls in love with his own image, and it's just a romance that doesn't end well for anybody. But I thought it was an interesting chance to interrogate power. How much power does Echo have when the king of the gods is telling her to do something? And how unfortunate that women are pitted against each other in stories like this.

AHL: Greek mythology feels particularly bad for this. You know, I think about Medusa, who is raped by Poseidon in Athena's temple. Athena punishes Medusa, not Poseidon, for desecrating her temple. Saying that it's Medusa's beauty that caused her rape, Athena makes her ugly as a punishment. It does feel like there is this misplaced anger in Greek mythology where women very rarely hold men accountable.

JFM: That's probably the way men would like it. In Silvia Federici's book, she talks a lot about how, before early modern witch hunts, women lived more communally and worked together. They did chores together. The witch hunts separated women from each other. They banned gossip, and they accused all women speaking to each other of gossiping. They didn't want women socializing with each other. Women needed to be at home working, they needed to be subservient. They couldn't talk or talk back. It's just a way in which women are pitted against each other in the structures we live under. It's about the consolidation of patriarchal power. And how can you rebel if you can't speak to someone else?

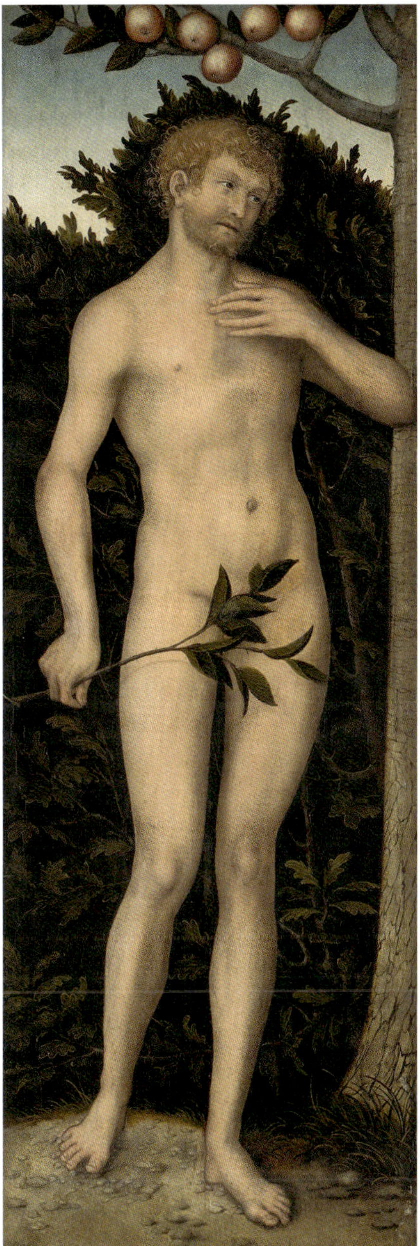
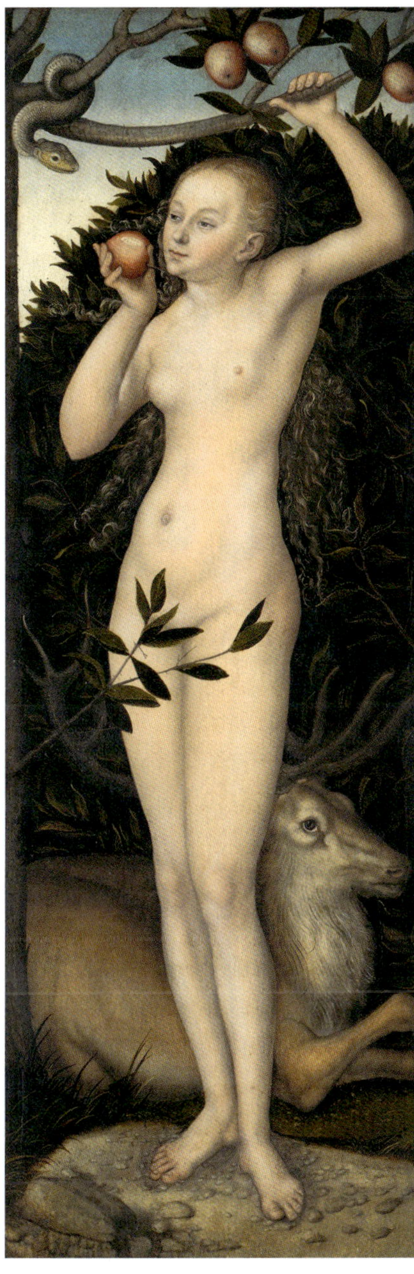

FIG. 30
Lucas Cranach the Elder
Adam and Eve
1533–1537

Federici argues that the witch hunts are how women were terrorized and brought to heel; women would see other women being publicly punished or murdered. It is ironic that the witch became the optimistic point of view in this exhibition, because Europe's witch hunts were an astounding episode of misogynist violence, with some historians estimating between 500,000 and a million women killed. This is femicide—the murder of women. What happened was that this craft of women, this knowledge of healing and the solidarity amongst women, became something to attack, and women became separated from their knowledge of the natural world. So I was looking back at maybe the before times, or reinterpreting these images of witchy women as positive from a feminist point of view, so that they are women who have agency, who are empowered, who take care of each other, and who have this connection to the natural world that nurtures them and cares for them, that they can use in a magical —or maybe not so magical—way.

AHL: It's interesting to ask: Was Judith not a witch?

JFM: Yeah, exactly. What about Eve? Then I realized that Lilith is the first witch, but isn't Eve also a witch?[40]

AHL: Absolutely. And she's punished for it. She craves more knowledge than she's given. She's aware of the limitations of her knowledge, and she seeks more knowledge, even if it means taking a risk.

JFM: Thinking about her desire for knowledge, you can look at the rise of witch hunts as the desire to deprive women of knowledge, even the knowledge of their own bodies, to strip it away. I was thinking of her and Adam, especially the way they're depicted in historical art: they're often standing nude figures, Eve and Adam, like the witches. Eve is also shown with the snake. Sometimes Adam and Eve are shown with animals (FIG. 30). Witches are also shown with animals. The sexuality of women is very troubling in the eyes of the people creating these paintings. Eve's sexuality is the whole problem, right? She wants knowledge. And this is a sin. So, in my work, I was asking: What if the knowledge she craved was the knowledge of, say, plants that would allow her to have sex with her husband for pleasure?

AHL: It's interesting to look at the sixteenth century for a second and think about what's happening then around groups of women. For instance, the Protestant Reformation does away with convent life. Convents are this amazing place of refuge. Where women can practise intellectualism, where women can write, women can publish. But also where women exist in a hierarchy of power where they are self-governing and self-sustaining. Luther famously married a nun (FIG. 31). He was a monk and he married a nun, and they symbolically and literally broke the structures of monastic life. I like that there's this deep fear of what's going on behind convent walls in that moment.[41]

JFM: I read that Luther said that all the nuns should come out of their convents and marry and reproduce, because that is God's will. Then he said, from some mistaken belief, that bearing children was healthy for women's bodies, and that if women don't, they'd suffer from a wandering womb. Effectively threatening that women who don't engage in intercourse and reproduction would get sick.[42] There's a quote attributed to him where he says that it's better for women to bear children to death than to not bear children at all. In his view, the way to fix femininity is to keep a woman pregnant, busy with children, tethered to the home and to the traditional structure of marriage, a role of subservience and parenting.

AHL: But at the same time there is this tremendous obsession with a woman's virginity.

JFM: I've been reading about the life of Artemisia [Gentileschi], who was raped, and I did not know there was such a legal emphasis placed on virginity at the time (around 1610). The laws against rape were not about the illegality of sexual violence. The crime of rape at that time was the taking of a woman's virginity.[43]

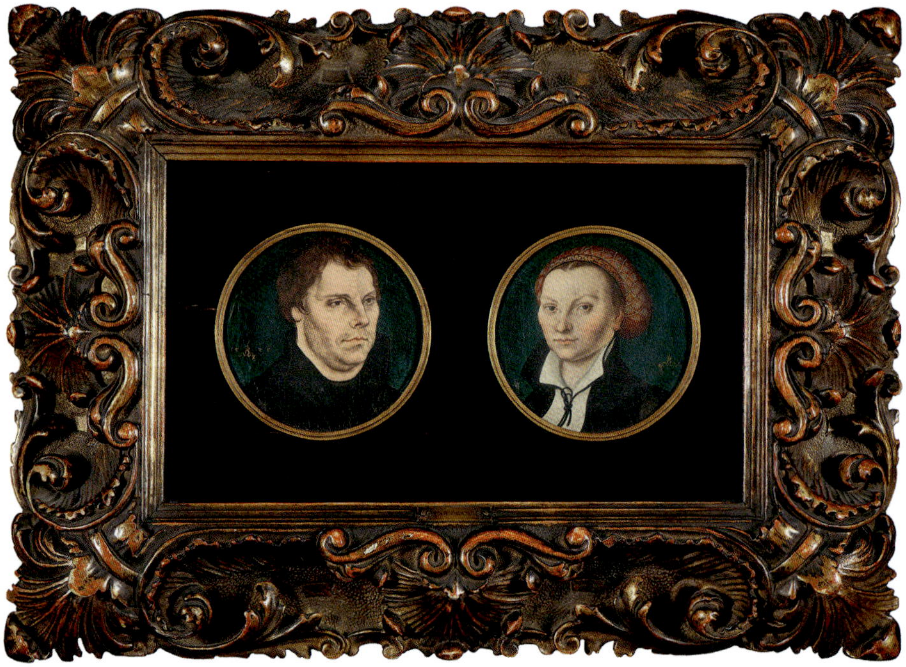

FIG. 31
Lucas Cranach the Elder
Portraits of Martin Luther and His Wife, Katharina von Bora
1472–1553

41 Martin Luther married Katharina von Bora in 1525. She was one of twelve nuns smuggled out of a Cistercian convent two years earlier.

42 This refers to a medieval concept called "The Wandering Womb." Essentially, medieval anatomists believed that the uterus was not fixed in place but migrated around the body, and in particular places caused maladies and misalignment. When the woman was gravid, however, the uterus rested in its correct place, and so the woman was most regulated and healthiest and happiest when pregnant.

43 In 1611, fellow artist Agostino Tassi raped Artemisia Gentileschi in her painting studio. When Tassi refused to marry Artemisia, her father, Orazio Gentileschi, took Tassi to court. The transcripts from the seven-month-long court proceedings survive and have been studied extensively. The judge ordered Artemisia to be tortured in case she had fabricated her story. While Tassi was found guilty, he was not punished.

44 Elizabeth S. Cohen published an analysis of the court transcripts in a 2000 issue of the *Sixteenth Century Journal*.

AHL: It essentially amounts to destruction of the father's property, right?

JFM: Yeah. In that time, the crime could be either "rape with consent," or rape as violent defloration. The word is *defloration*. When I was first reading this, I thought, "Oh, they cared about rape," because there were punishments associated with the crime. And then as I kept reading, I realized that, no, they did not care about women. This is something else. It was like you said: it was not really the crime against the woman that they were concerned about. It was the devaluing of that piece of property.

AHL: I believe the punishment sometimes was marrying the woman that they raped...?

JFM: That's what happens with Artemisia. She doesn't marry him, but she wants to. These cultural beliefs were so strong that the only way to save herself would be to marry her rapist. After he violently rapes her, she goes on to sleep with him willingly. And how willingly, is the question. Because it seems that she believes she had to do that in order to get him to marry her, which is what she needed to protect her status in society and to adhere to her religious values.

AHL: One of the reasons that we know so much about Artemisia's life is because the transcripts from her trial survive in the archives.[44] The fact that we can read that alongside this huge body of work by one of the greatest painters of the seventeenth century is just surreal. What does she mean for you? When you think about her paintings of women like Judith, for instance. What kind of place does she occupy in your psyche?

JFM: I admire her and her work so much. She's so tremendously talented, a better painter than her dad, much better than a lot of her peers. She isn't just an unusual figure—a successful woman painter when there were so few—she's one of the best painters who ever painted. When you look at her paintings (FIG. 32), you can feel things from a female perspective. You can see that, say, a boob has weight because she observed real breasts, probably on her own body. She depicted these stories we have been discussing, where women are victimized or where women are empowered. The paintings don't ever feel objectifying to me. Sometimes on my way to the studio in the morning, I will be hoping that something dried well overnight, and I'll say a little prayer to the gods of oil painting for their assistance. Recently, I've just been calling on Artemisia.◆

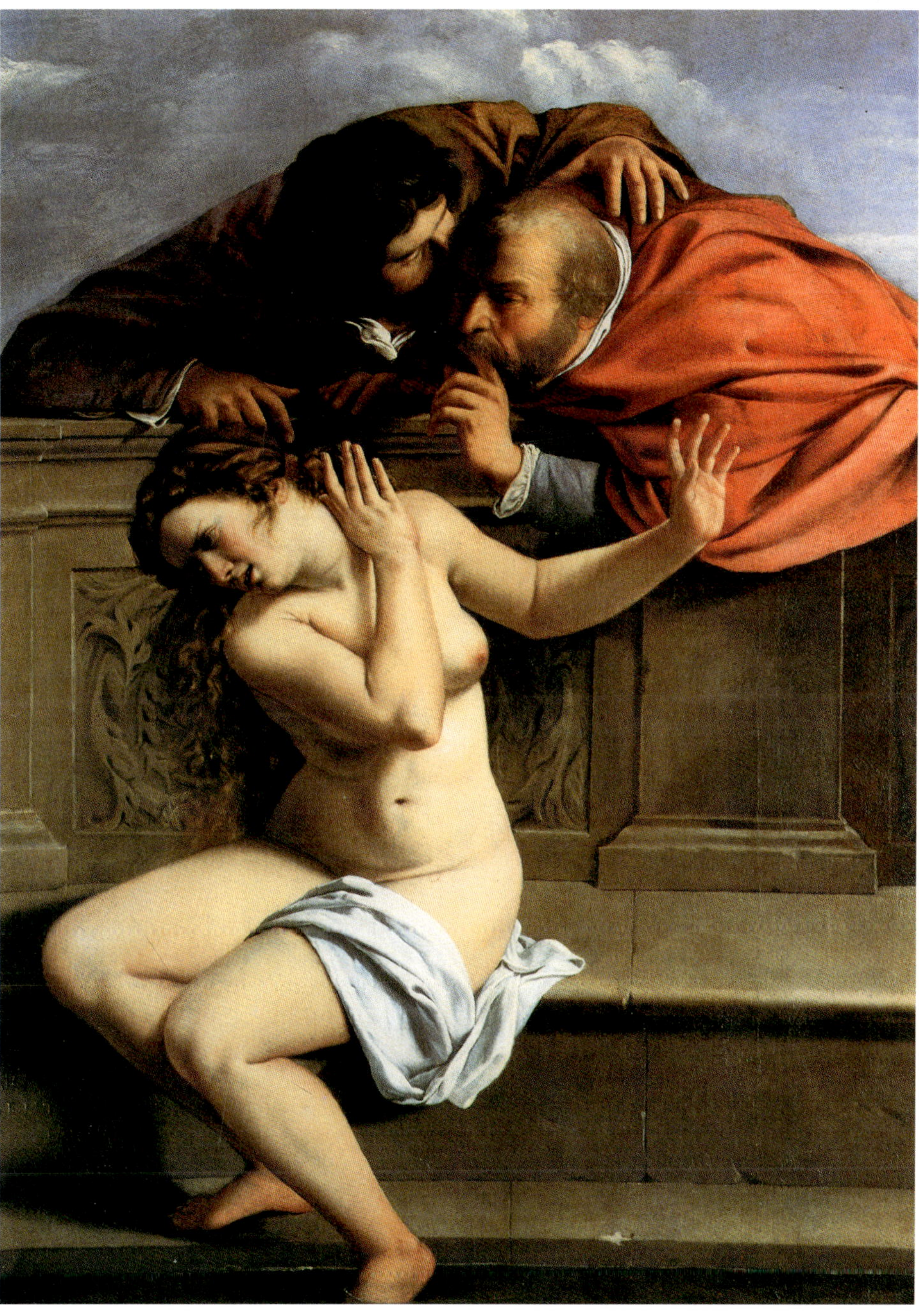

FIG. 32
Artemisia Gentileschi
Susanna and the Elders
1610

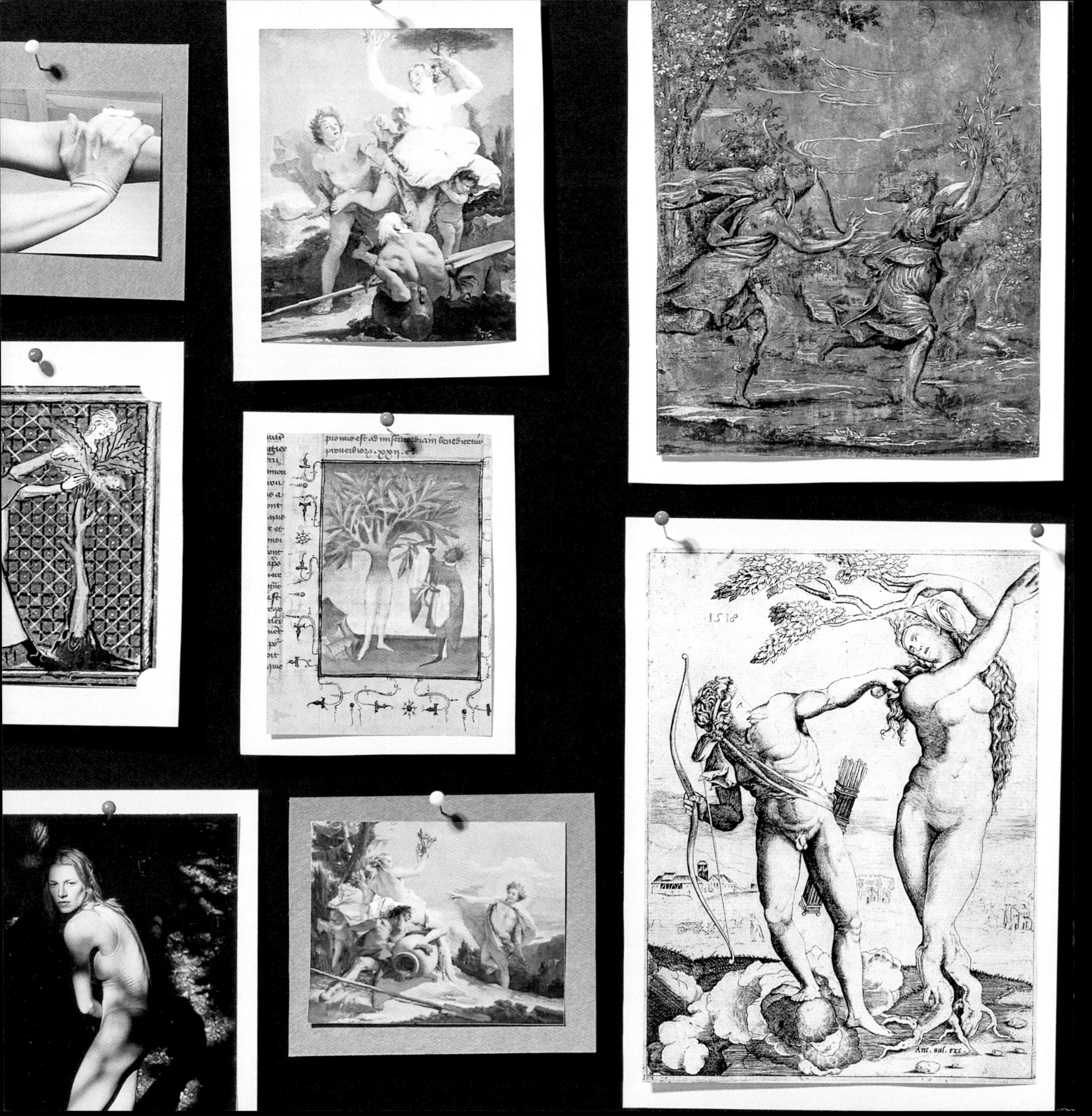

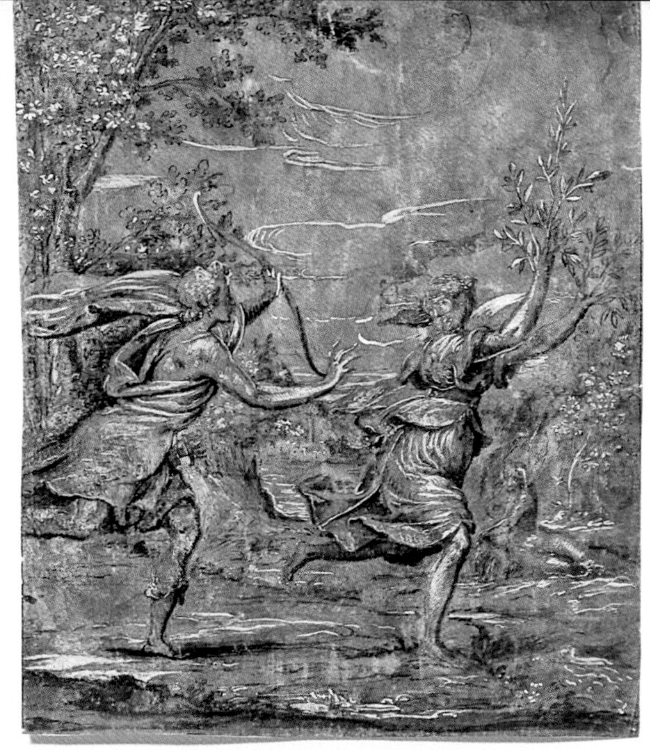

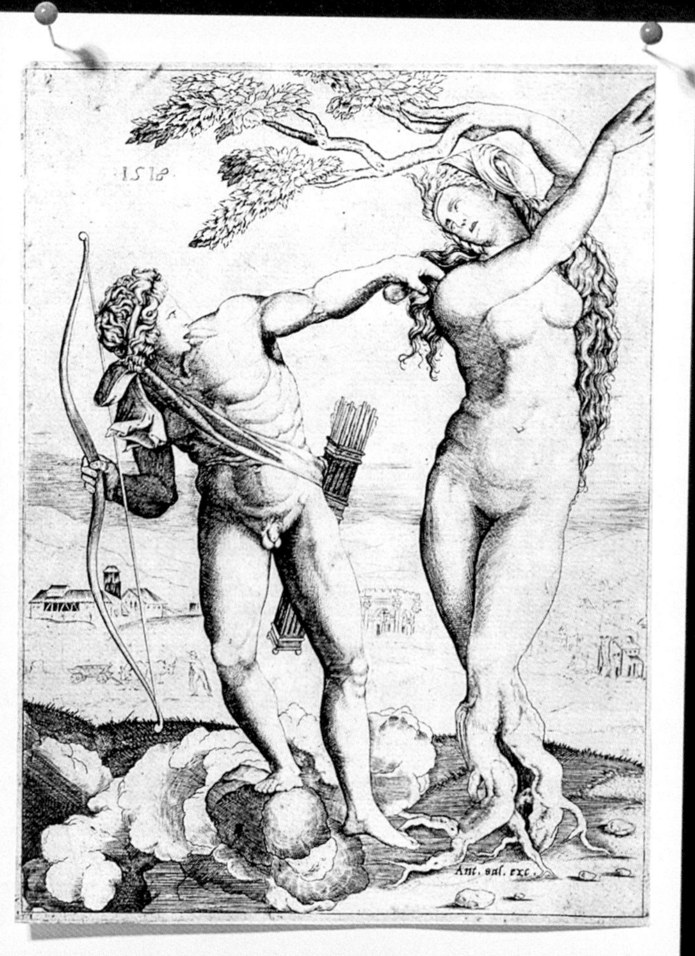
1518
Ant. sal. exc.

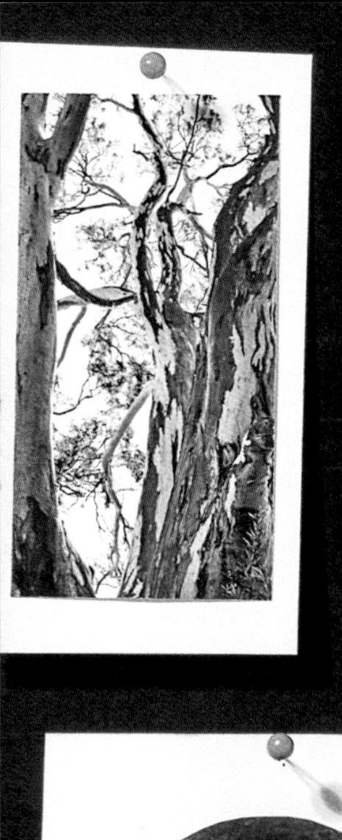
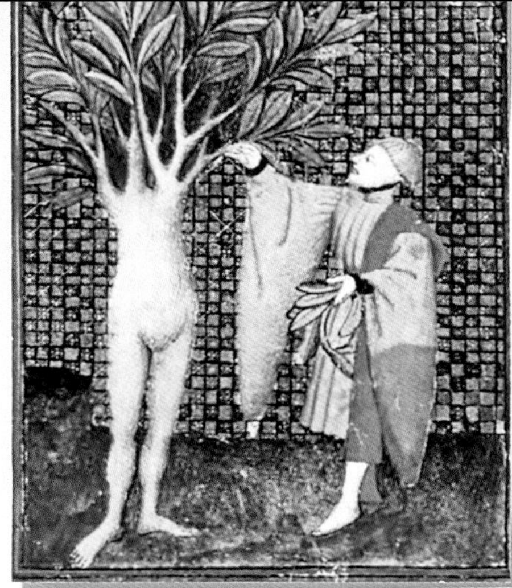
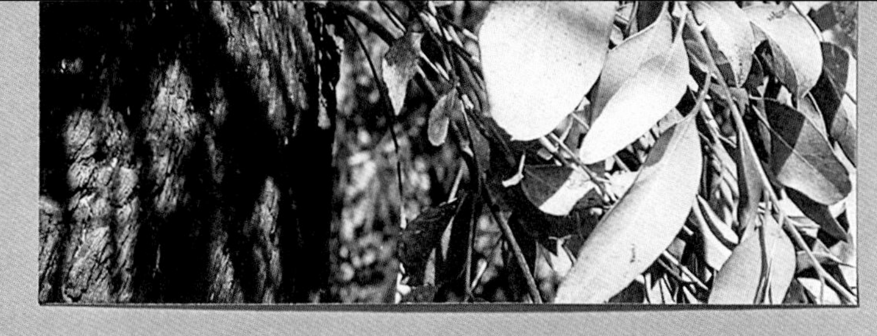
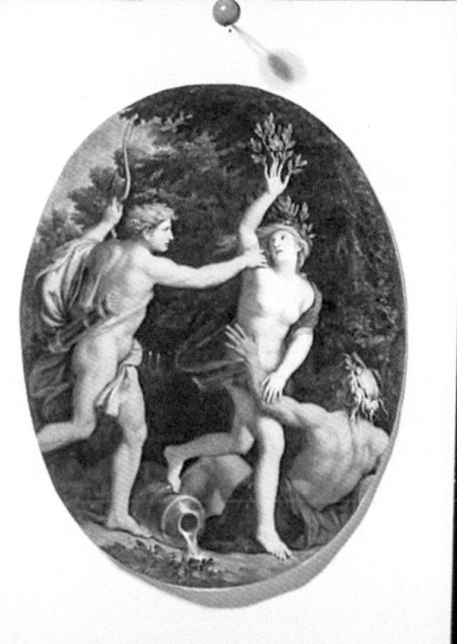
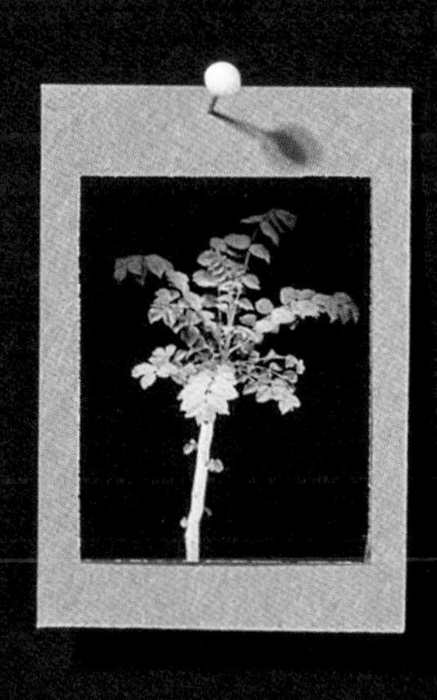
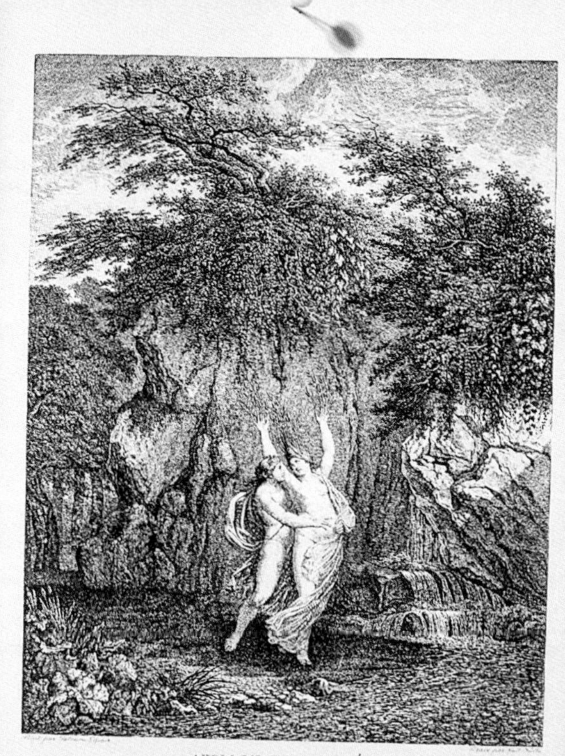
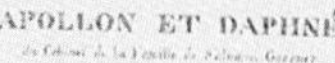
APOLLON ET DAPHNÉ
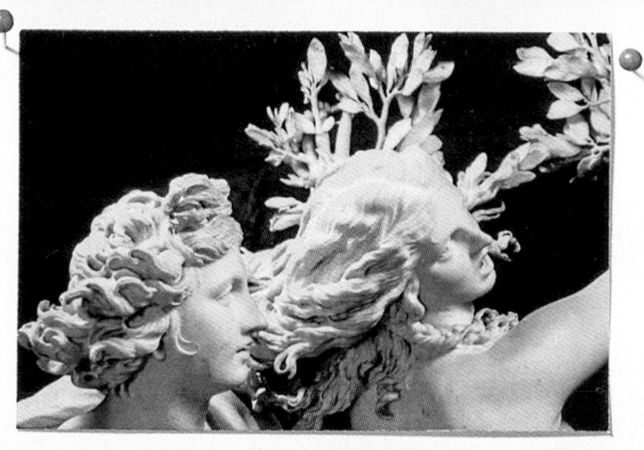
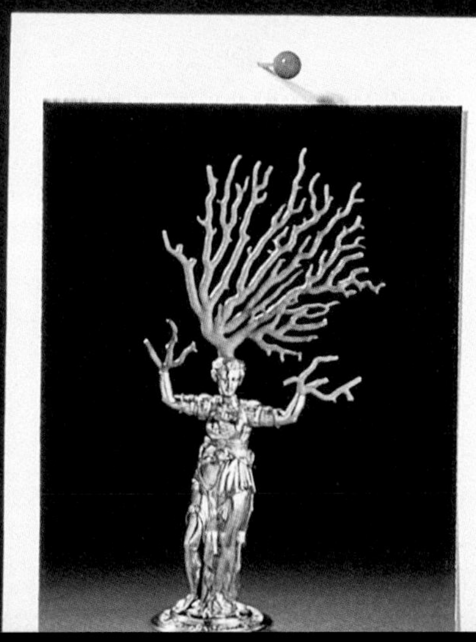
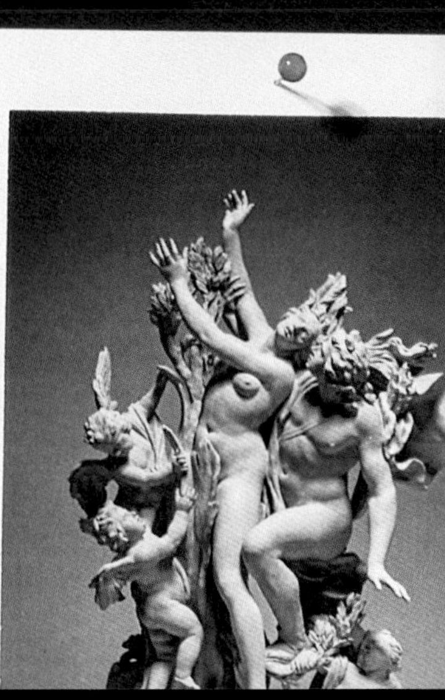

Carmen Maria Machado

It Seemed to Him

I. Fires too subtle for my thought.

Here she is, as she always is, Daphne—*daughter*, *virgin*, *first beloved*—stumbling into the path of Phoebus. Phoebus, *proud*, Phoebus, *great*. Phoebus, who wronged Cupid (*vengeful* Cupid, *undaunted* Cupid, *impish* Cupid). Cupid, with two arrows:

dull, lead, repelling love *sharp, gold, exciting love*

It could have been otherwise. It could have been *daughter* and *virgin* and *first beloved* incandescent with want. Daphne as we see her, spreading for heaven. Leaping from peak to peak for a taste of what thrilled her—the pierce of radiance. The touch of the god of poetry of dance the touch of the *god of glorious light.*

But no. Lead to Daphne, lovely. Gold to the god of contempt.

II. The joys of chase.

Daphne did not need a reason but Cupid gave her one. She longs to stay a virgin (one *who denies the joys of love*). She begs her father to allow her *modesty*. Dearest father, she says, *let me live*. (So much to do, so much to do. A list as long as a tree is tall, and it grows by the hour.) Like so many daughters, she would rather *live* than *love.* Like so many fathers, he promises what he cannot give. Because her beauty *prevails* against her *will.* (What do we call it, what do we call it?)

And as the *stubble of the field flares* (tsk tsk, it happens) and the *stacked wheat* is *consumed by flames* (every day, it seems), so the *bosom* of Phoebus is *consumed*. (He is *consumed* but he still has notes. Her hair would be perfect if *properly arranged*.) (He didn't need the arrow but it's how the story will go.)

The god of light calls to the living virgin Daphne. He tells her to calm down. Yes, the *lamb leaps from the raging wolf.* Sure, *from the lion runs the timid faun.* Of course, the *prey* flees from their *natural enemy.*

But not now. Not this time. Daphne, *beloved*, why do you run?

It Seemed to Him by Carmen Maria Machado was originally published in conjunction with *Spotlight: Jesse Mockrin* at The FLAG Art Foundation, New York, NY (2025).

Carmen Maria Machado is the author of the bestselling memoir *In the Dream House* and the award-winning short story collection *Her Body and Other Parties.* Her essays, fiction, and criticism have appeared in *The New Yorker*, *The New York Times*, *Granta*, *Vogue*, *This American Life*, *The Believer*, *Guernica*, and elsewhere.

III. She seemed most lovely.

Her flight made her beautiful. *Zephyrs* stirred her *garments*. The *wind* caressed her *hair.* He is *greyhound.* He is *mad with love*. He *rushes*. She *flees.* He *gains.* He *follows* and *permits her no rest*. *Spent*, she cries out to her father (useless) and her mother (better). She offers up her *body* and her *beauty*. No prison worse than his desire. Anything to be free. (Fathers have a way of misunderstanding what mothers do not.)

We are close to her now. (She lets us wants us to see to know.) *Bark* crawls down her arms her torso her thighs like gauntlets like armor like silk. (She suffers in triplicate.) *Branches* sprout from her fingers. (She twists and writhes and spirals.) She sees him, she *sees him*. She looks at us. Her hair becomes as *leaves*.

(So literal, father. So correct and yet so perfectly utterly wrong.)

Rooted, she takes her first and final breath.

IV. It seemed to him.

Any man can love a tree. (She is still *slender* has knots and clefts and lost her imperious mouth.) His hand *lingers* on her trunkchest. (How many times in her life? Too many to number.) He *clings* to her *branch*arms like *twine*. (Every day, at least.) Her bosombark *throbs*. (With what depends on the teller.) He puts his *mouth* to the *wood* of her. (Does she *shrink from every kiss*, or is it the breeze that stirs her?)

Phoebus always did love a monologue. He always adored having the last word.

Treebride. Nymphet of the forest. Chosenmine. You can no longer speak so I will speak for you. You cannot give me your body and so I will take it. In honor of your honor I will strip your leaves and wear them on my brow. I will *wreathe* you around my *quiver* and my *lyre*. And as I will remain everyoung, your leaves will never leave and will belong to men if there are men.

See? She's nodding.

as a girl she had imagined the fullness of love   she had spoken endless unbroken verse into the gloaming or twilight or dusk   she had stripped her*self* and wore her*self* and beheld her*self*   she loved her hair the color of wheat or soil or blood or pitch   she had been so good with a bow she would sing to the birds, to the water, to her mother   she was her own and only

it is, of course, only the wind

Plates

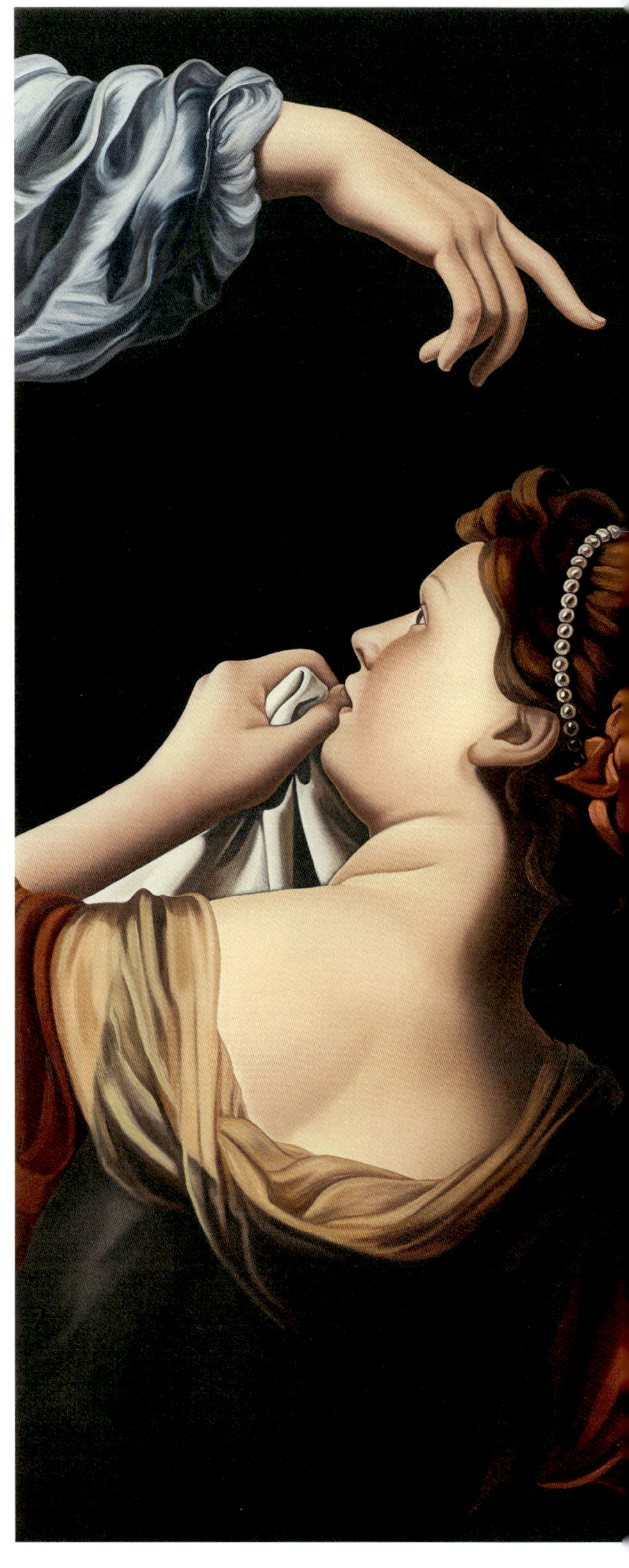

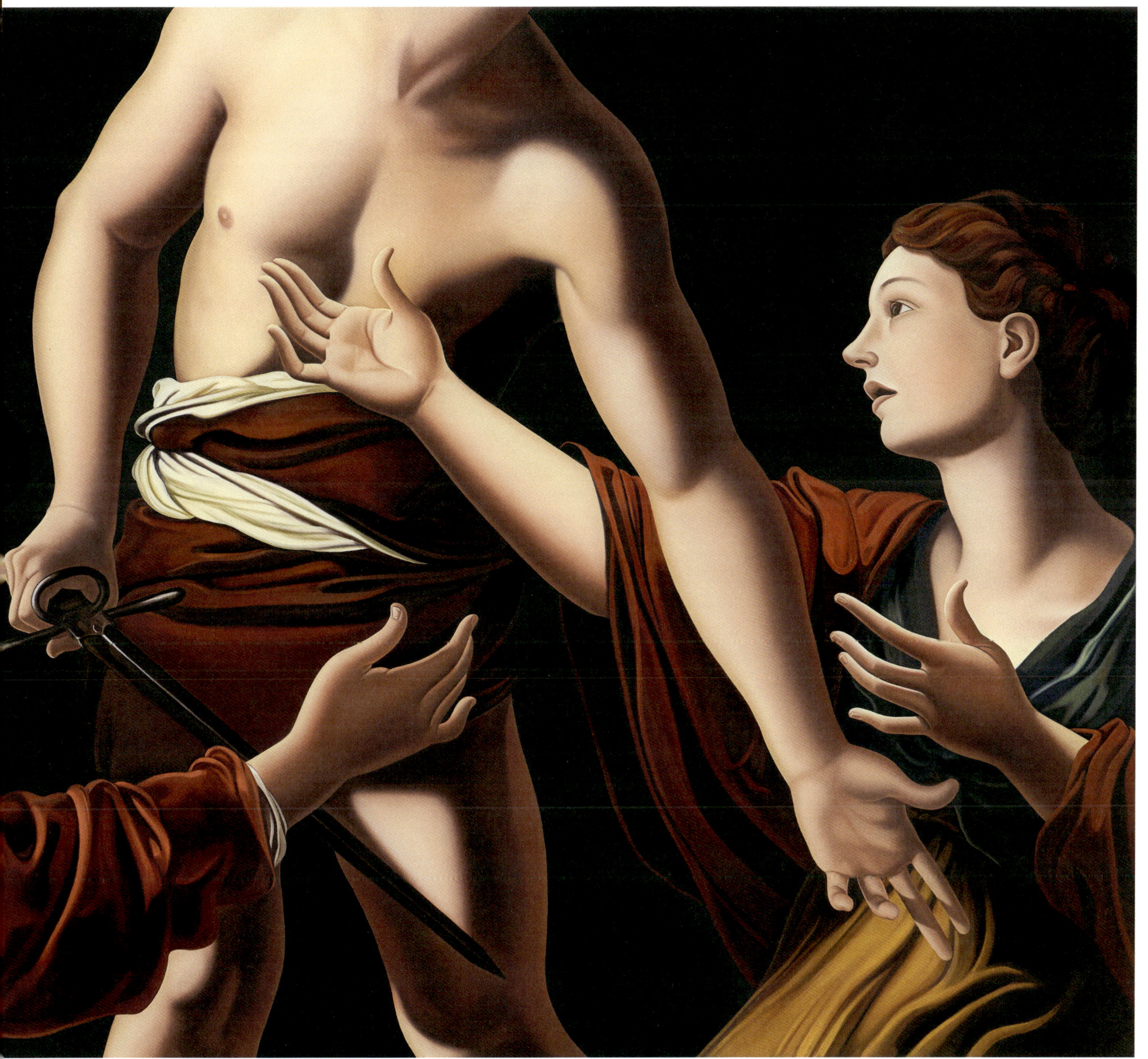

Fracture 2024

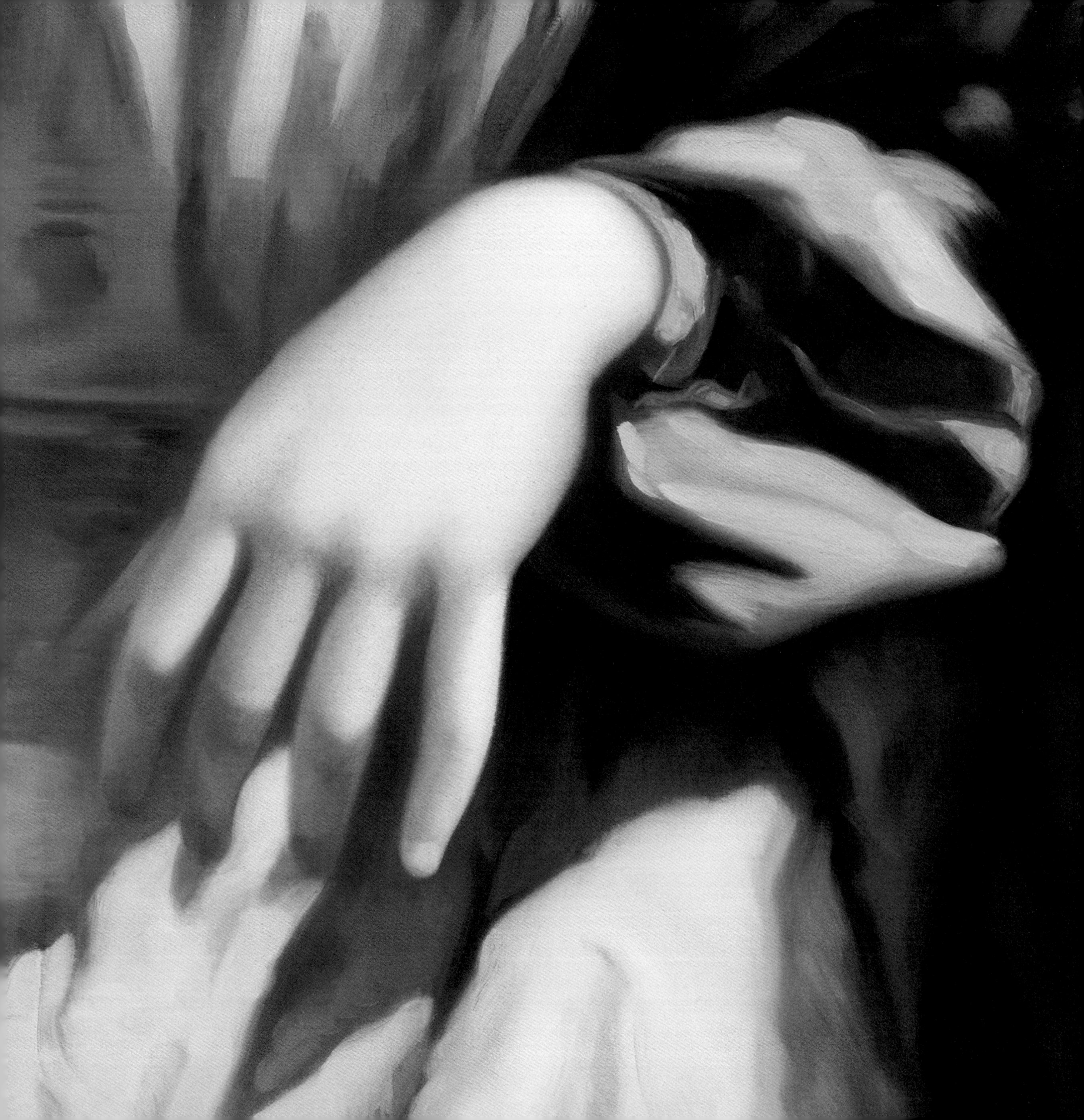

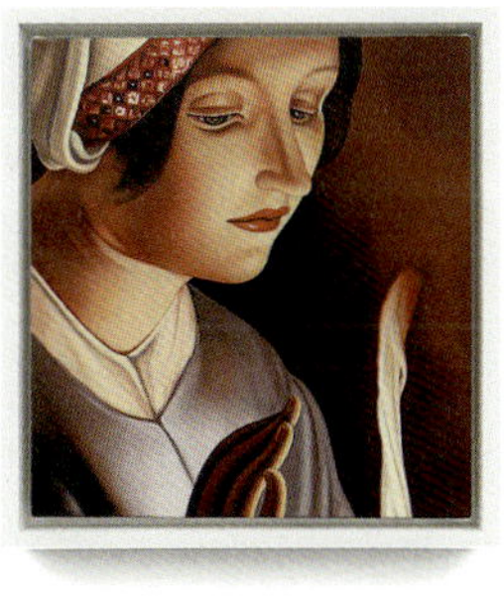
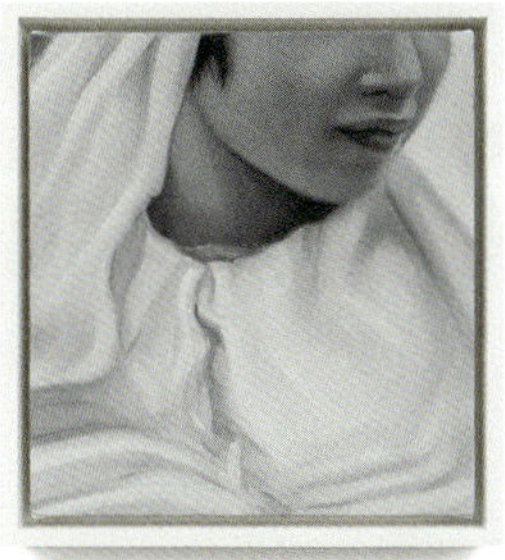
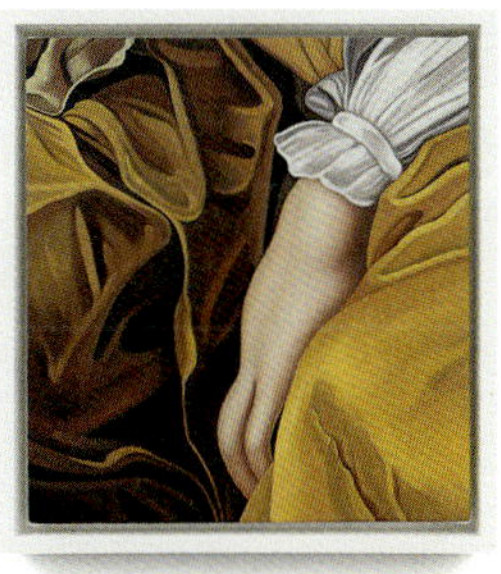
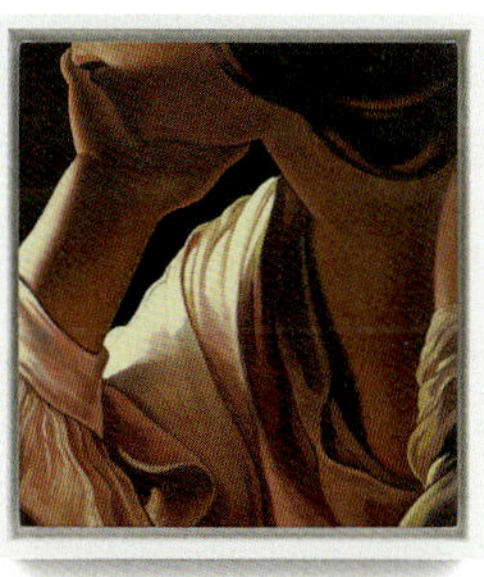
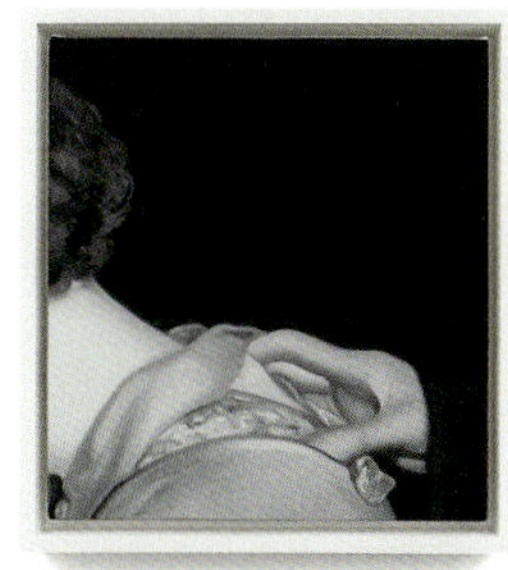
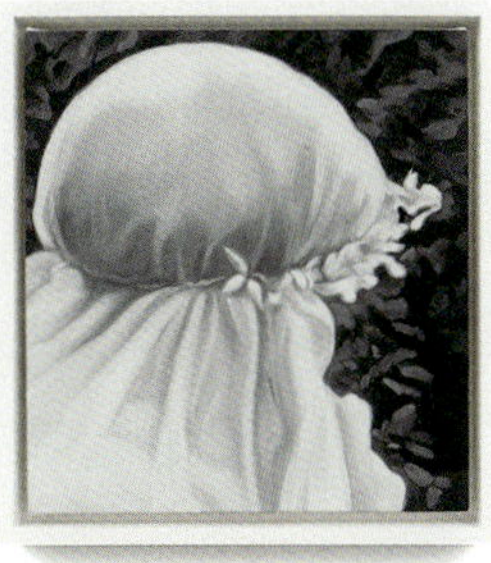
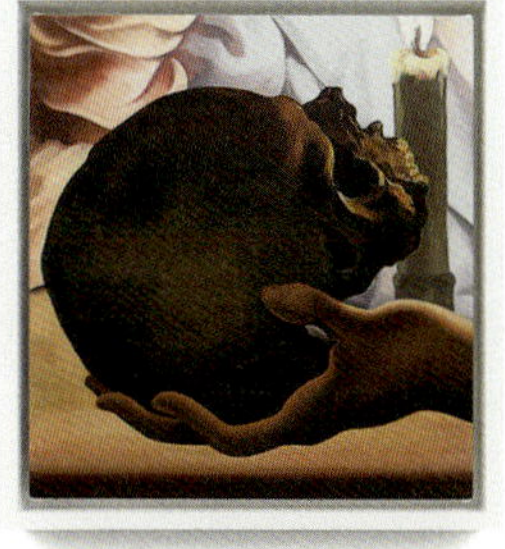
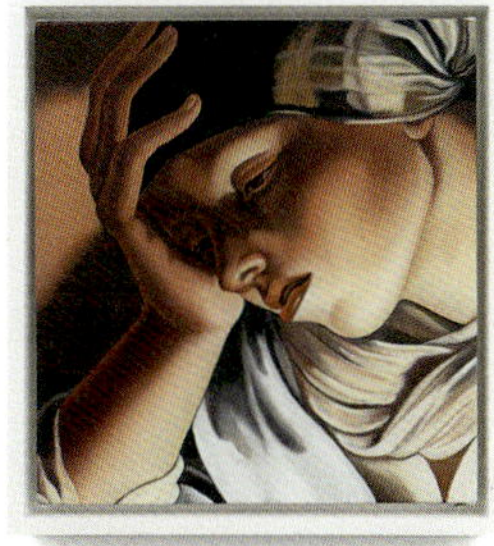
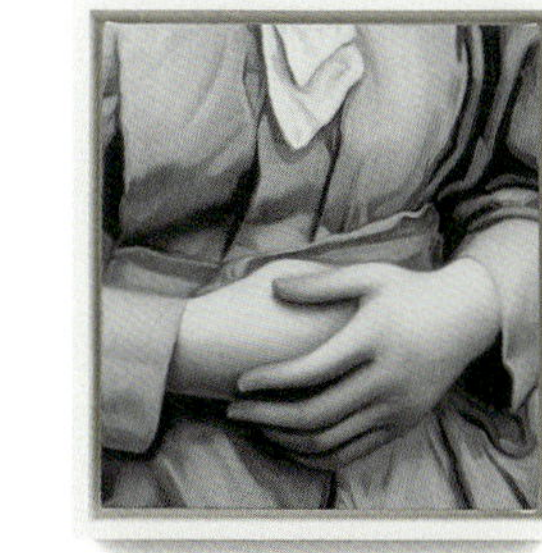
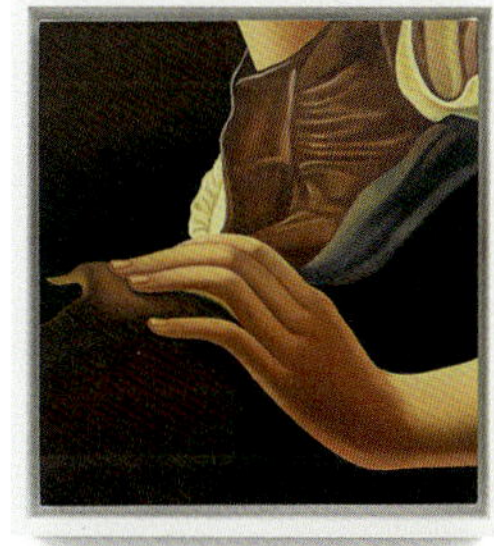
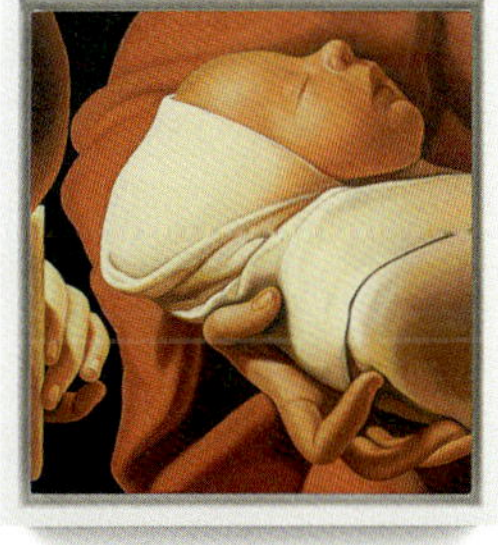
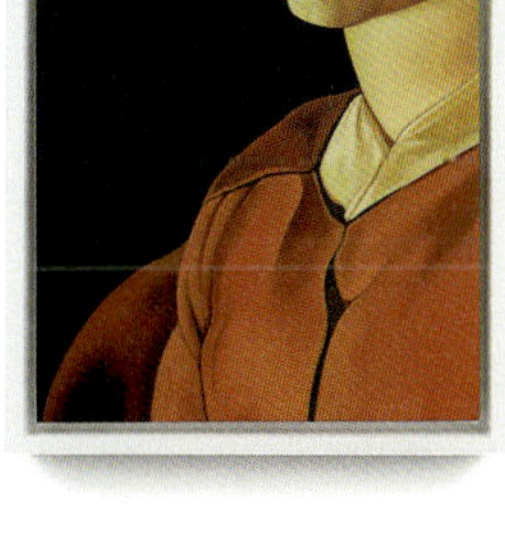
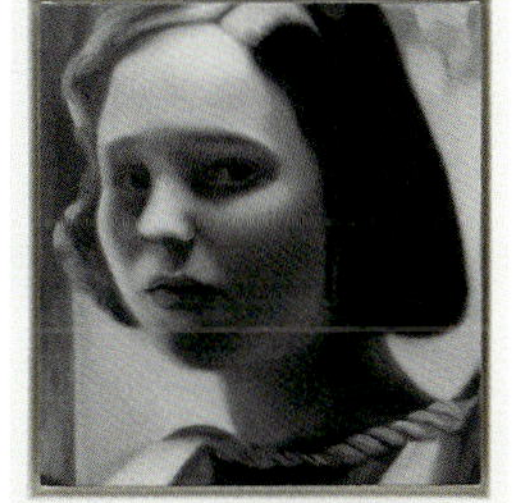
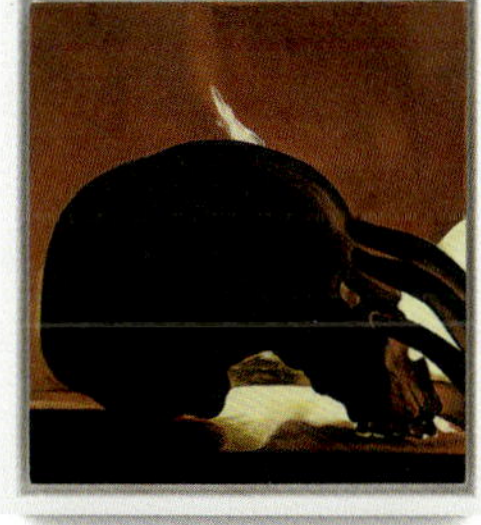
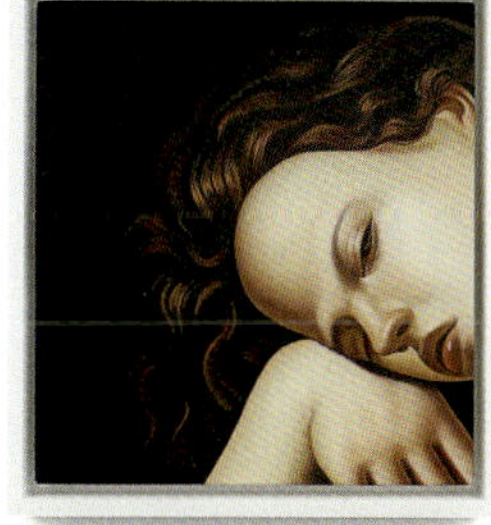
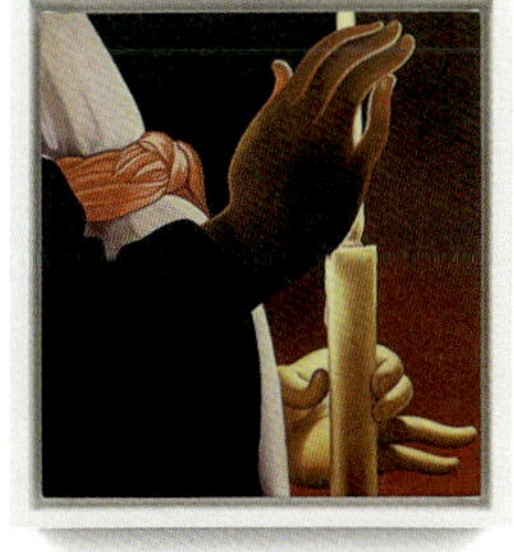
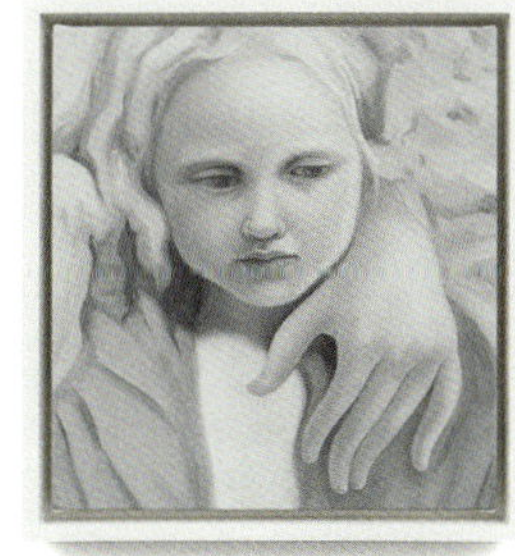
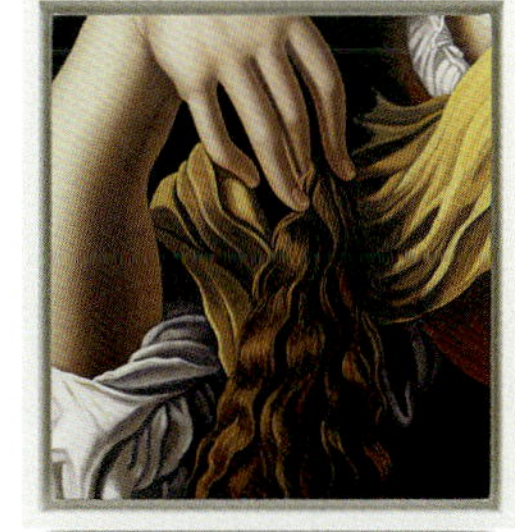
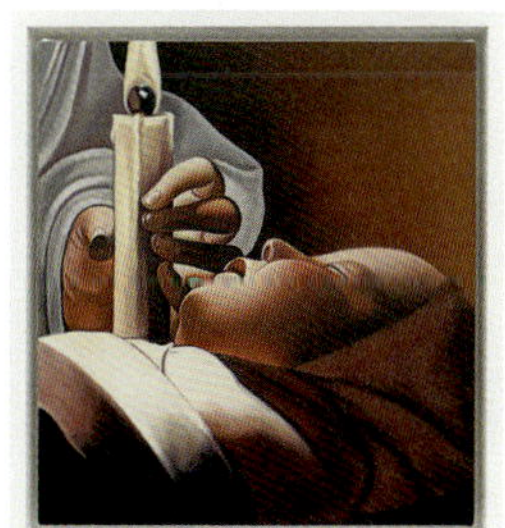
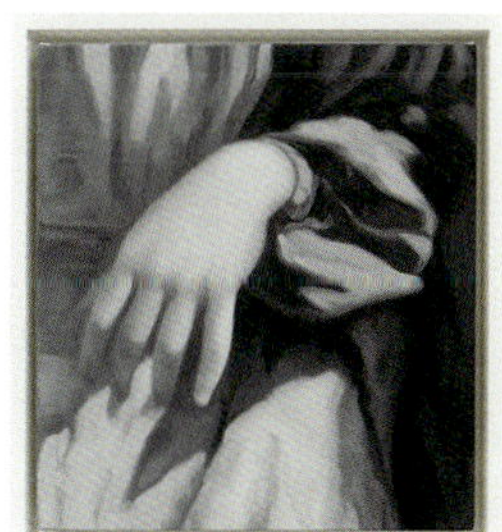

Bitter Seeds 2024

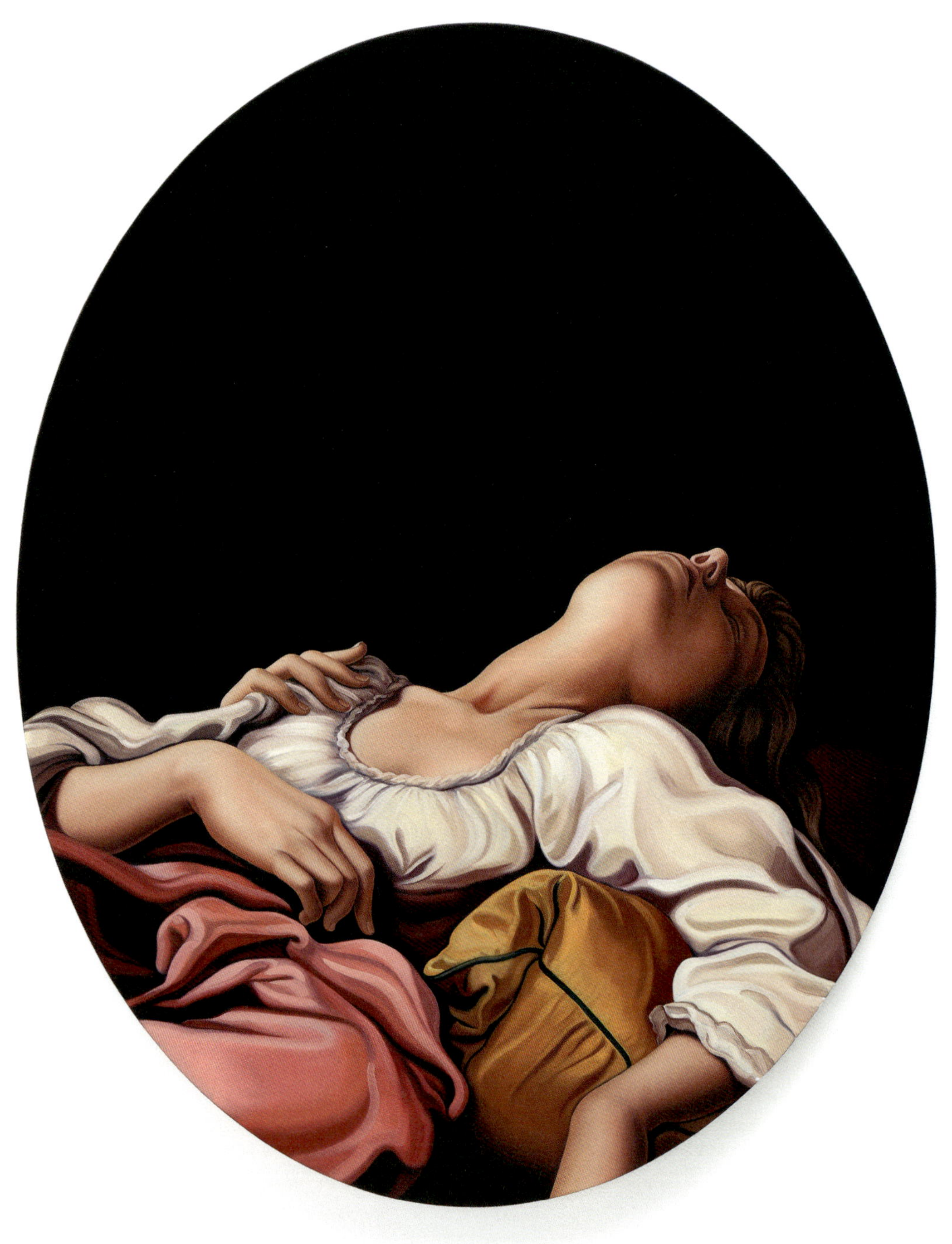

Longing 2025

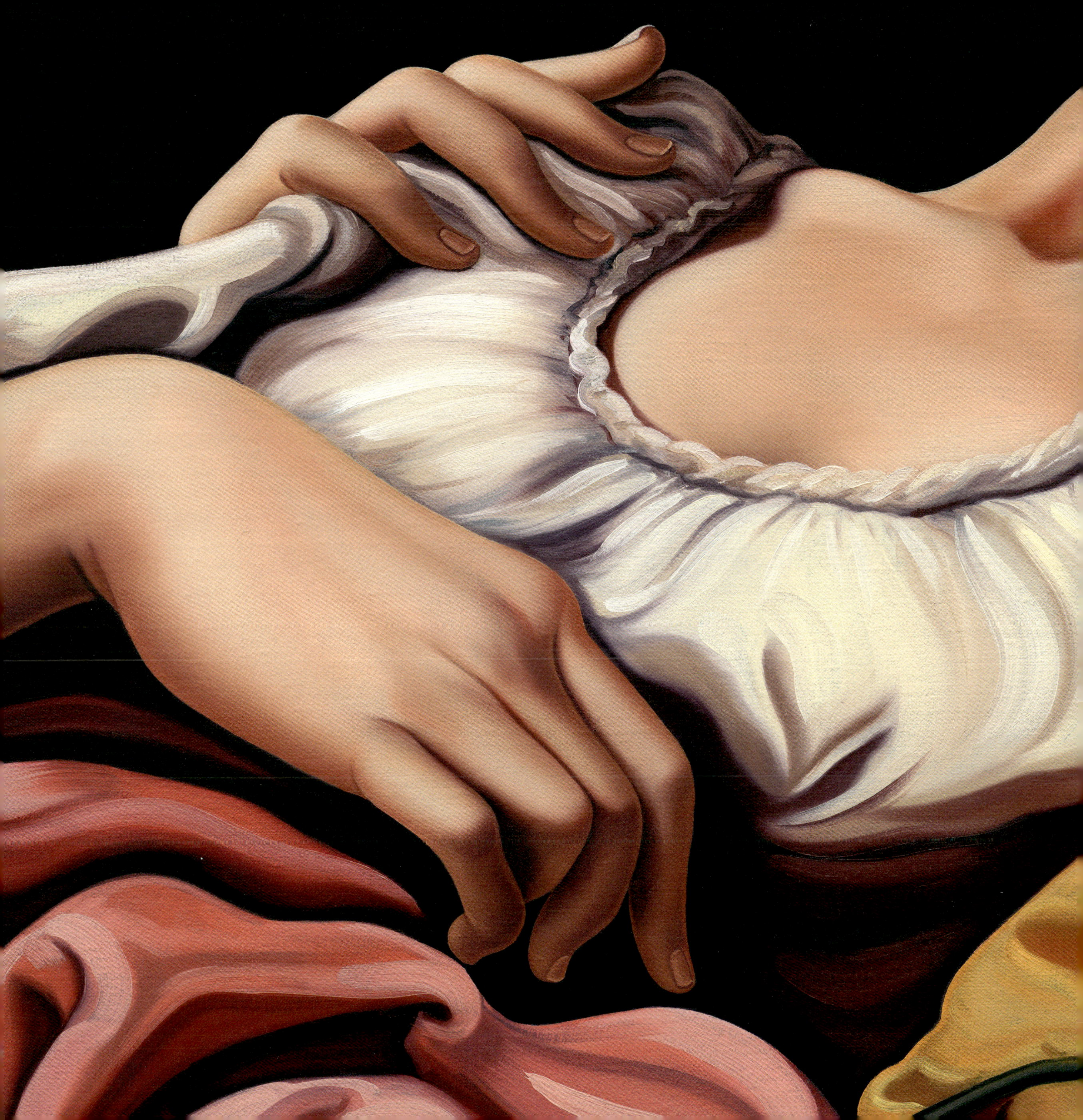

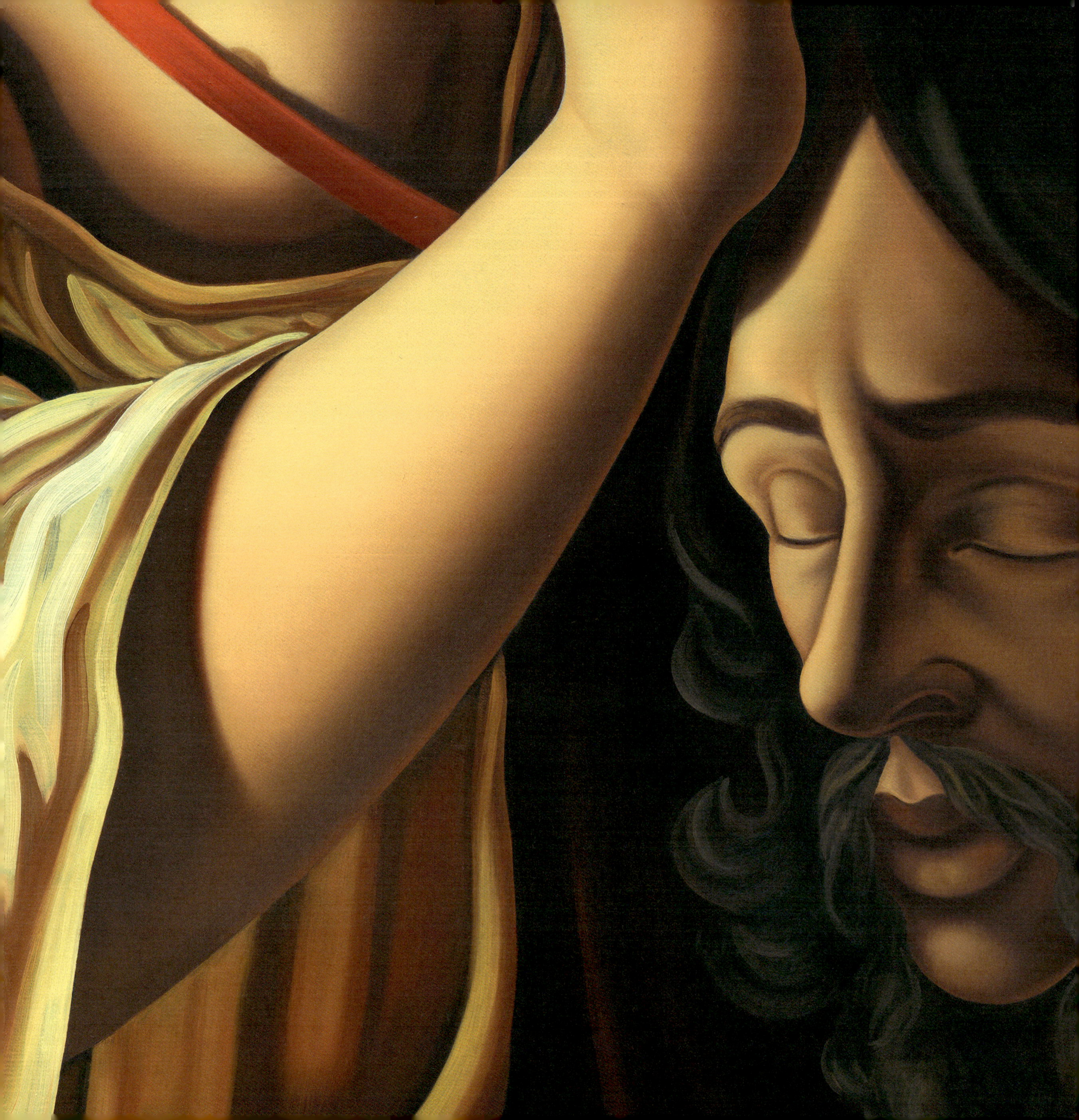

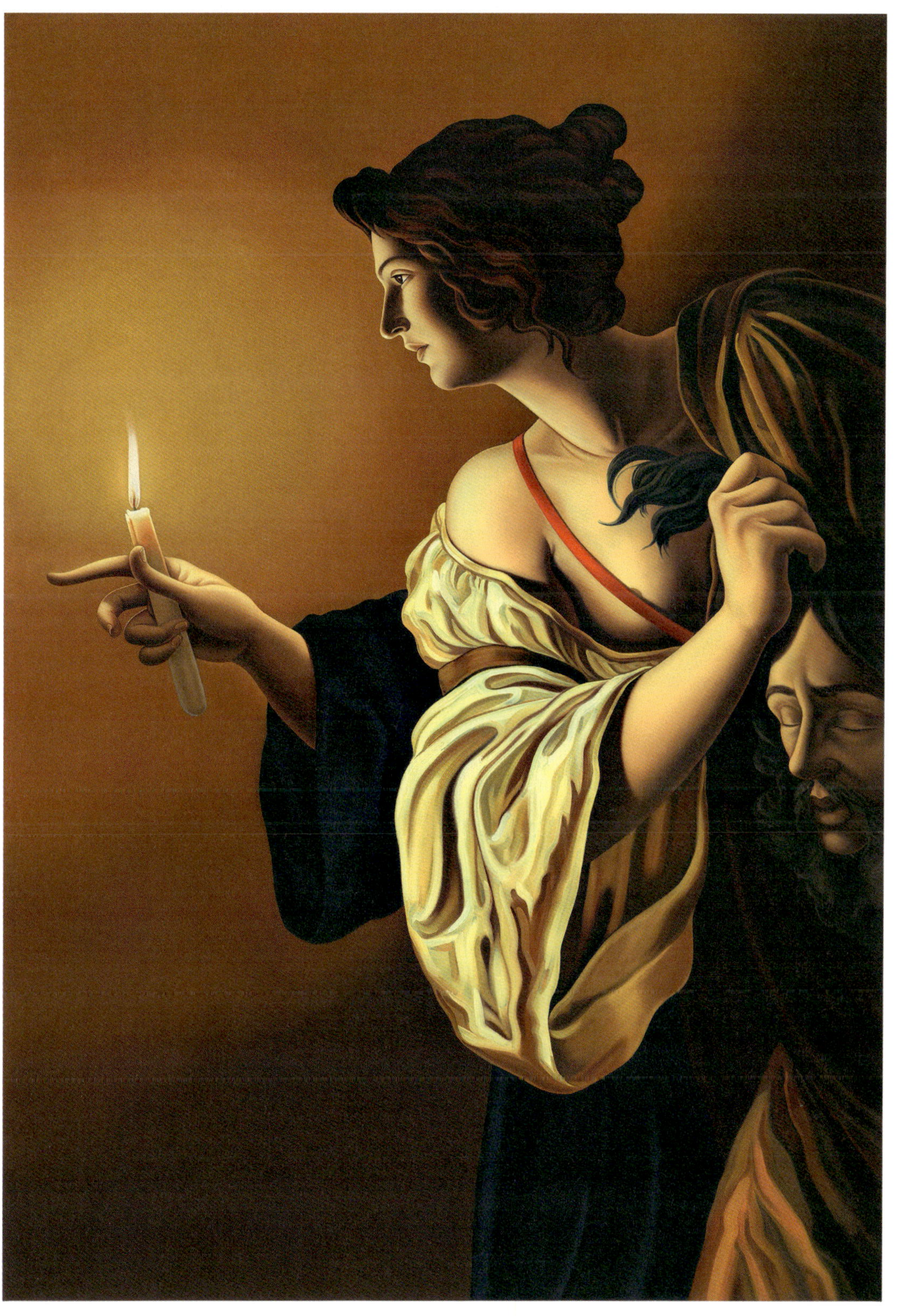

By her hand 2025

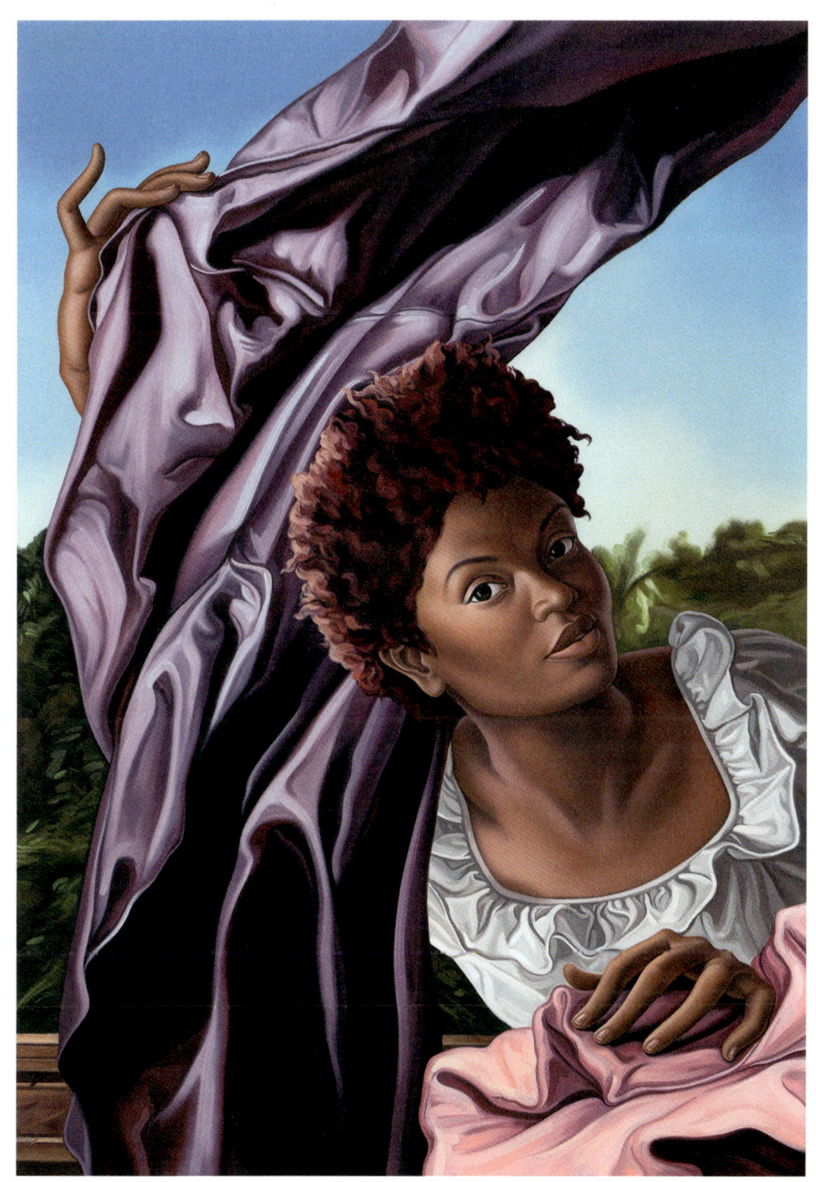
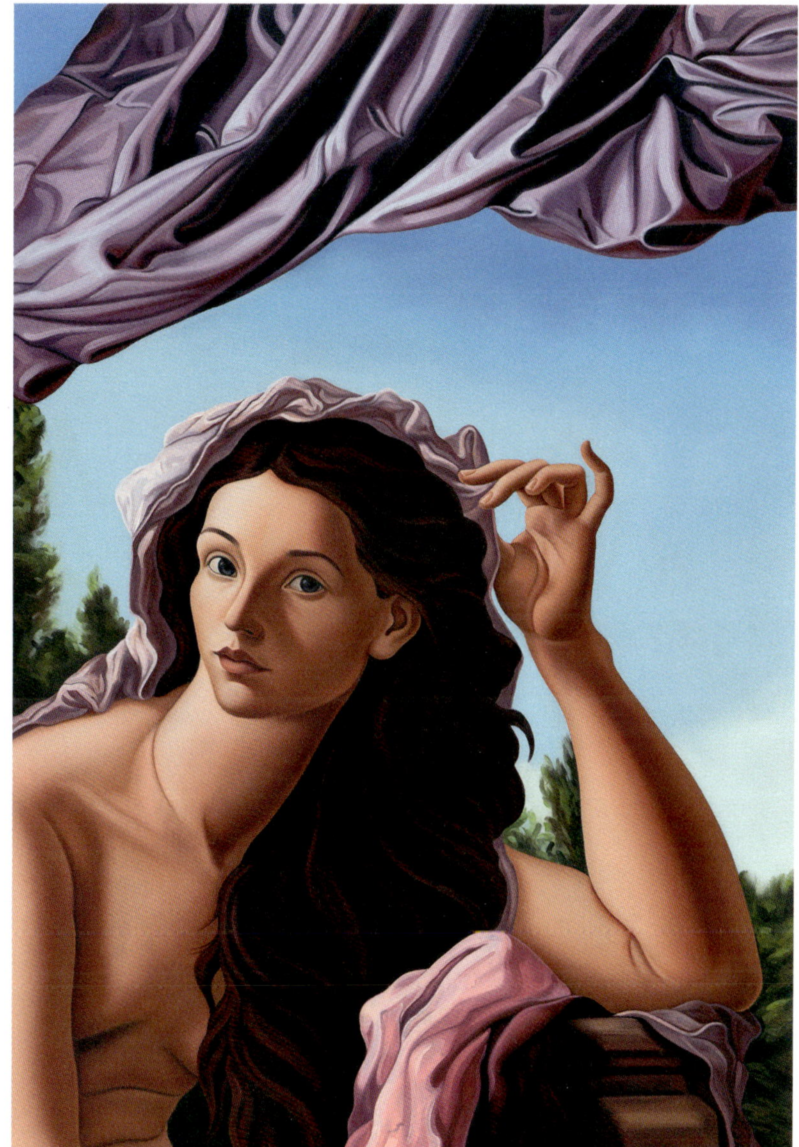

Witness 2025

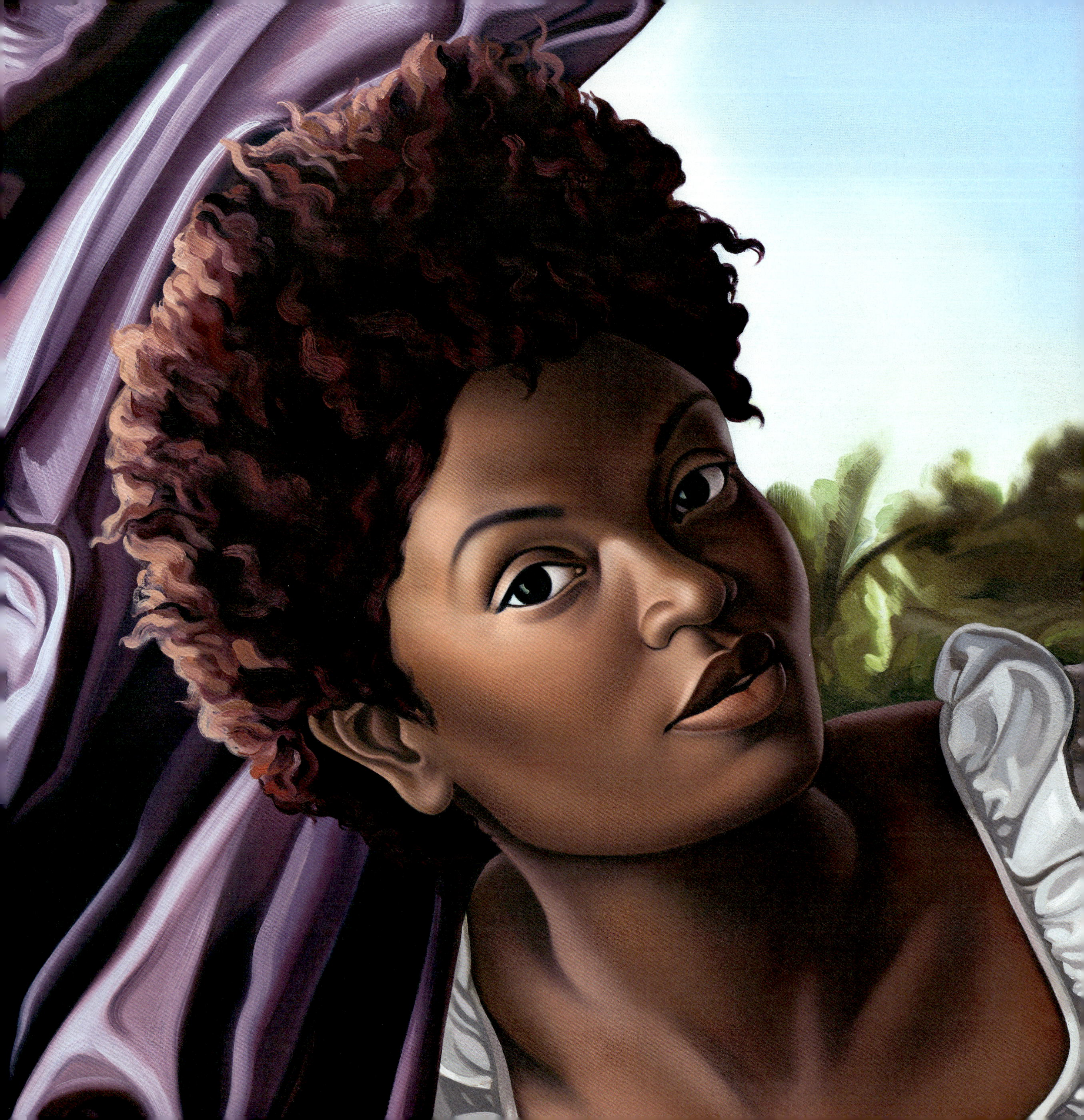

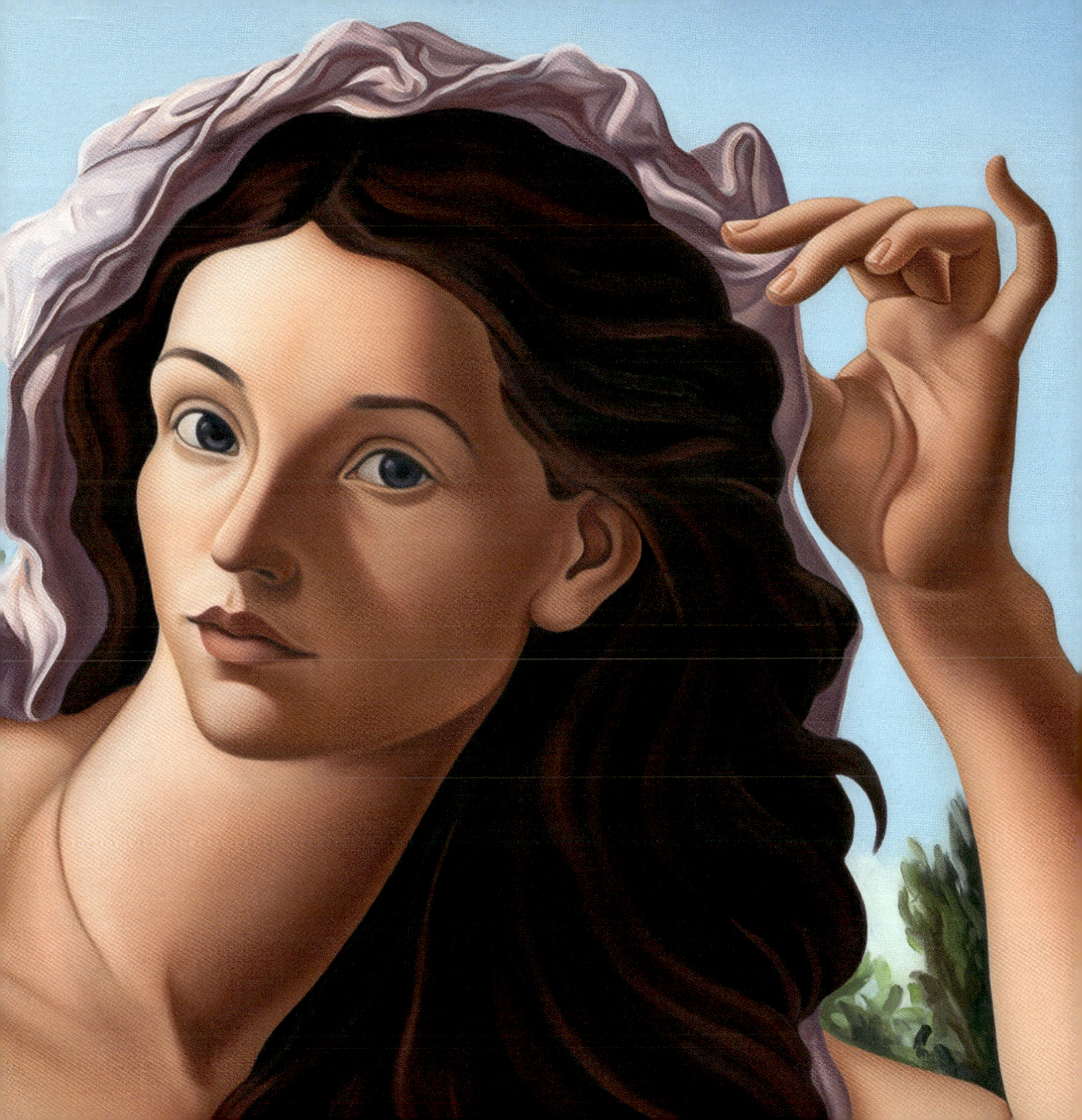

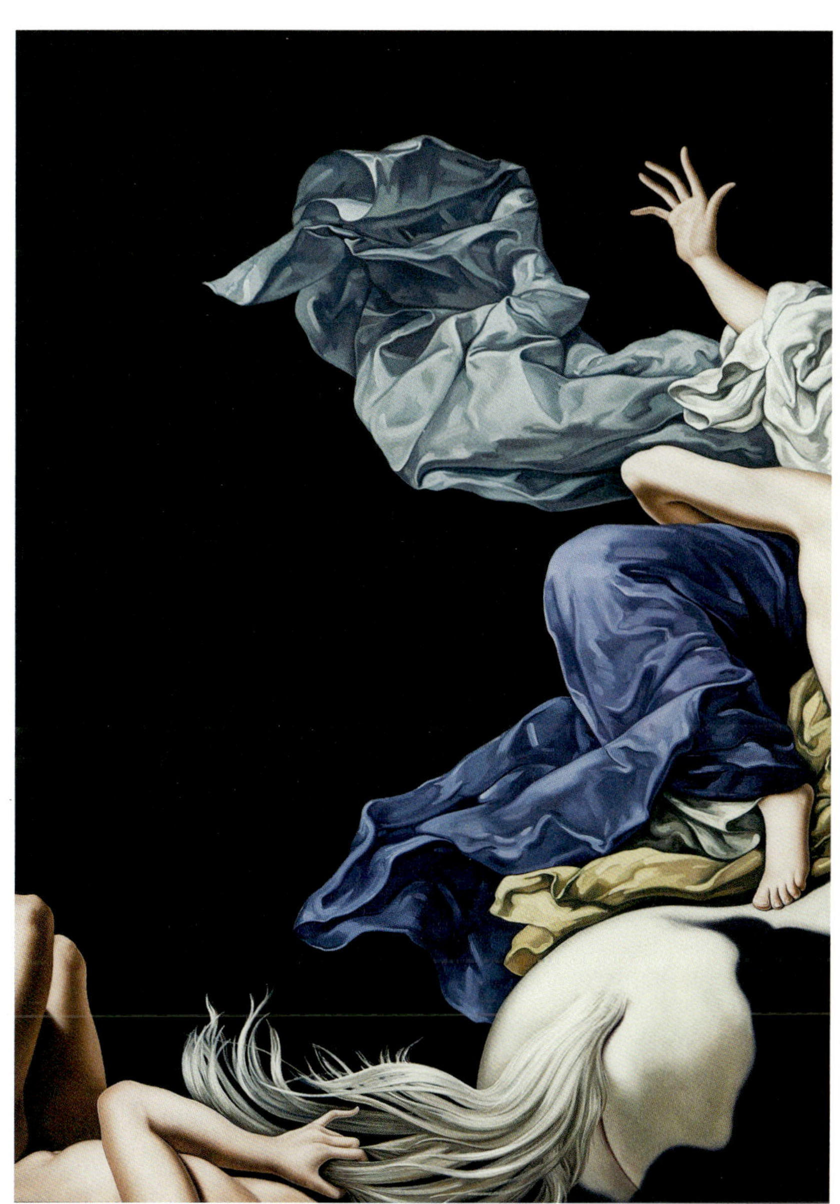

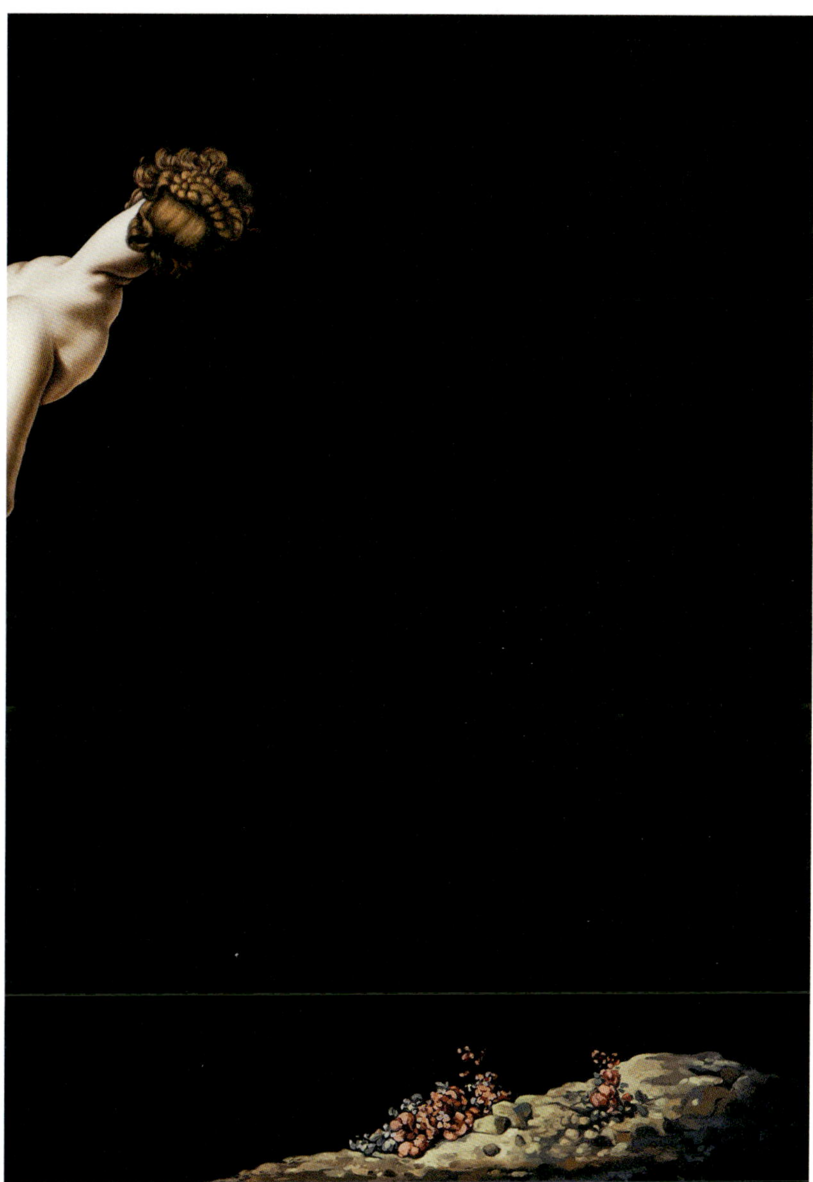

In mid-stream 2017

The Descent 2024

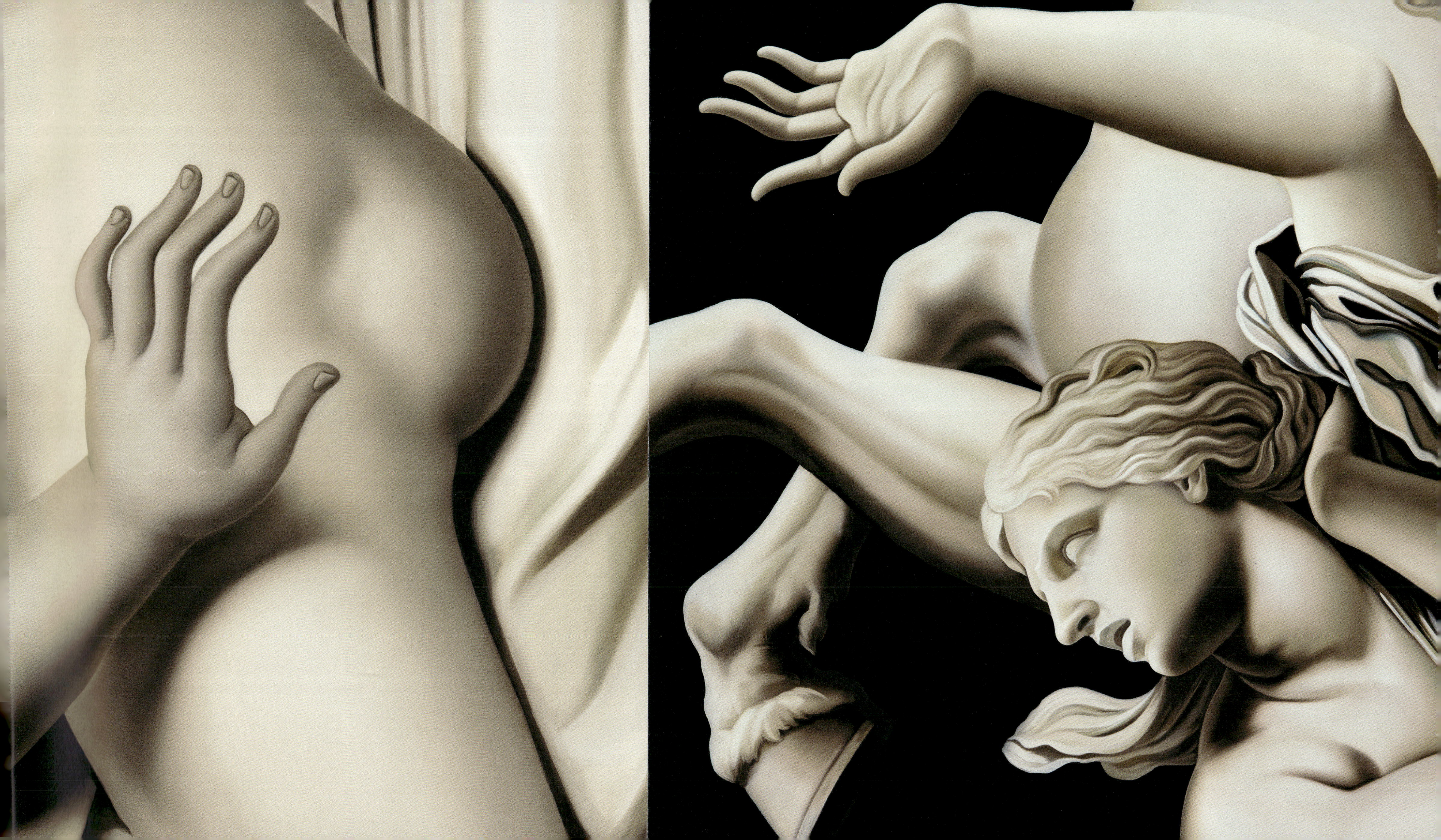

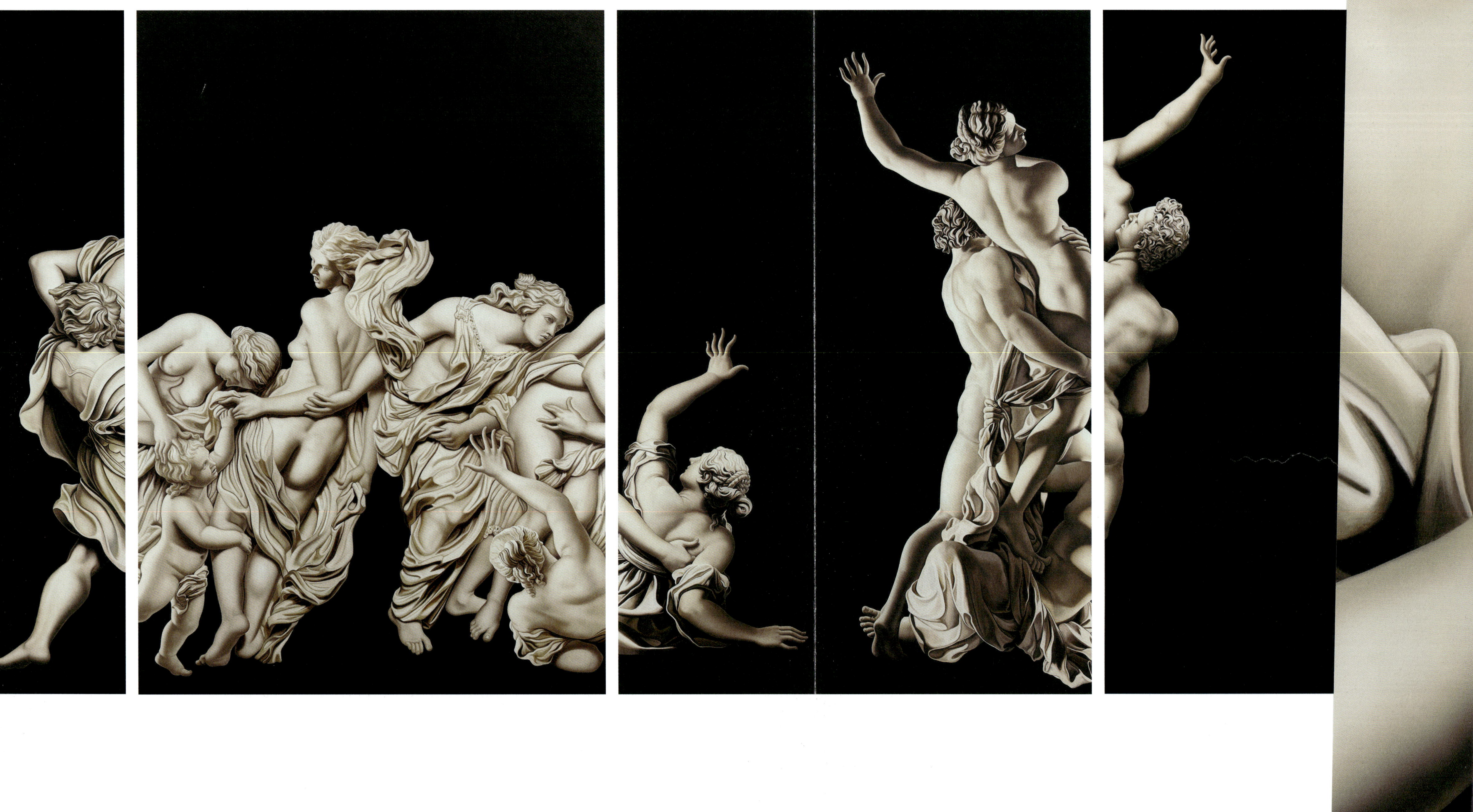

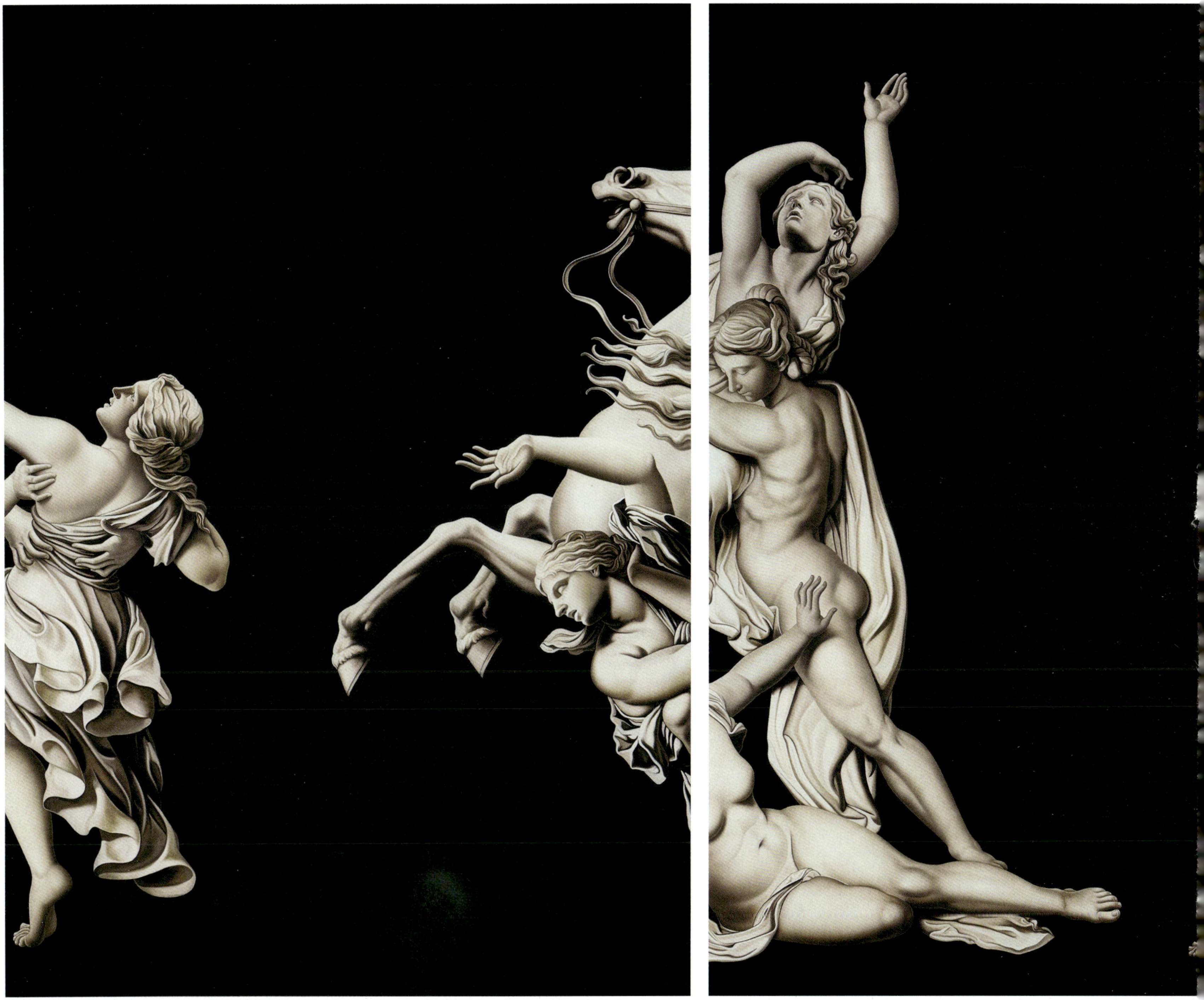

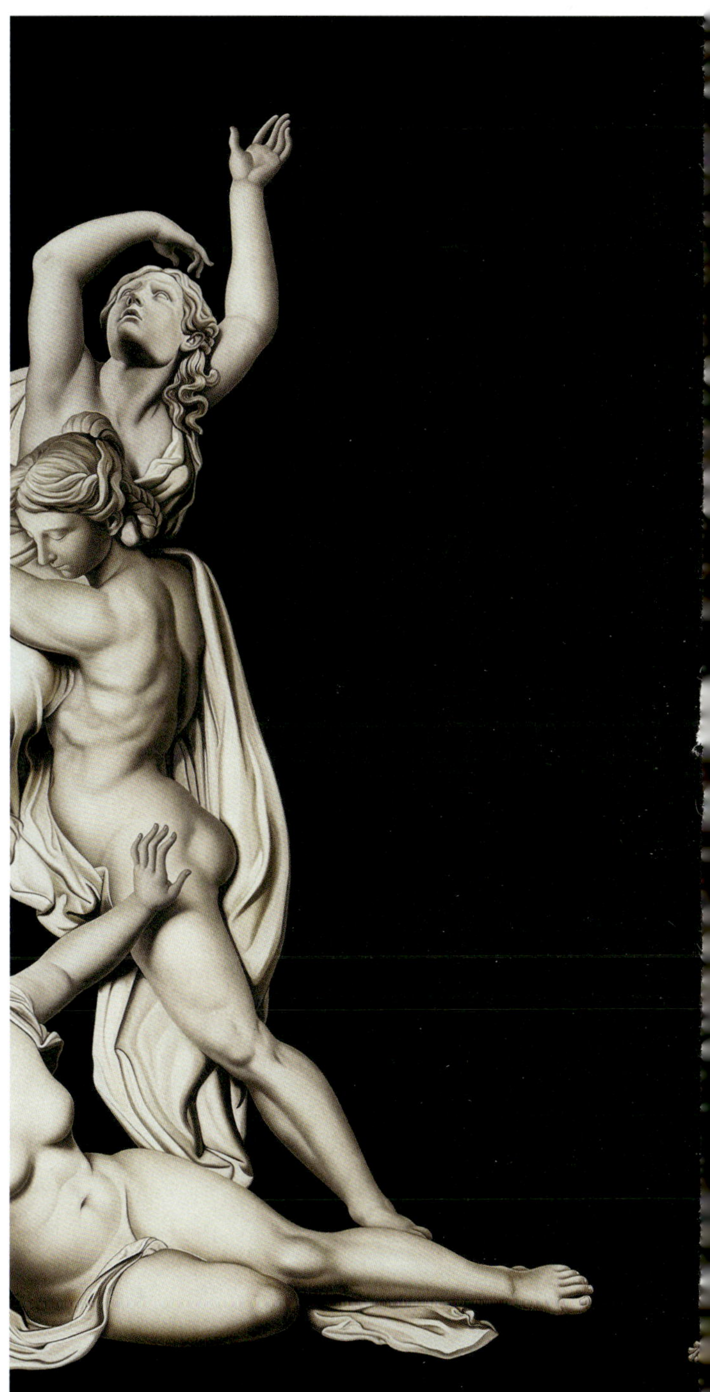

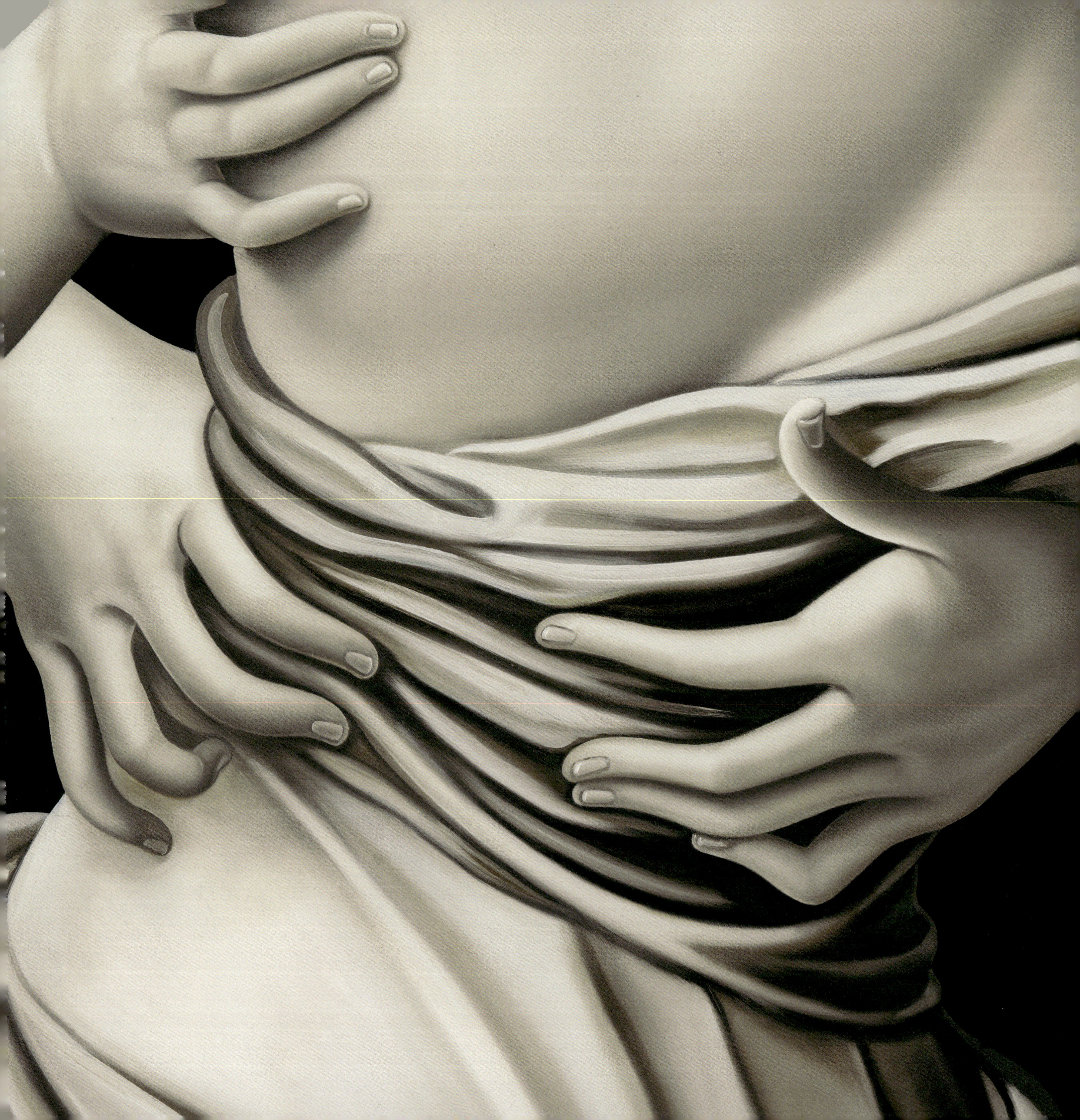

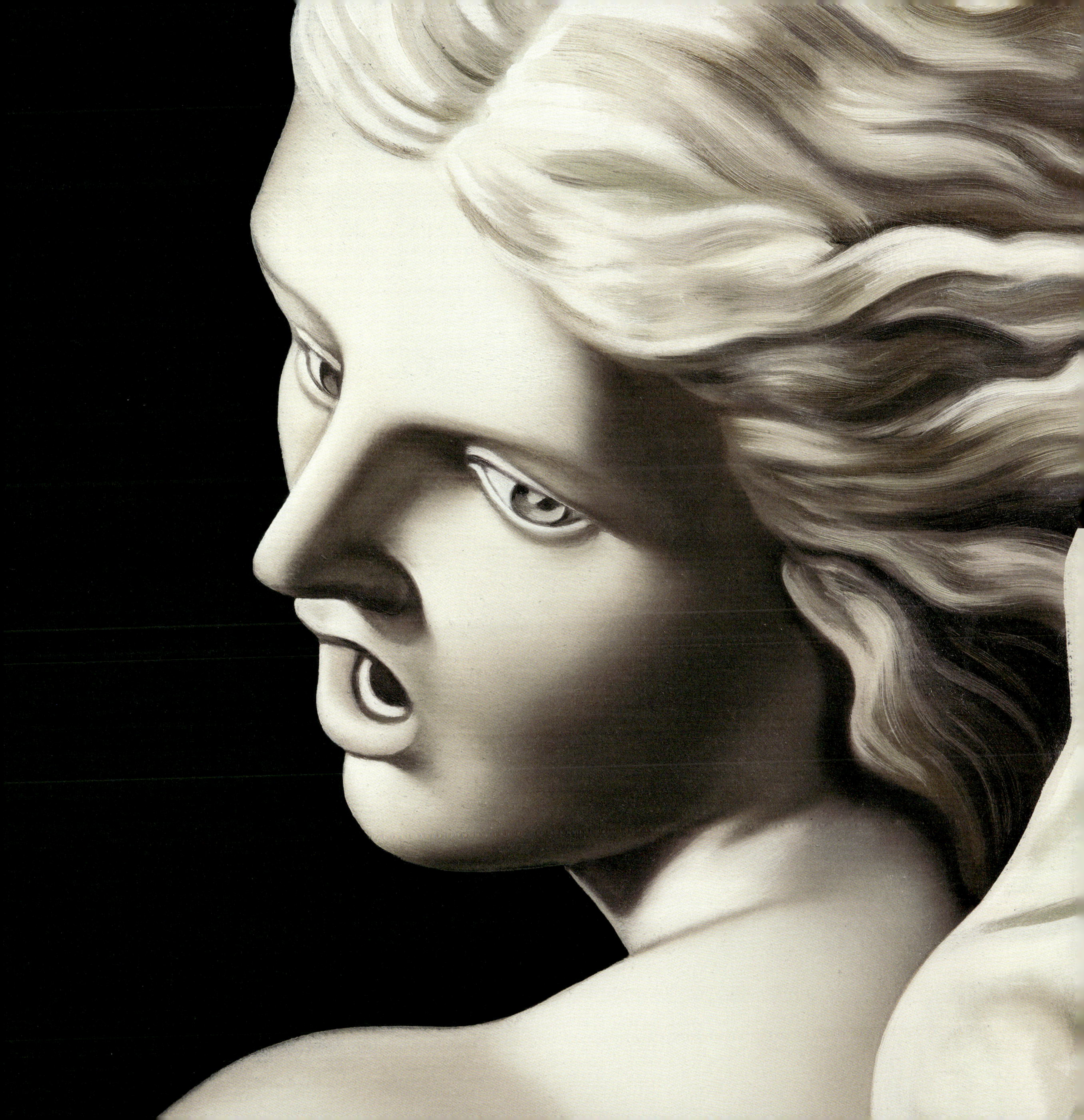

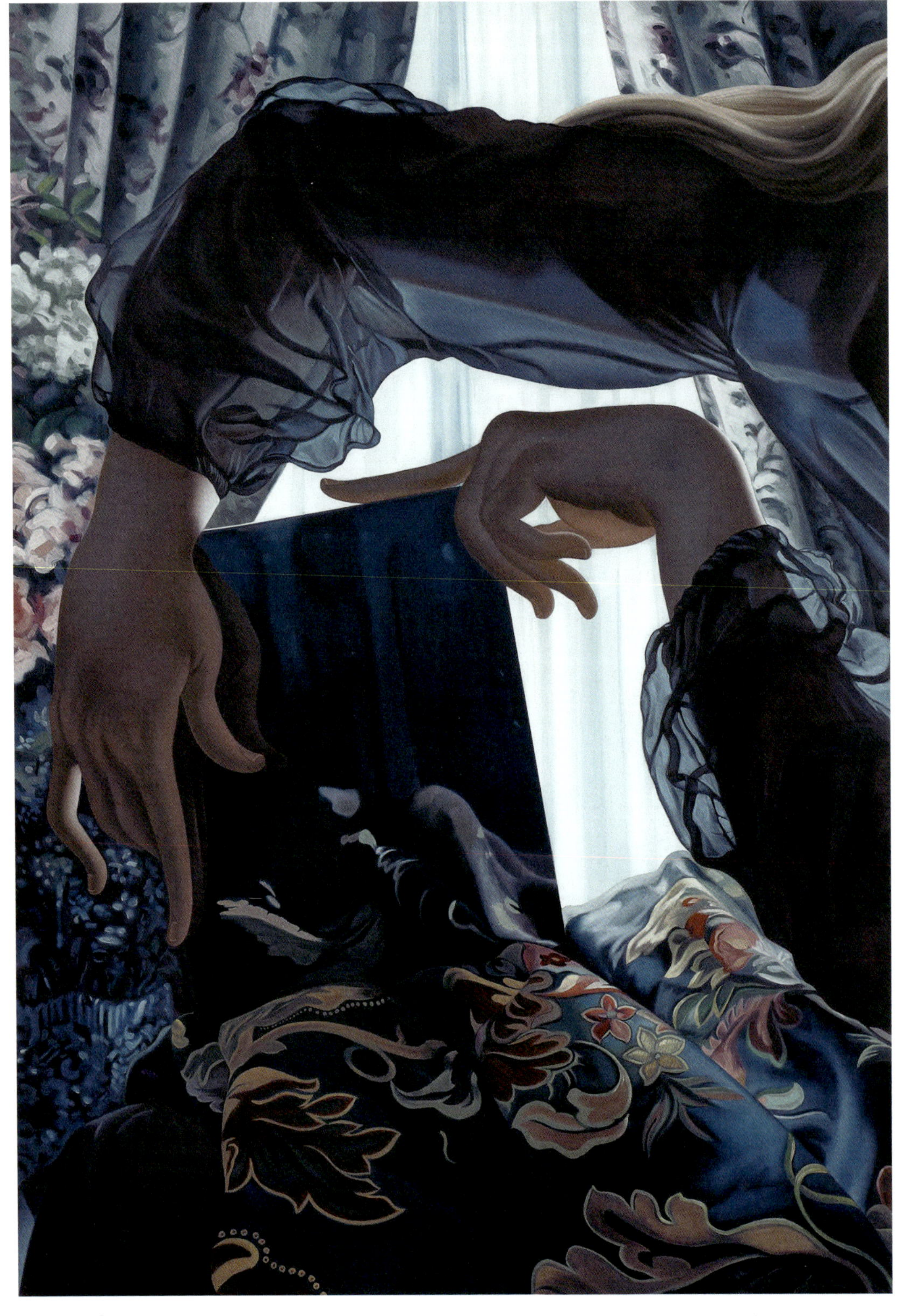

Divination 2023

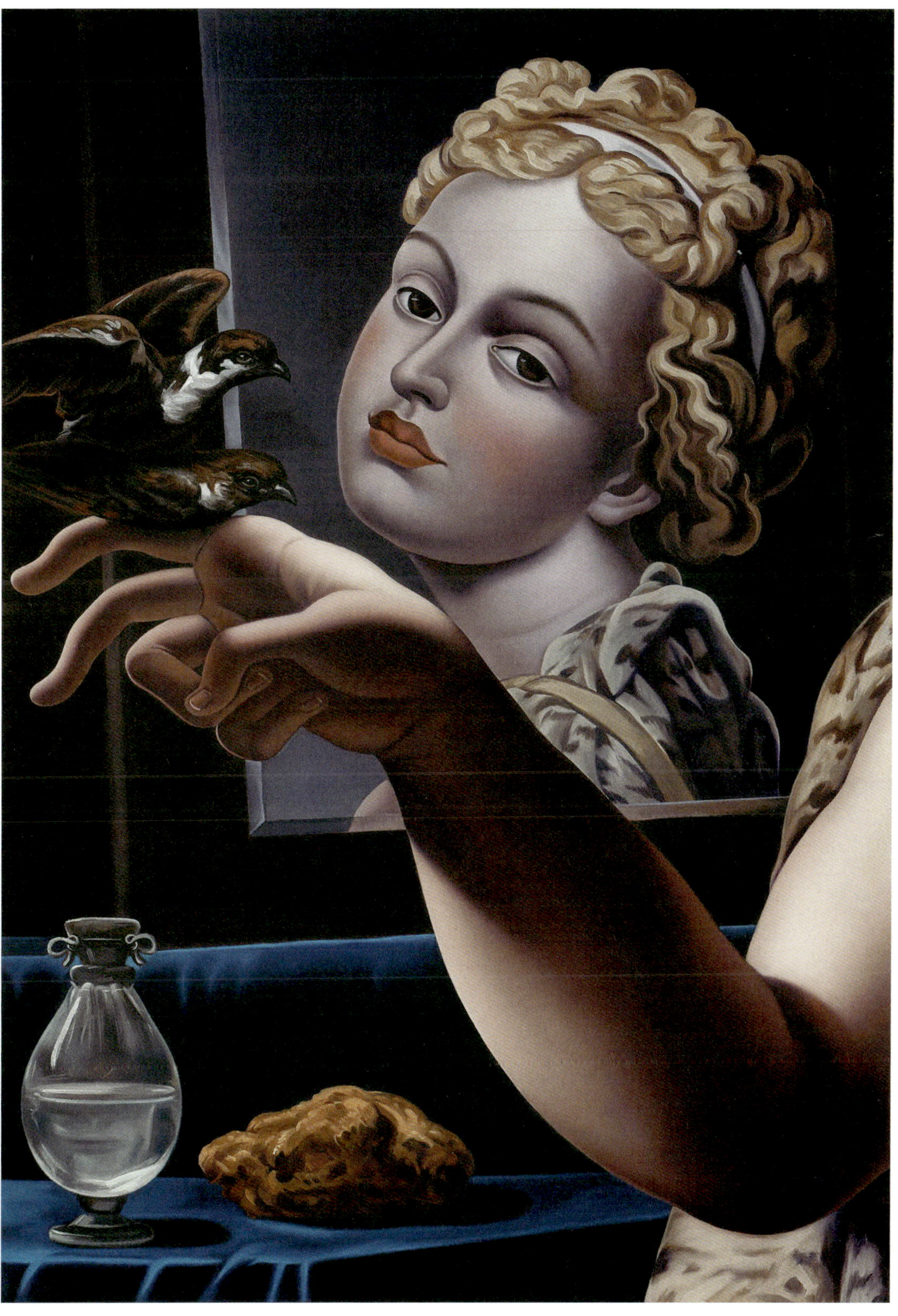

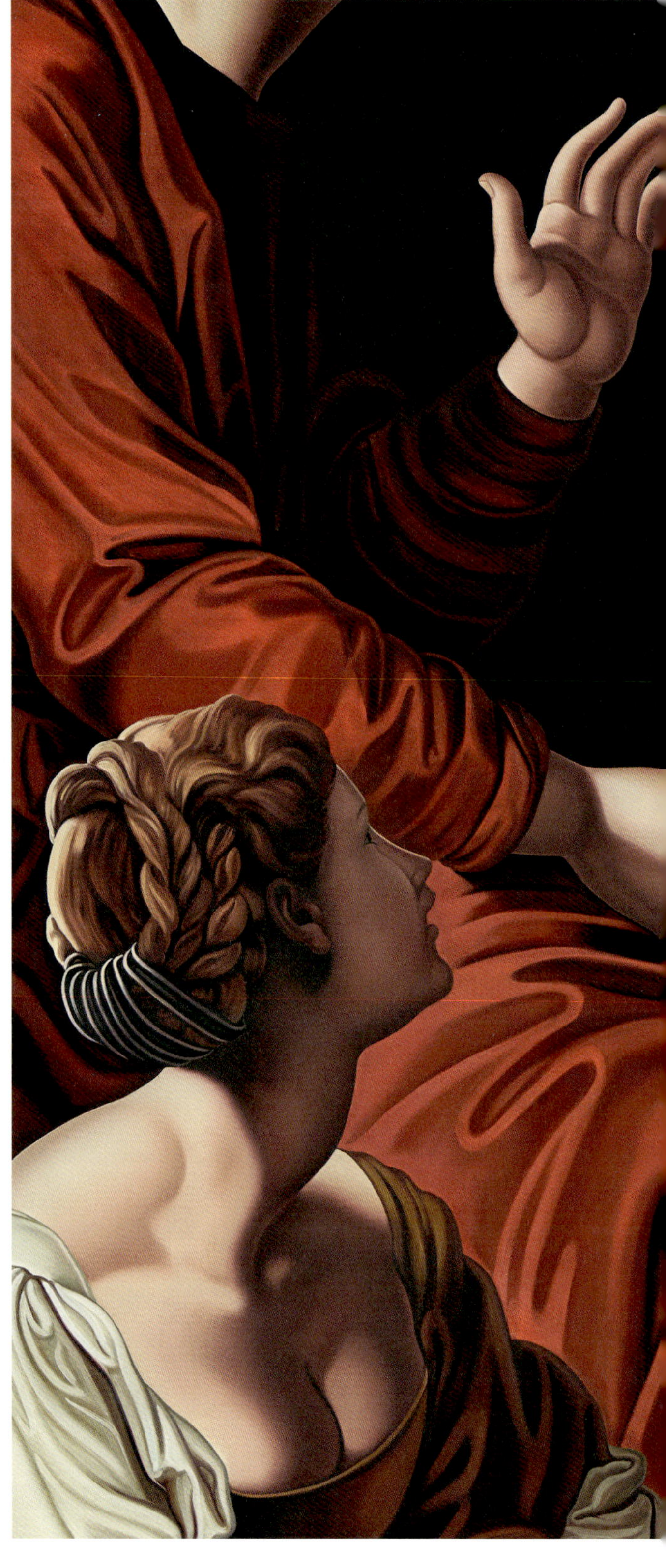

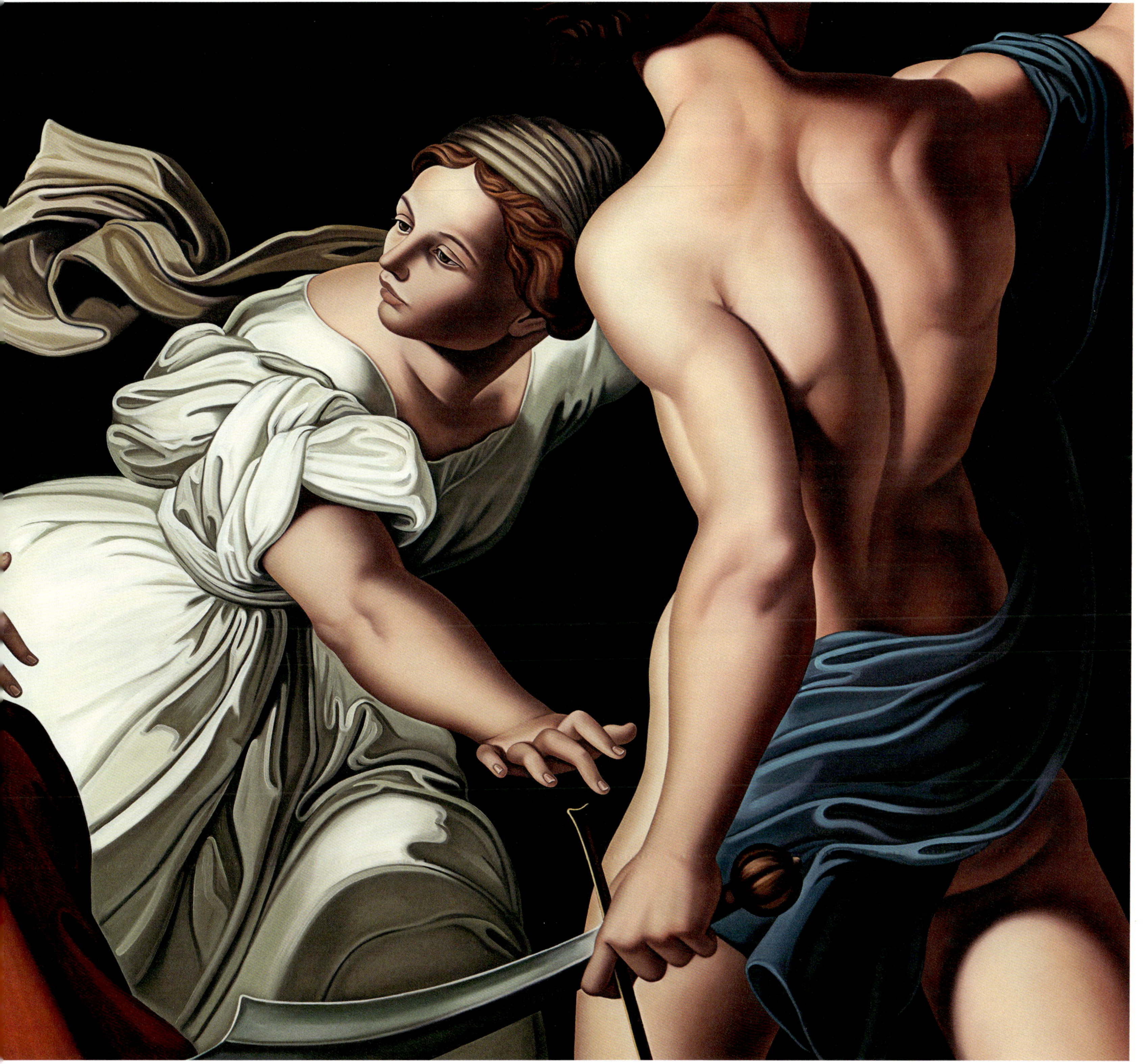

Outcry 2024

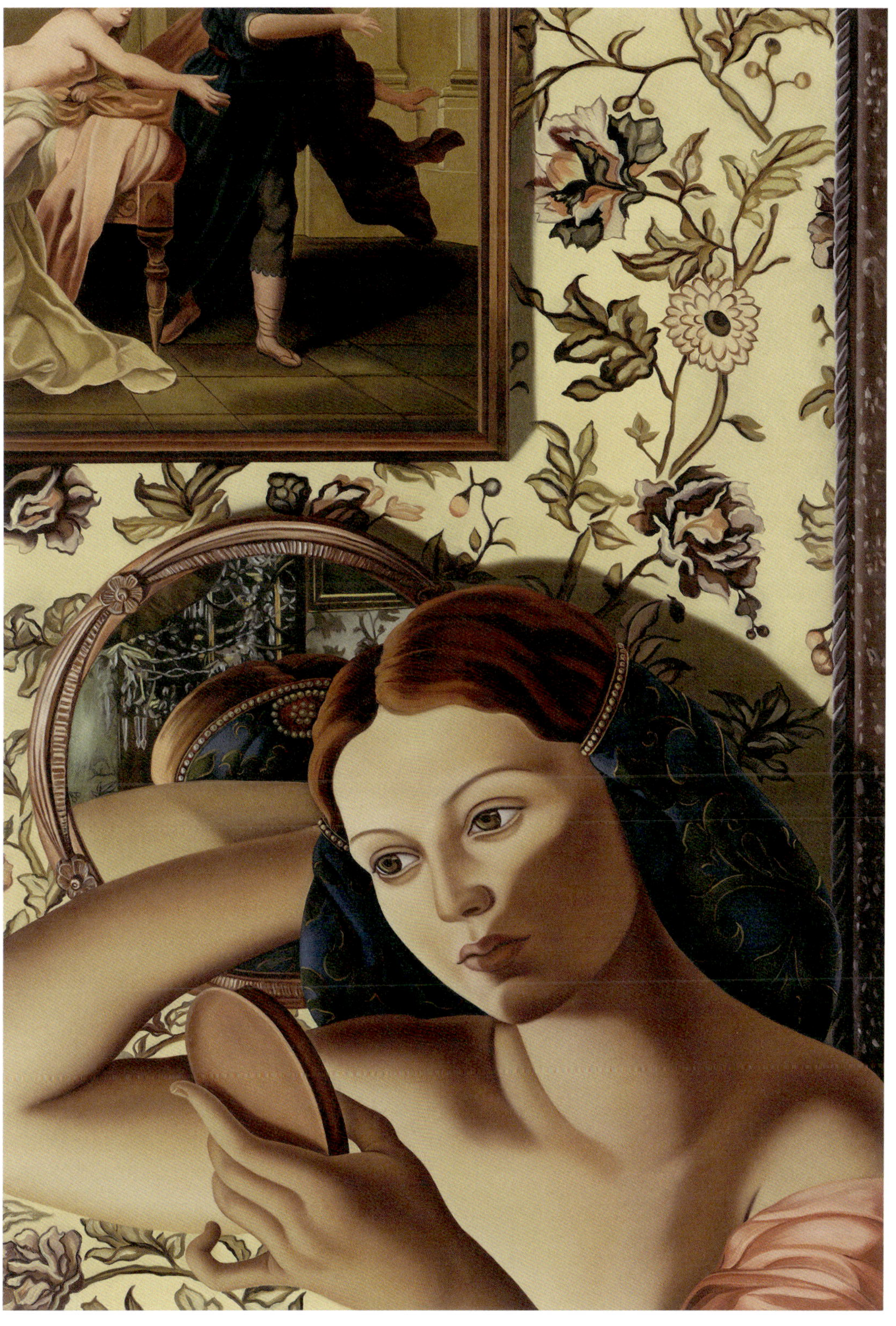

Herself unseen 2023

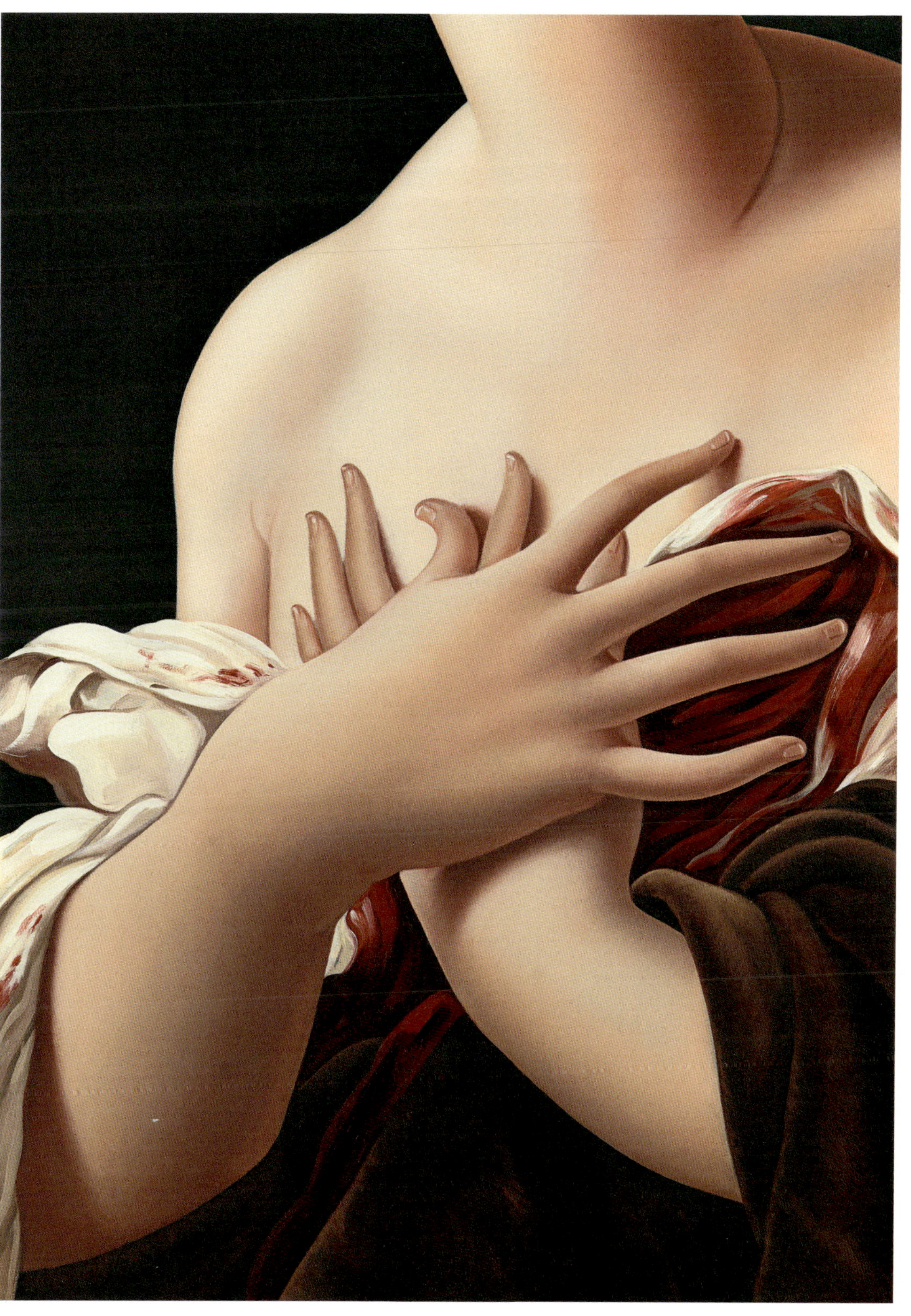

Unyielding 2023

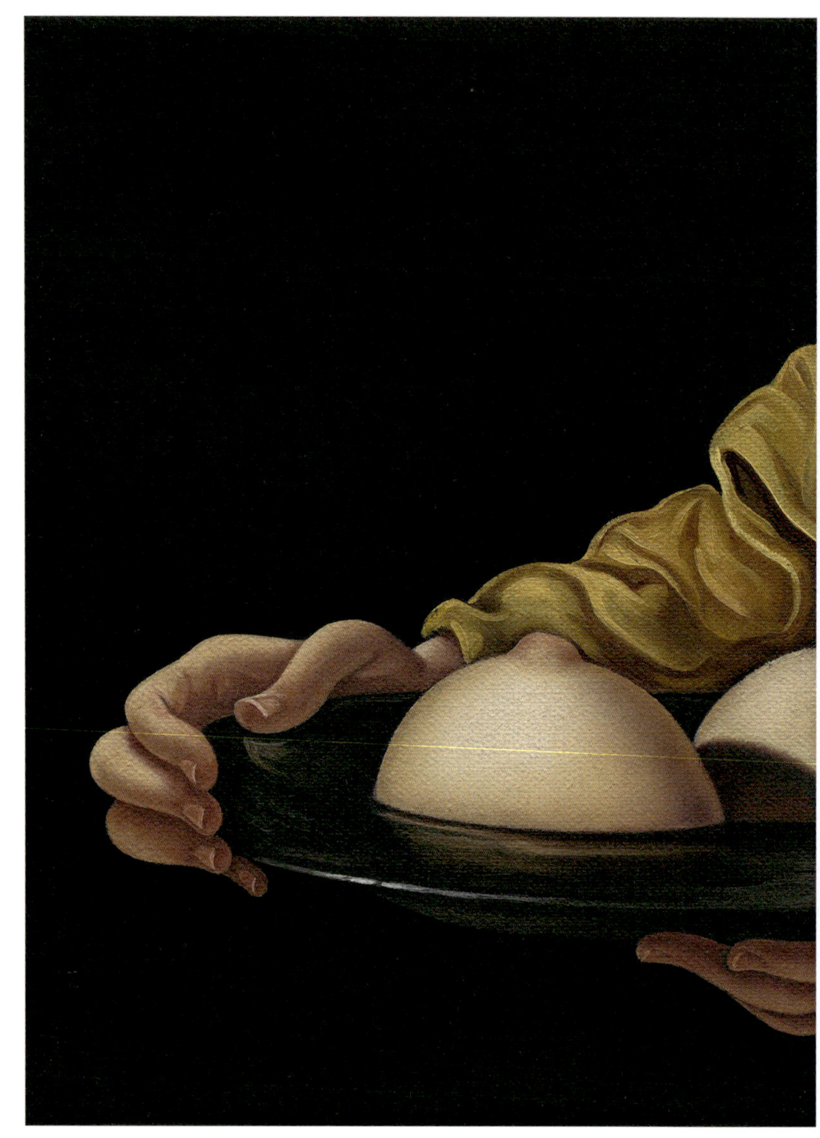

Plunder 2024

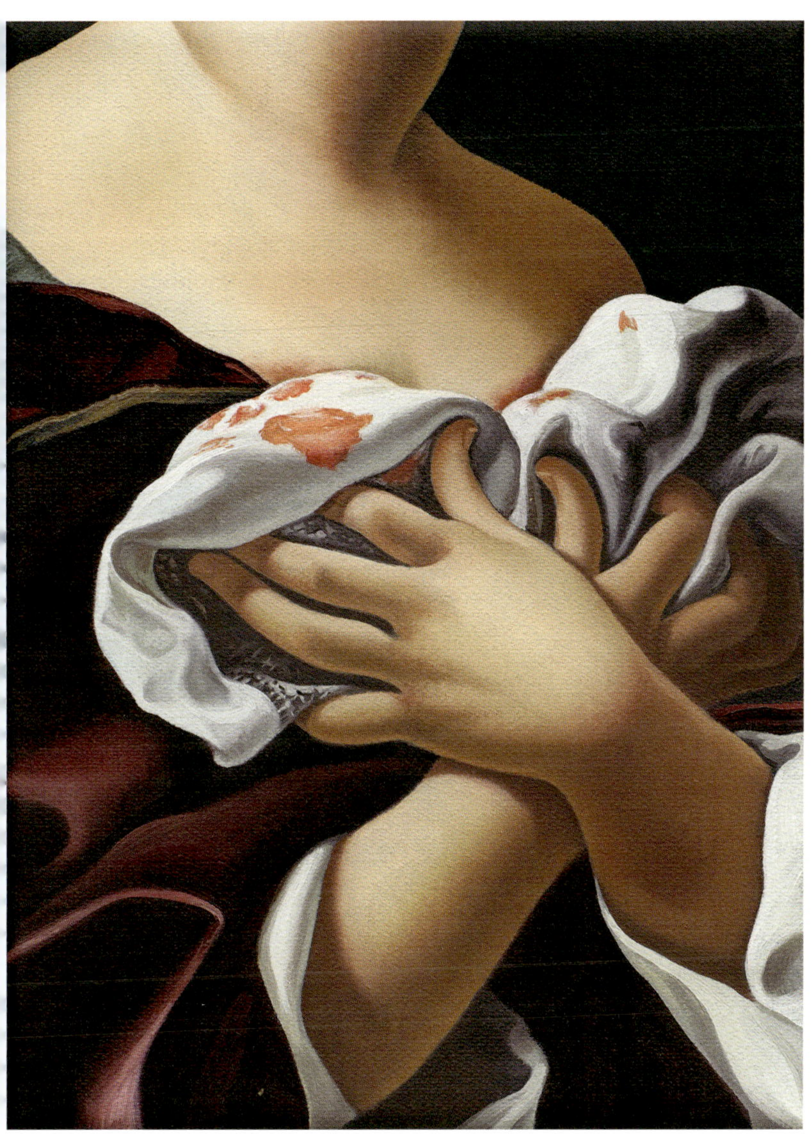

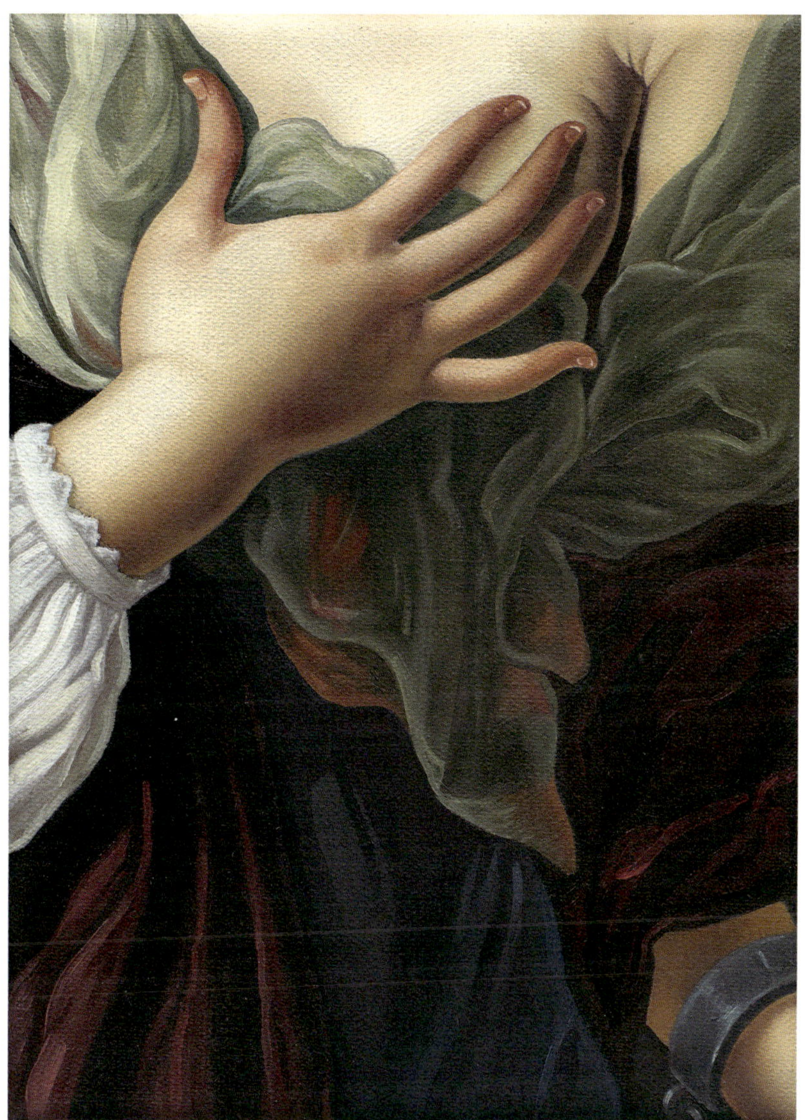

Despoil 2024

Revere 2024

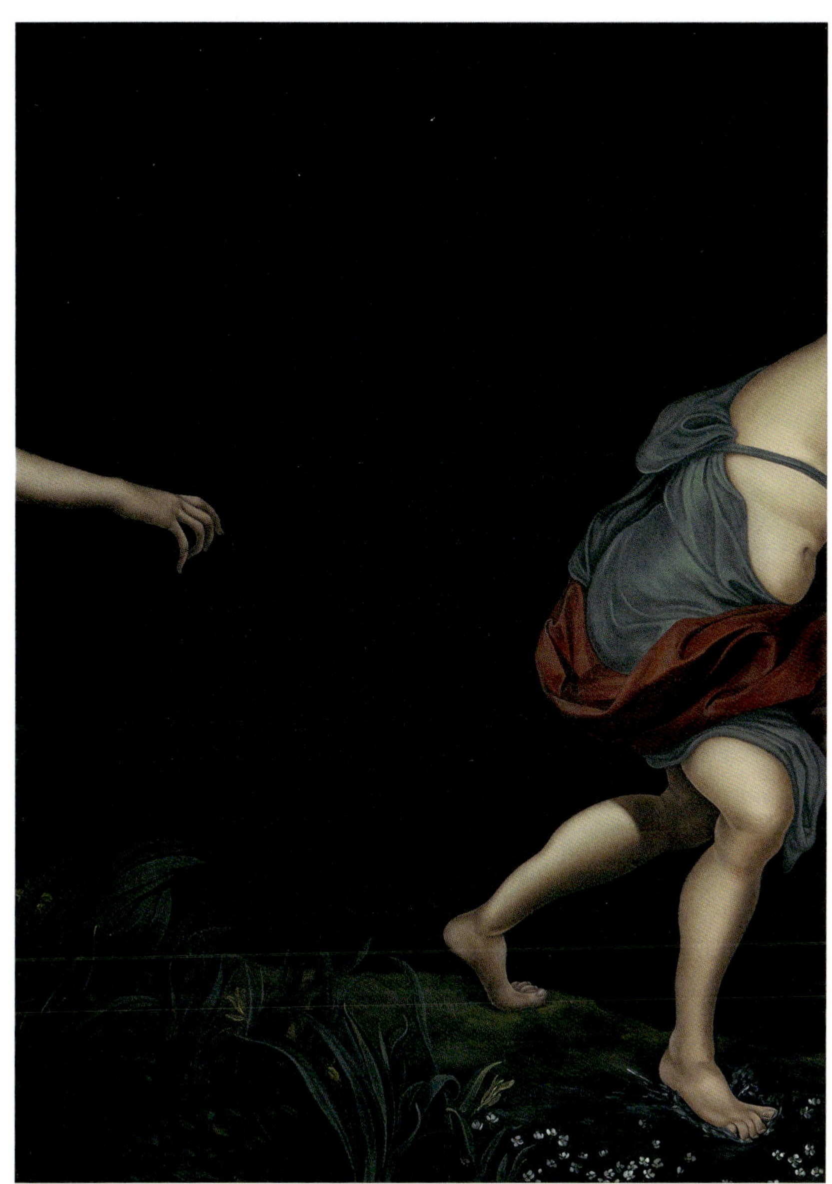
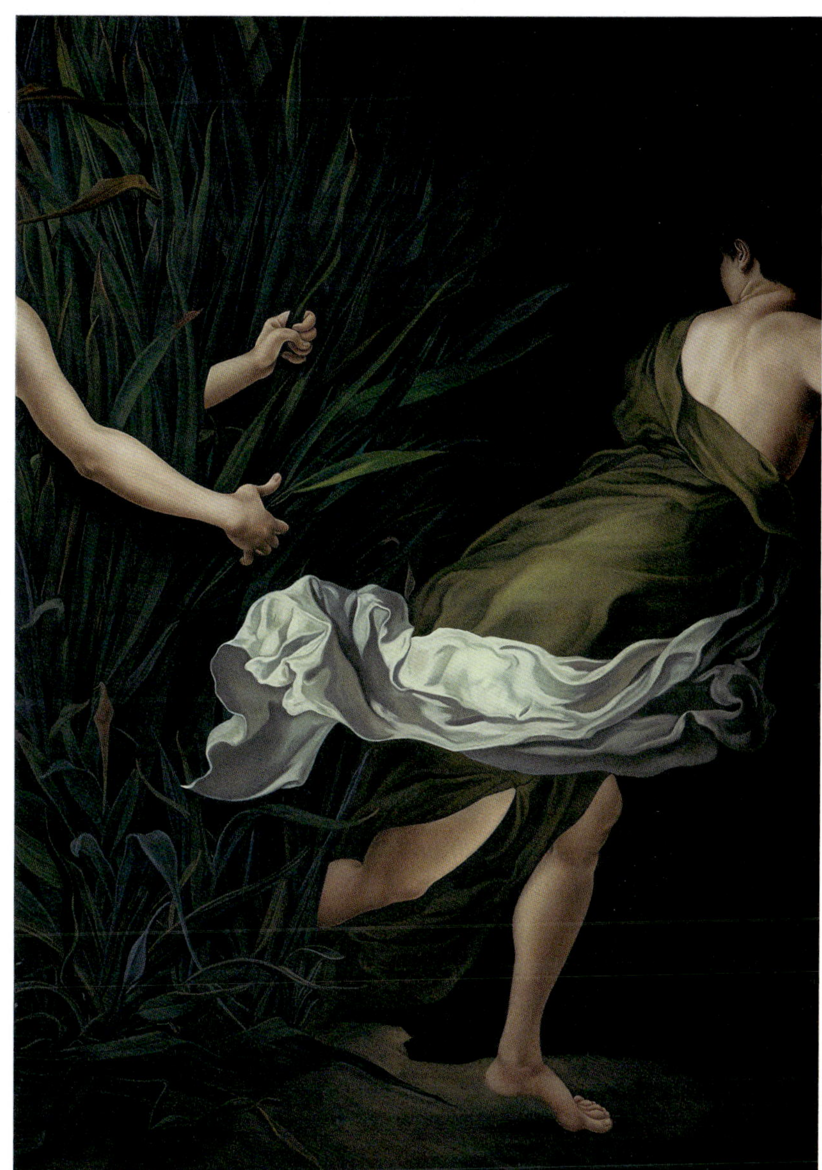

Syrinx 2018

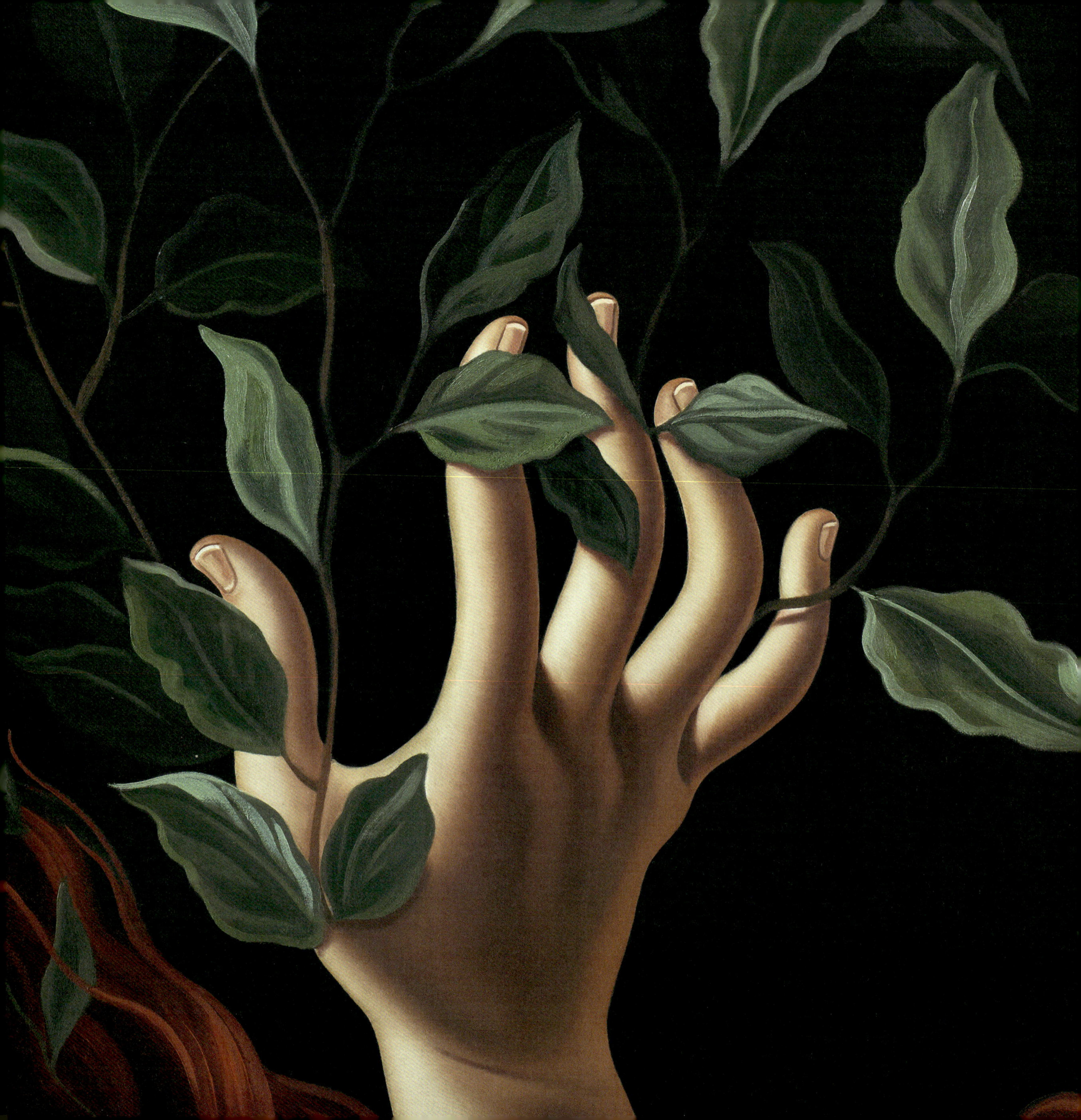

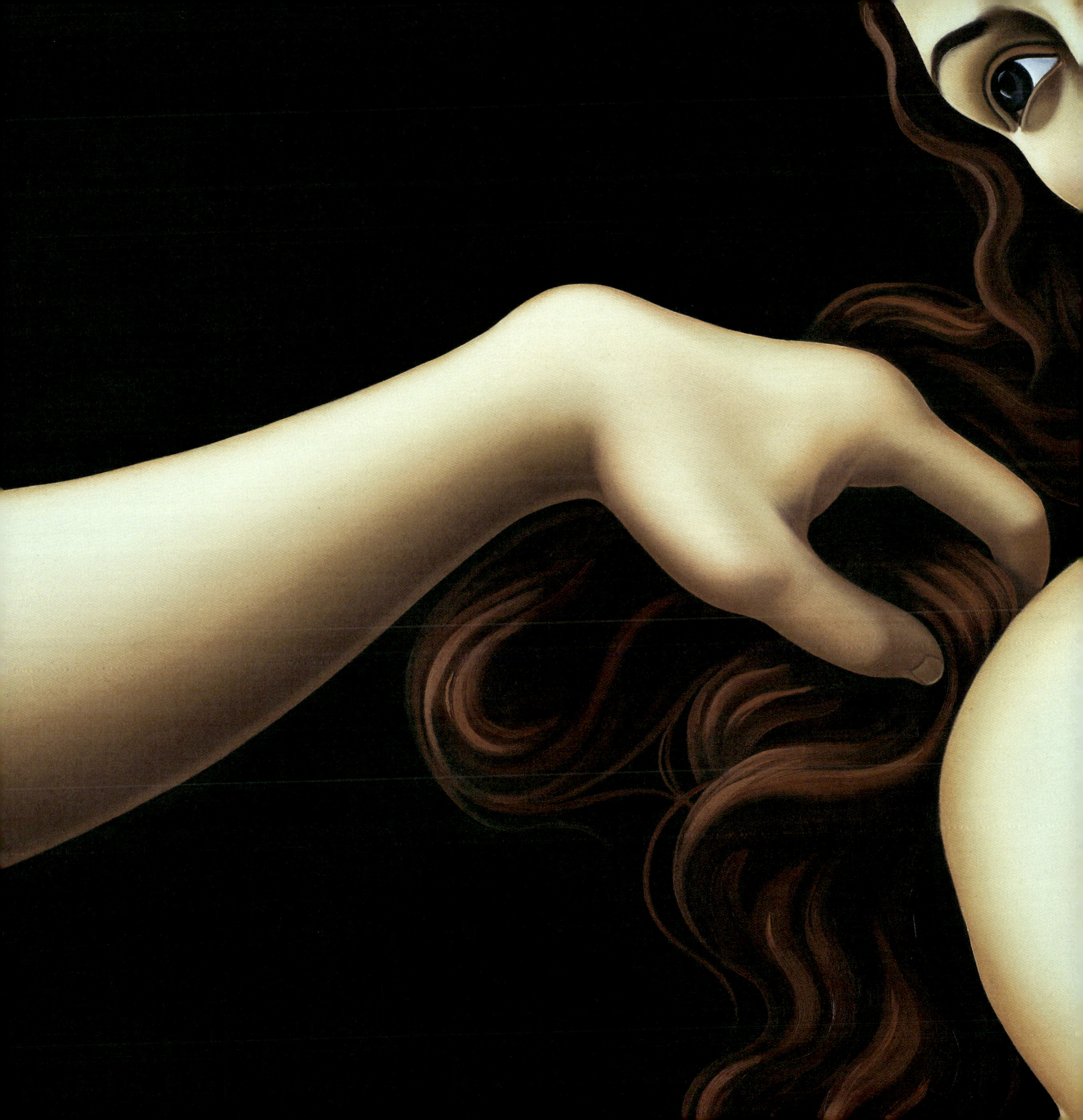

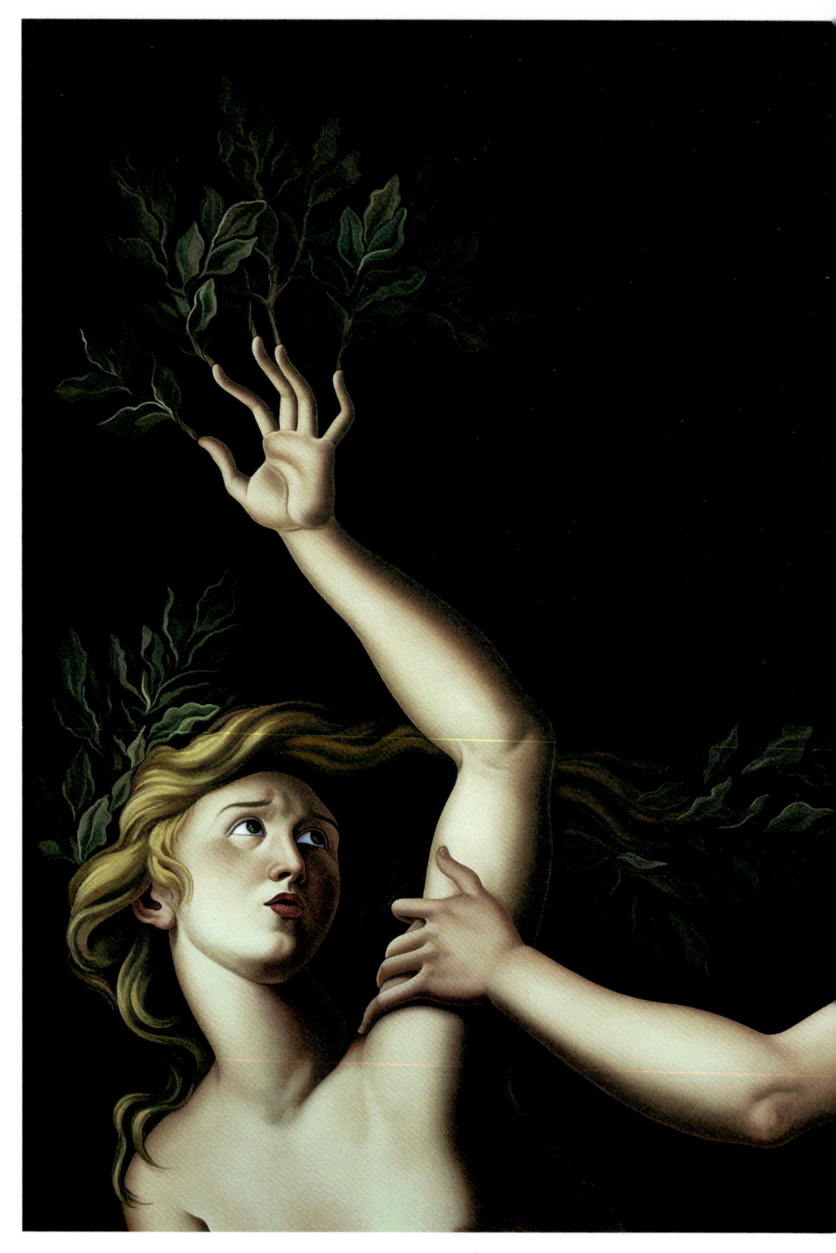

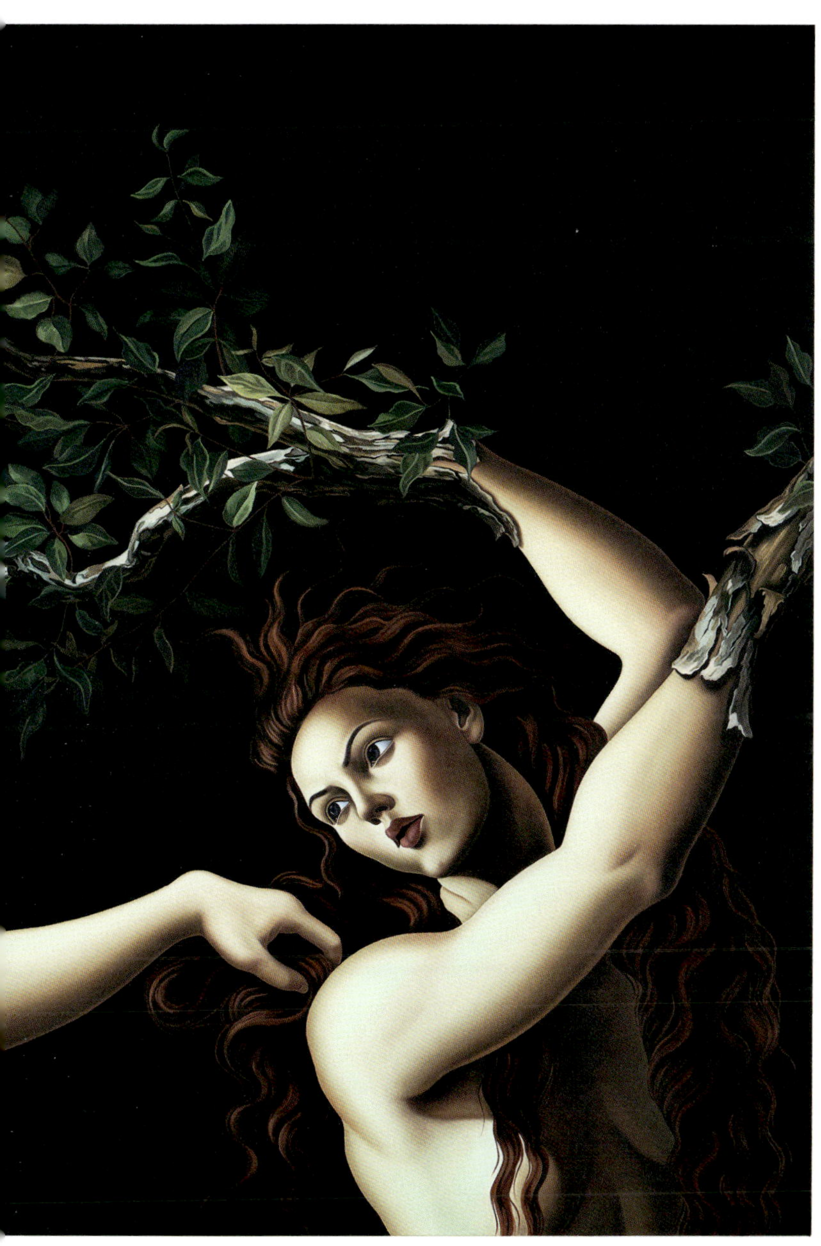

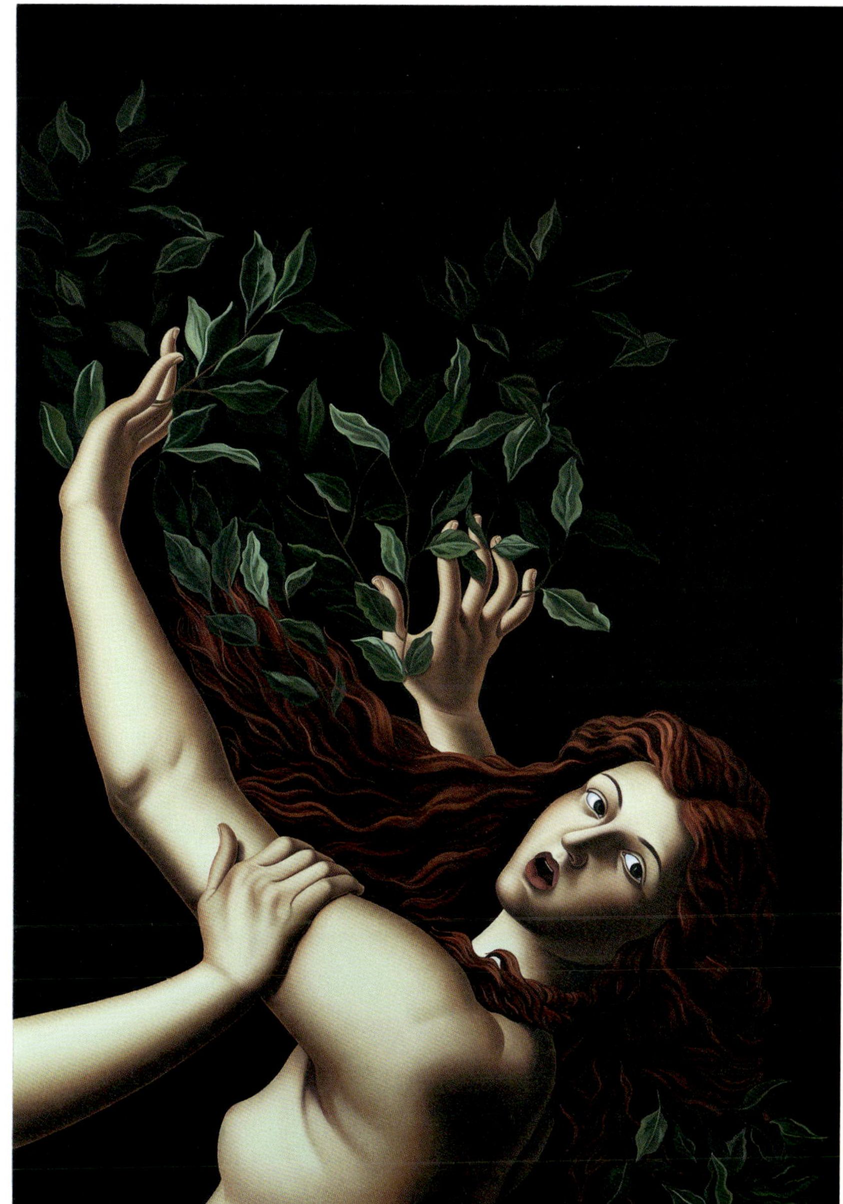

A story told this many times becomes the forest 2025

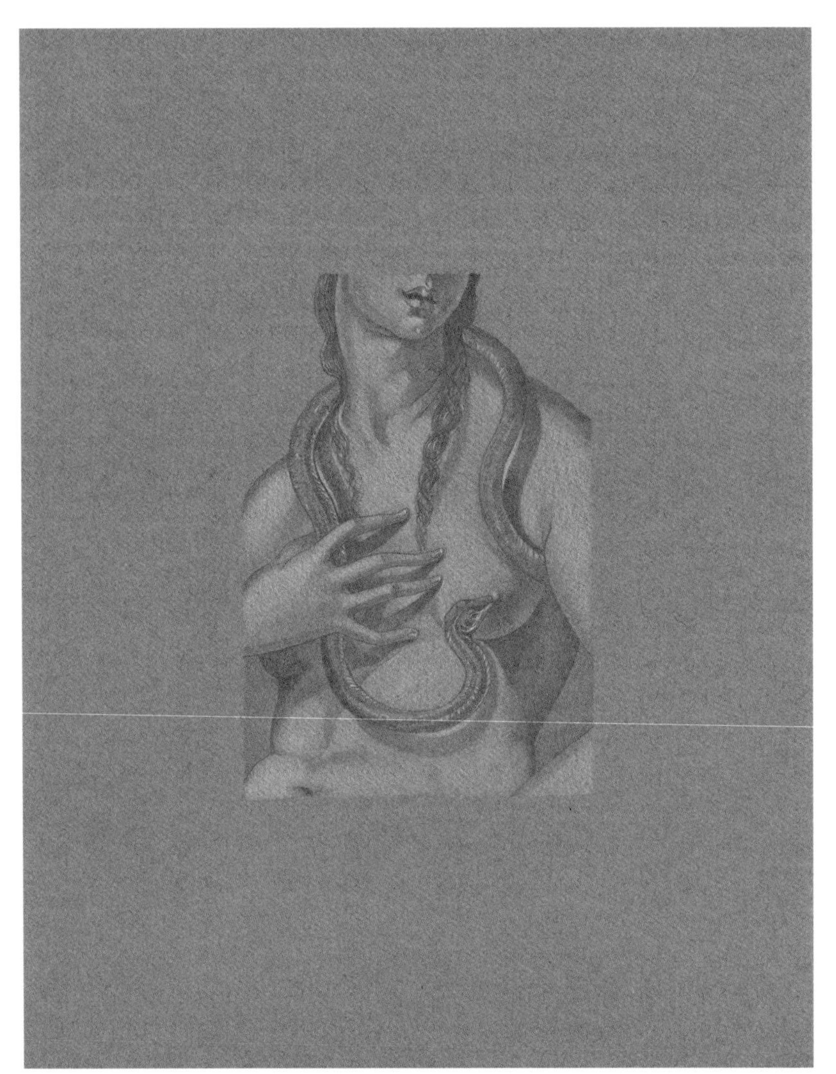

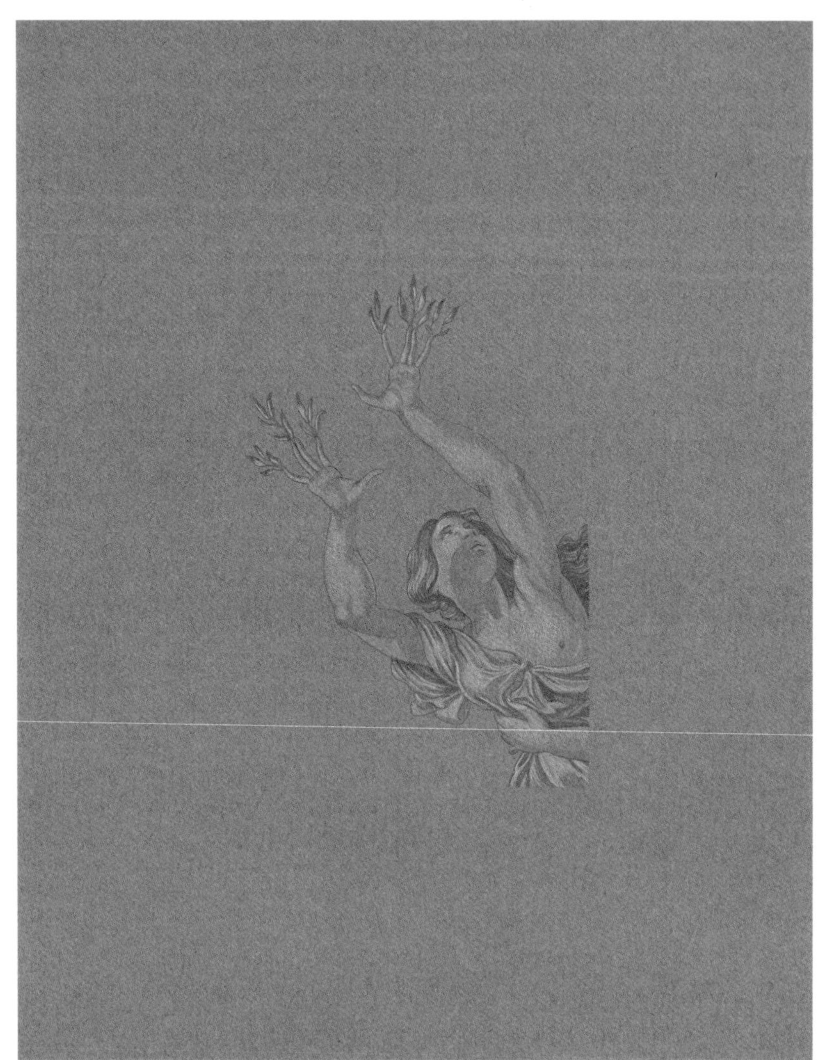

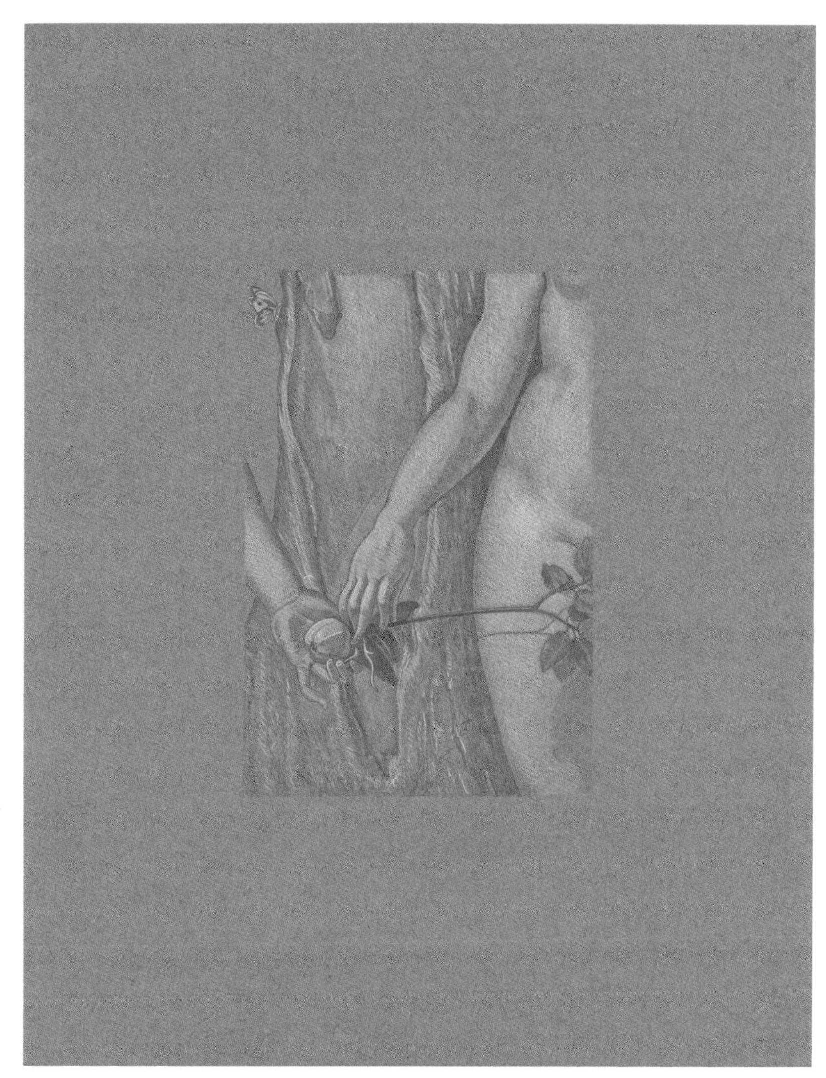

Selection of drawings from *Echoes* series 2025

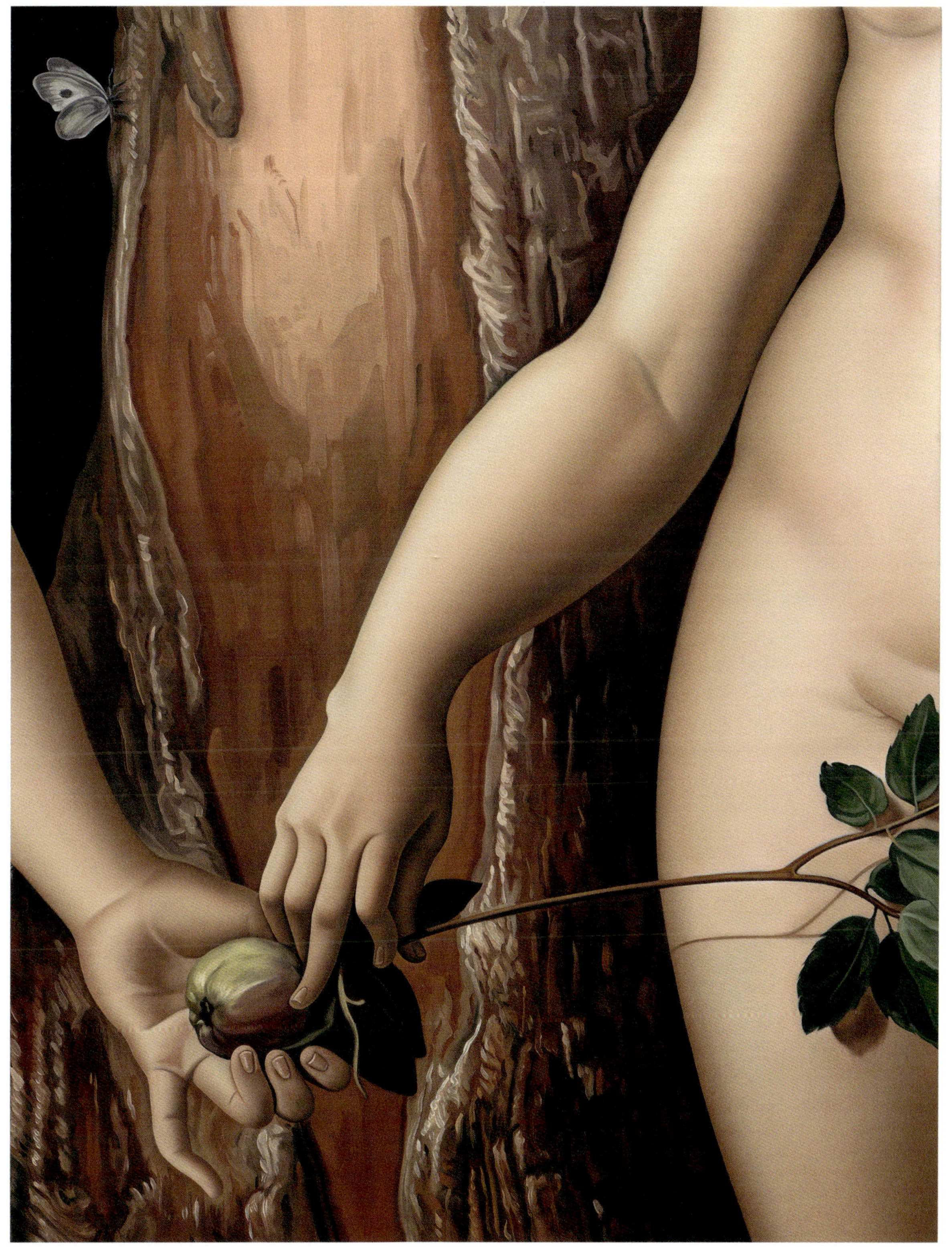

Forbidden Fruit 2025

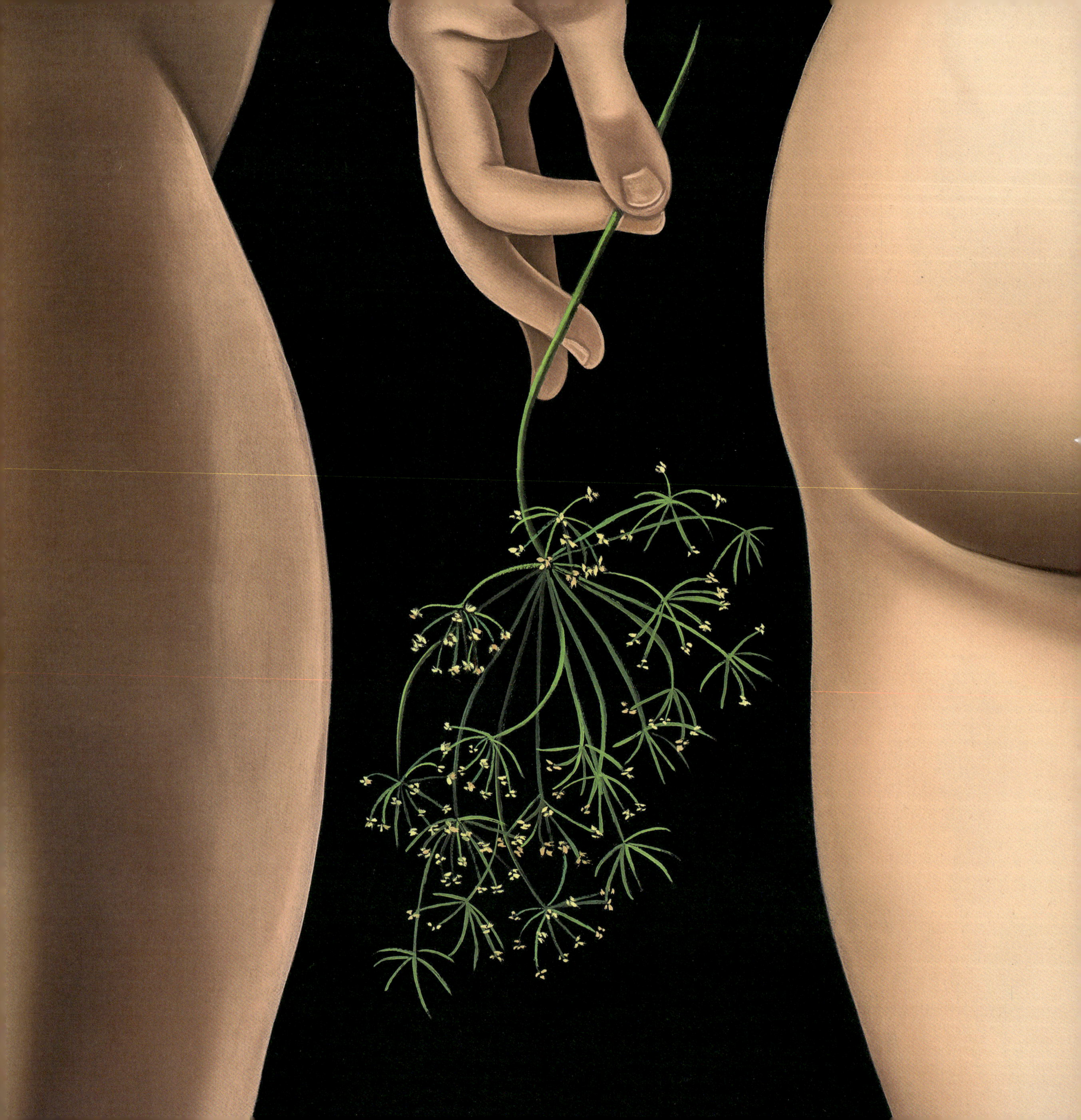

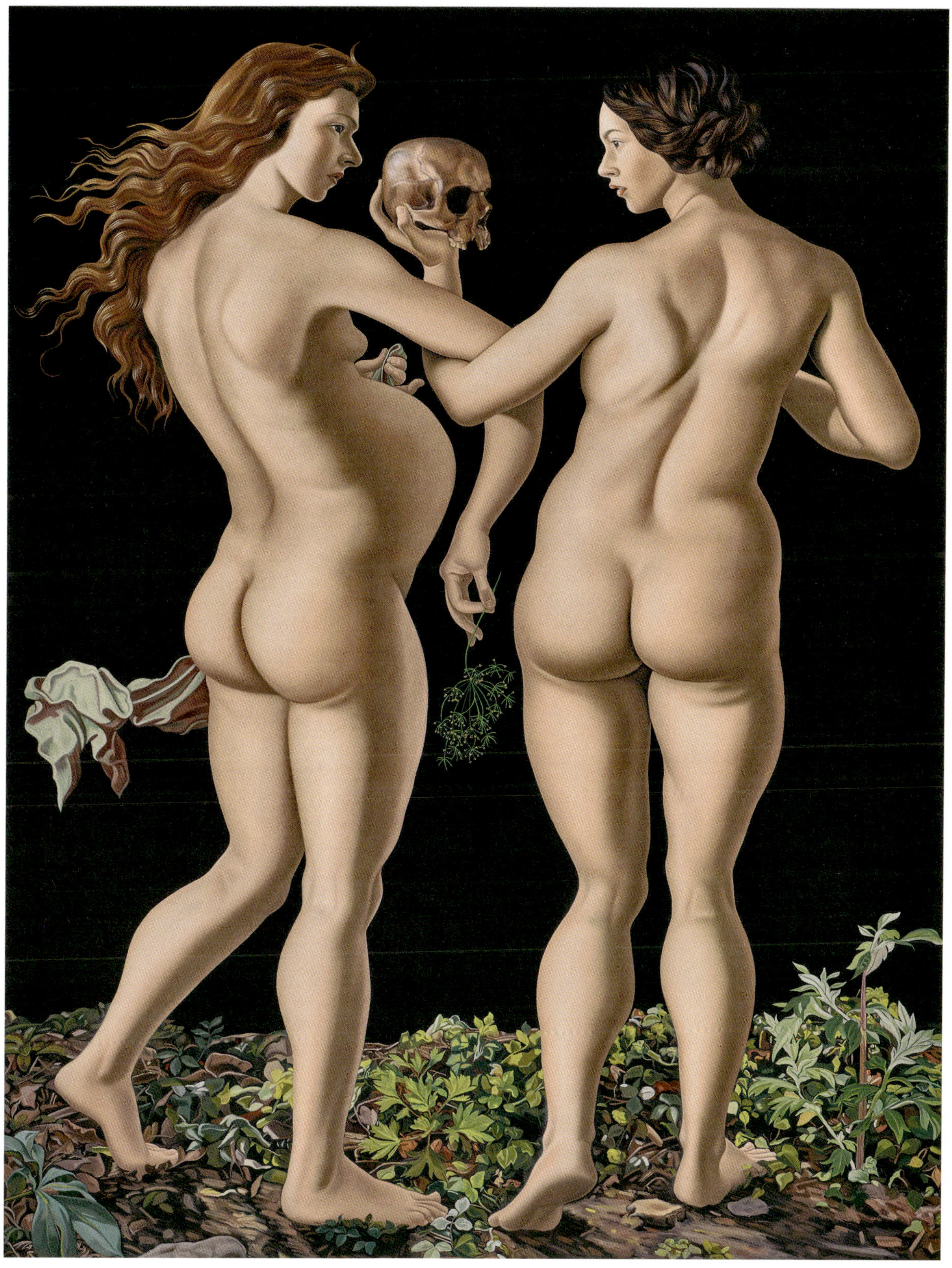

Natural Order 2025

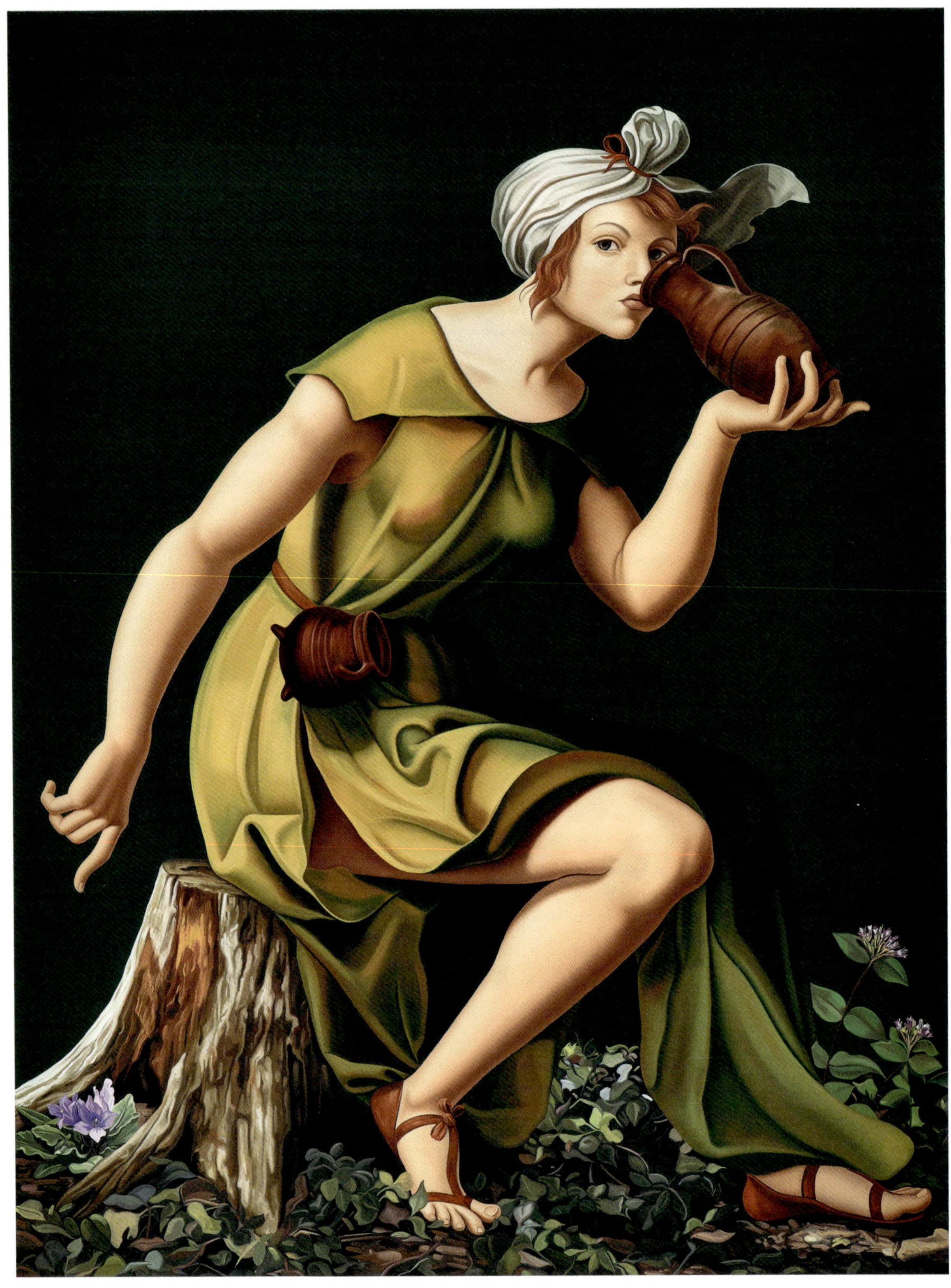

Old Magic 2025

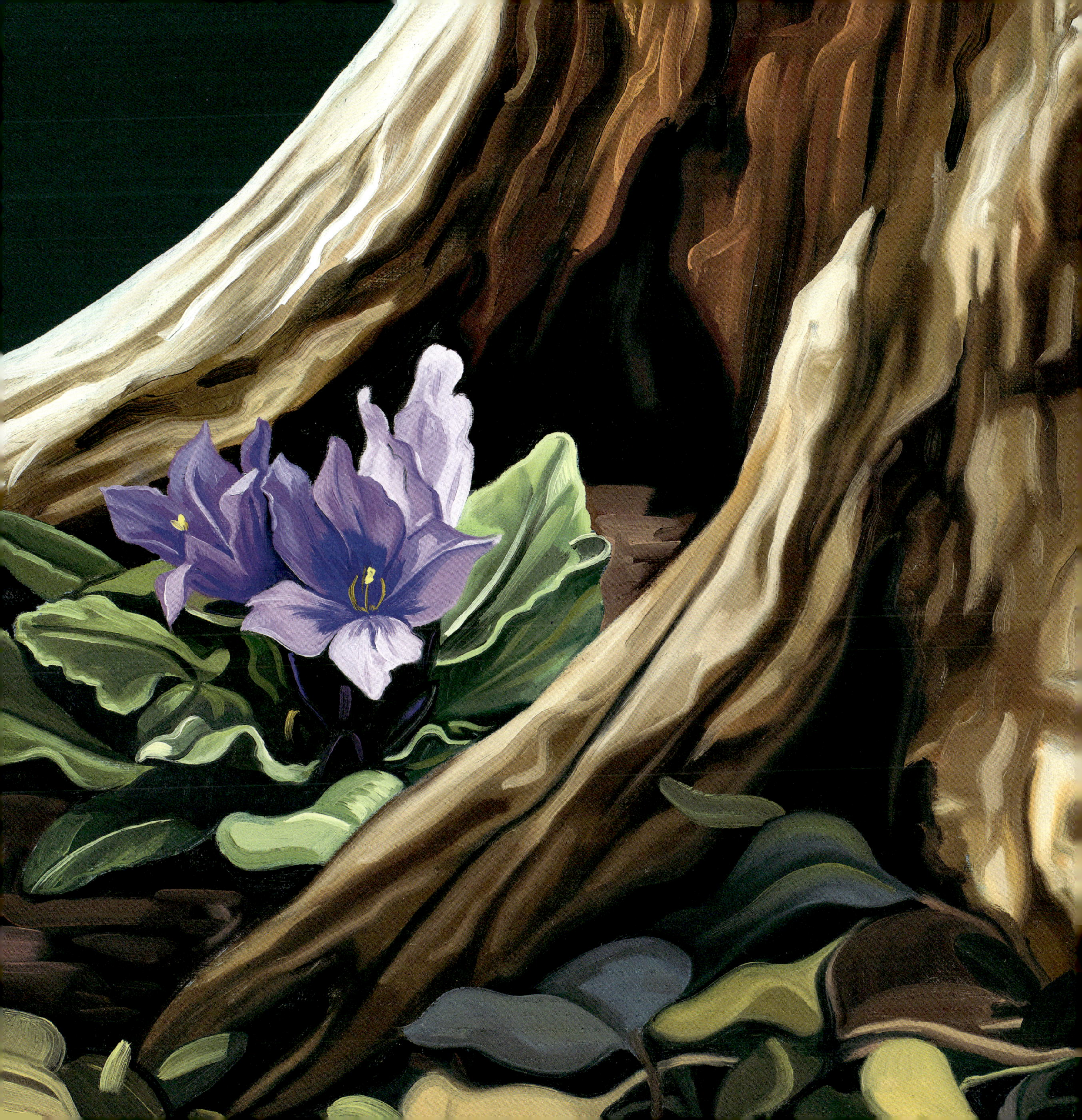

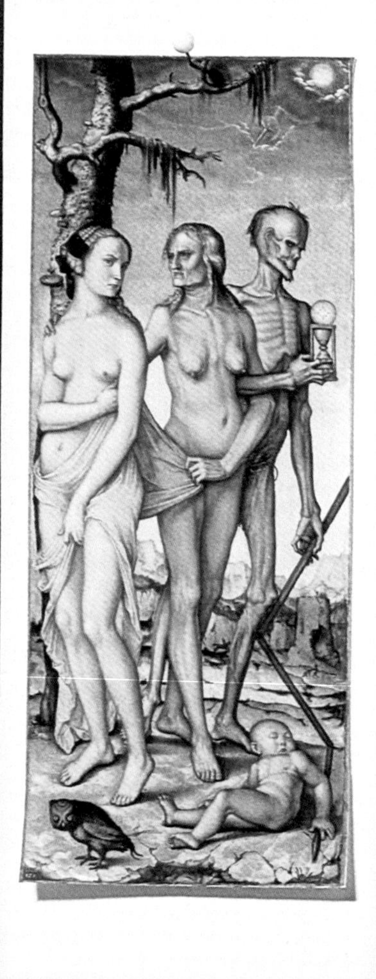

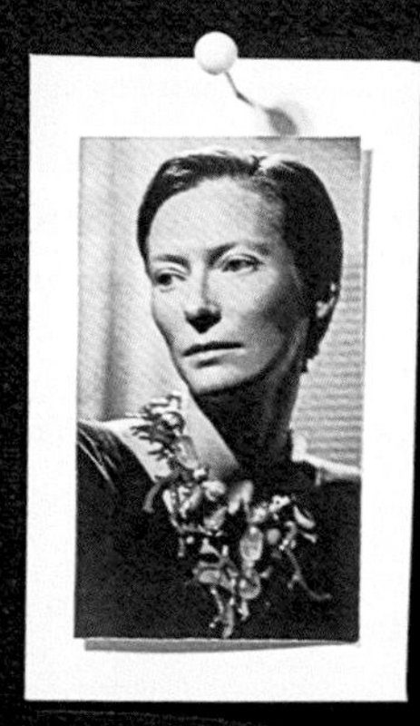

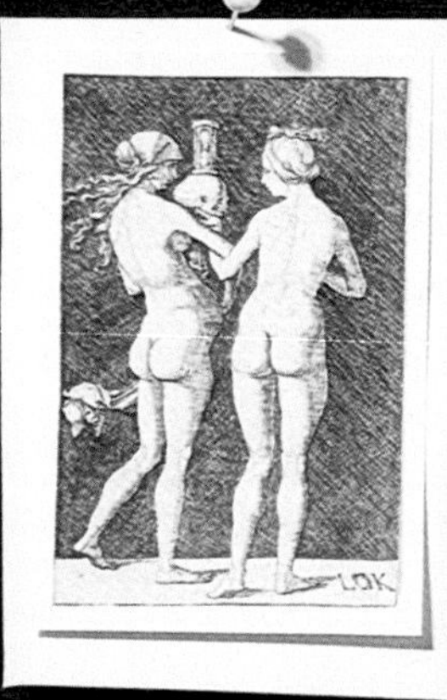
LDK

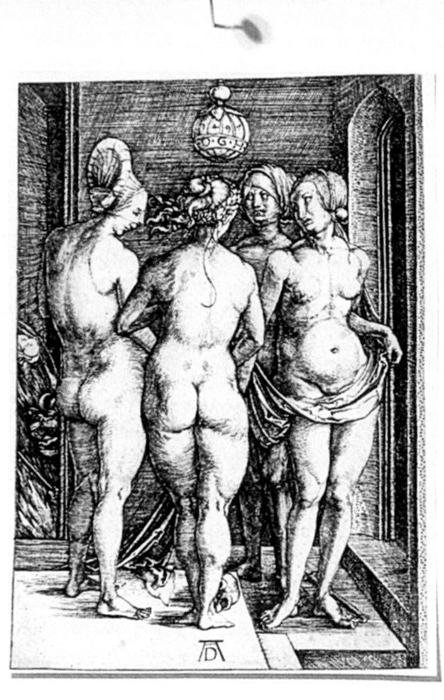

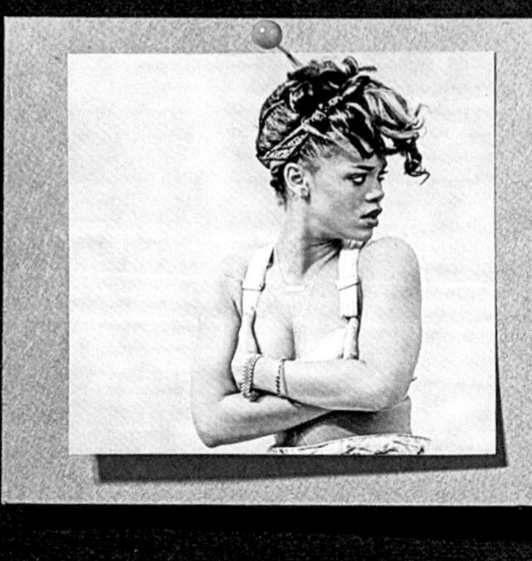

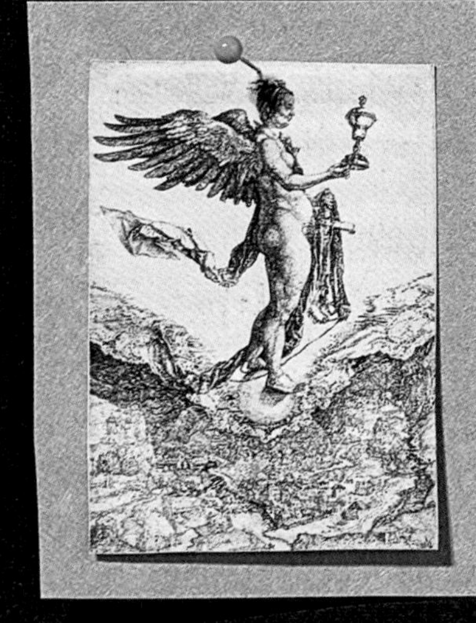

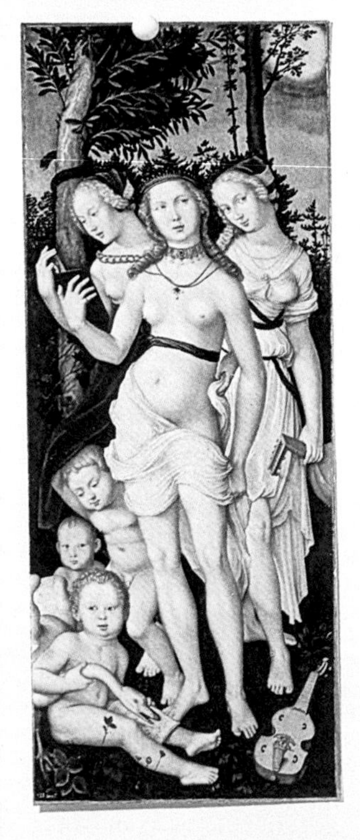

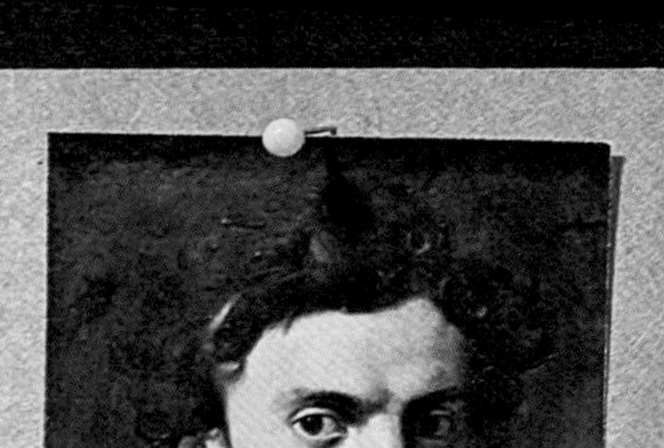

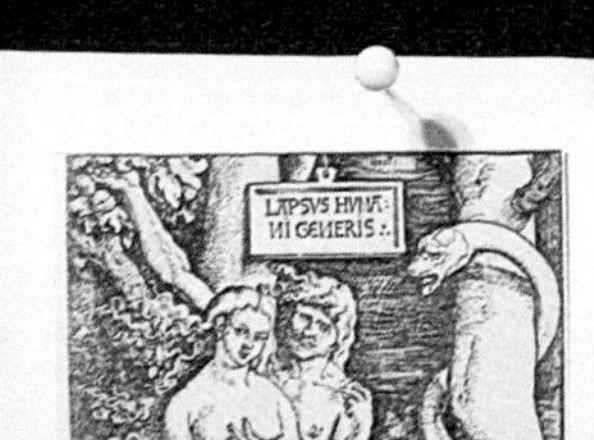
LAPSVS HVMA-
NI GENERIS

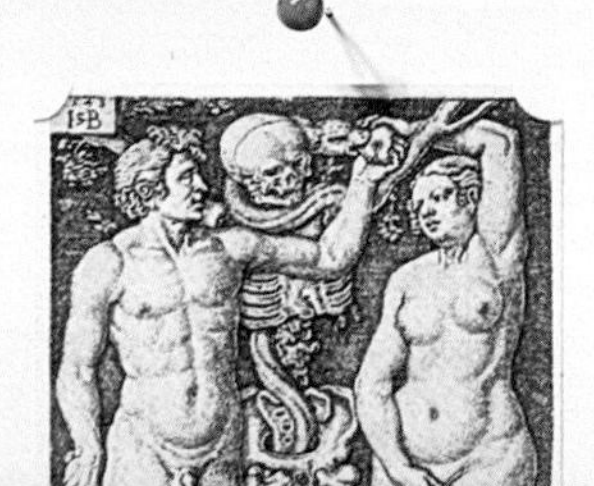

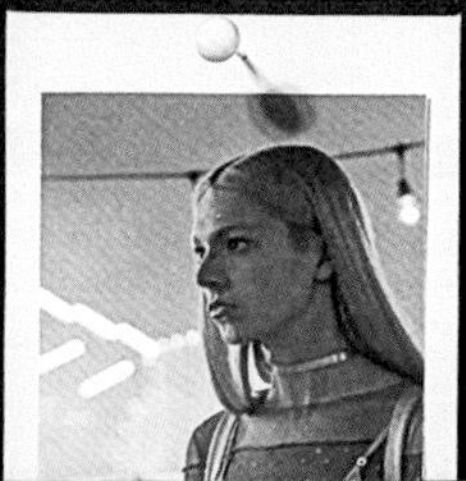

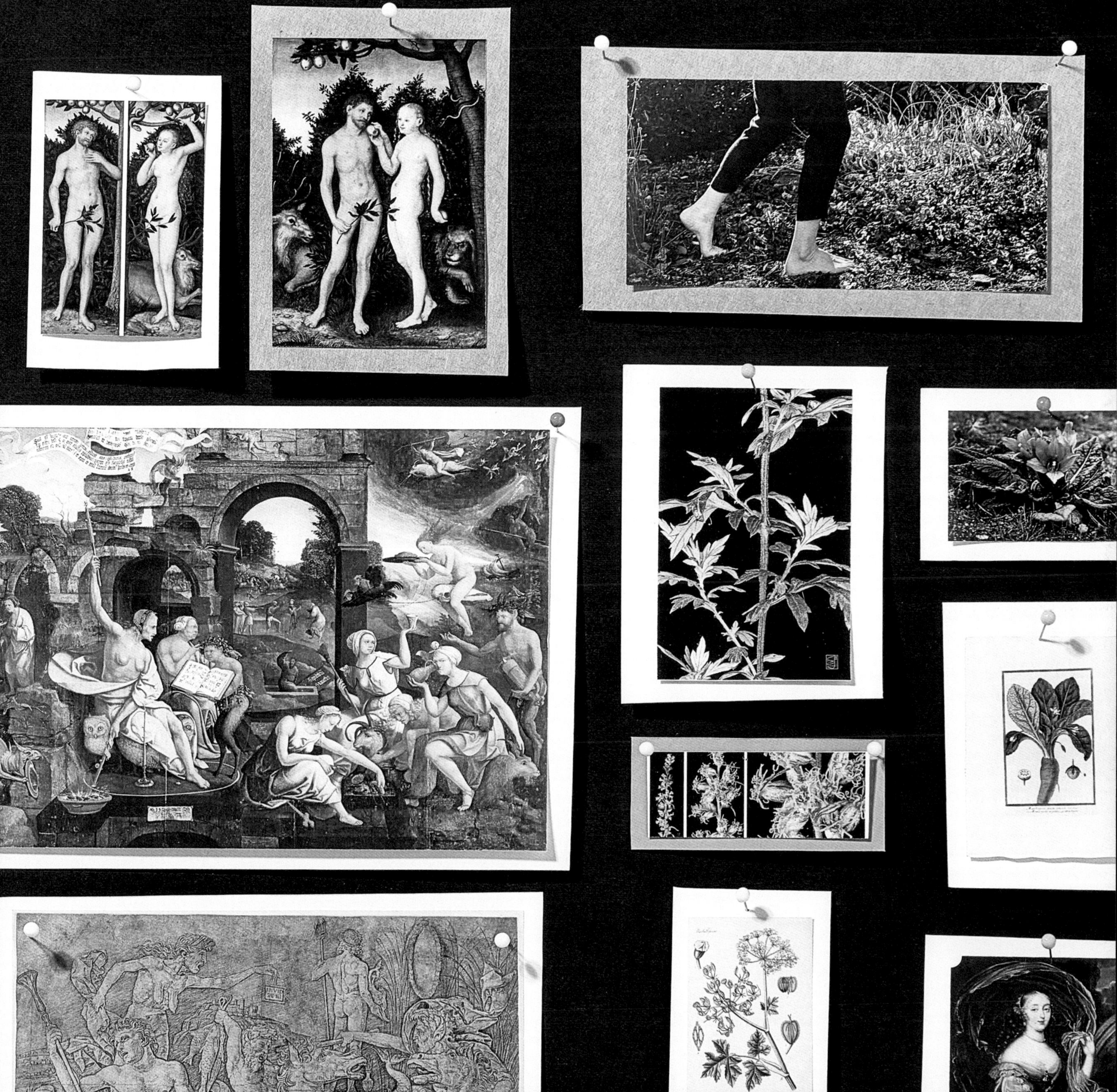

List of Works Exhibited

Jesse Mockrin
born Silver Spring, Maryland,
United States, 1981

A cry is heard
2025
oil on linen
109.2 × 83.8 cm
Courtesy of James Cohan,
New York
not illustrated

A story told this many times becomes the forest
2025
oil on linen, three panels
124.5 × 83.8 cm (each);
124.5 × 251.5 cm (overall)
Collection of Mark and
Louise Nelson,
Sydney, Australia
Photo: Izzy Leung
Pages 82–85

Behold/Beholden
2025
oil on cotton
160 × 106.7 cm
Courtesy of James Cohan,
New York
not illustrated

Bitter Seeds
2024
oil on linen, twenty panels
28.3 × 25.4 cm (each);
134.6 × 157.5 cm (installed)
On loan from the collection
of Hooman and Tiffany Dayani
Photo: Dan Bradica
Pages 1, 4, 21, 54–55

By her hand
2025
oil on cotton
124.5 × 83.8 cm
Private collection,
Columbus, Ohio
Photo: Dan Bradica
Pages 58–59

Despoil
2024
oil on cotton
17.8 × 12.7 cm
Johnson Shufro Collection,
New York
Photo: Dan Bradica
Pages 8 & 79

Divination
2023
oil on cotton
94 × 63.5 cm
Private collection
Photo: Marten Elder
Page 70

Series of *Echoes* drawings
2025
graphite and coloured pencil on paper
30.5 × 22.9 cm (each)
Courtesy of James Cohan,
New York

Echoes 1
Photo: Dan Bradica
Page 86 (left)

Echoes 2
Photo: Dan Bradica
Page 87

Echoes 3
Photo: Dan Bradica
Page 86 (right)

Echoes 4–8
not illustrated

Exhibition
2023
oil on cotton
73.7 × 50.8 cm
Private collection,
courtesy Kristy Bryce Art Advisory
Photo: Marten Elder
Page 71

Forbidden Fruit
2025
oil on linen
76.2 × 50.8 cm
Collection of the artist
Photo: Dan Bradica
Pages 23 & 89

Fracture
2024
oil on linen
91.4 × 142.2 cm
Art Gallery of Ontario
Purchase, with funds from
the F.P. Wood Fund, 2025
2024/390
Photo: Phoebe D'Heurle
Pages 12–13, 52–53

Heartsick
2025
oil on linen
109.2 × 83.8 cm
Courtesy of James Cohan,
New York
not illustrated

Herself unseen
2023
oil on cotton
94 × 63.5 cm
Collection Glenn and
Amanda Fuhrman NY,
courtesy The FLAG Art Foundation
Photo: Marten Elder
Page 75

In mid-stream
2017
oil on linen, two panels
188 × 129.5 cm (each);
188 × 259.1 cm (overall)
Private collection, Los Angeles
Photo: Karl Puchlik, image courtesy
of the artist, Michael Kohn
Gallery, Los Angeles,
Night Gallery, Los Angeles, and
James Cohan, New York
Page 65

Longing
2025
oil on linen
109.2 × 83.8 cm
Collection of Julie Montague
Photo: Dan Bradica
Pages 56–57

Natural Order
2025
oil on cotton
177.8 × 132.1 cm
Collection of Nish and Ali de Gruiter
Photo: Nik Massey
Pages 90–91

Old Magic
2025
oil on cotton
152.4 × 111.8 cm
Private collection
Photo: Nik Massey
Pages 92–93

Only Sound Remains
2025
oil on linen
198.1 × 144.8 cm
Courtesy of Circa 1881
Photo: Dan Bradica
Pages 14 & 17

Outcry
2024
oil on linen
91.4 × 142.2 cm
Collection of Amy and Drew McKnight
Photo: Phoebe D'Heurle
Pages 2–3, 72–73

Plunder
2024
oil on cotton
17.8 × 12.7 cm
Johnson Shufro Collection,
New York
Photo: Dan Bradica
Pages 9 & 78

Revere
2024
oil on cotton
17.8 × 12.7 cm
Johnson Shufro Collection,
New York
Photo: Dan Bradica
Page 79

Sleepless night
2025
oil on linen
81.3 × 110.5 cm
Courtesy of James Cohan,
New York
not illustrated

Syrinx
2018
oil on linen, two panels
172.7 × 119.4 cm (each);
172.7 × 238.8 cm (overall)
Collection of Ellen and
Jamie Copaken, Kansas City
Photo: Marten Elder
Page 81

The Descent
2024
oil on linen, five panels
228.6 × 157.5 cm (each);
228.6 × 787.4 cm (overall)
Collection of Sally Taylor
and Ralph Tawil
Photo: Phoebe D'Heurle
Pages 66–69, 112–113

*Tribute (Plants Used in the Past
for Conception, Contraception
and Abortion: meadow rue,
echinacea, parsley, doubtful
knight's-spur, larkspur, hellebore,
mint, silver knapweed and sunflower)*
2025
oil on linen
94 × 63.5 cm
Courtesy of James Cohan, New York
not illustrated

Unyielding
2023
oil on canvas
33.7 × 22.9 cm
Collection of Robert Simon,
New York
Photo: Phoebe D'Heurle
Page 77

Witness
2025
oil on cotton, two panels
94 × 63.5 cm (each);
94 × 127 cm (overall)
Collection of Robin and
Vanessa Delmer
Photo: Dan Bradica
Pages 61–63

Exhibited in conjunction with the following works from the Art Gallery of Ontario collection and The Thomson Collection:

Jacques Belly (after Annibale Carracci)
Apollo and the Cumaean Sibyl
date unknown
etching and engraving on paper
21.7 × 21.6 cm
Art Gallery of Ontario
Presented in memory of
W.R. Johnston, 1950
82/88

Giacinto Calandrucci
The Ecstasy of St. Theresa
date unknown
pen and brown ink with traces
of white over black chalk on paper
24.1 × 18 cm
Art Gallery of Ontario
Gift from the Estate of R. Fraser Elliott,
2005
2005/200

Jacopo de' Barbari
The Three Prisoners
c. 1505
engraving on paper
15.7 × 9.6 cm
Art Gallery of Ontario
Gift of Mr. Vincent Tovell, 1986
86/295

Albrecht Dürer
Nemesis
c. 1502
engraving on paper
33.3 × 22.9 cm
Art Gallery of Ontario
Gift of Dr. and Mrs. R. Ian Hector, 1989
89/398

Ignaz Elhafen (ivory);
Octavian Cocssel (silver)
Tankard: The Abduction of
the Sabine Women, and Samson
and the Lion
1697
ivory, gilded silver
30.5 × 22.9 × 16.5 cm
The Thomson Collection
at the Art Gallery of Ontario
29189

Giovanni Battista Foggini
The Rape of Orithyia by Boreas
before 1702
bronze
height: 54.5 cm
Art Gallery of Ontario
Purchased from the collection of
Margaret and Ian Ross with
assistance from the Volunteer
Committee Fund, 1982
82/71

Giovanni Battista Foggini
The Rape of Proserpine by Pluto
before 1702
bronze
height: 54.5 cm
Art Gallery of Ontario
Purchased from the collection of
Margaret and Ian Ross with
assistance from the Volunteer
Committee Fund, 1982
82/70

Guercino (Giovanni Francesco Barberi)
A Witch, Two Bats,
and a Demon in Flight
c. 1610–1666
pen and brown ink,
brown wash on paper
11.7 × 25.7 cm
Art Gallery of Ontario
Purchased as a gift of
the Trier-Fodor Foundation, 1986
86/194

Italian, sixteenth century
Apollo Pursuing Daphne
1500s
pen and brown ink, green wash
and gouache on green prepared
paper
27 × 21.6 cm
Art Gallery of Ontario
Gift of Sidney and Gladye Bregman,
1999
99/883

Carl Wilhelm Kolbe the Elder
(after Salomon Gessner)
Apollo and Daphne
1805–1811
etching on paper
61.8 × 46.3 cm
Art Gallery of Ontario
Gift of Philip R.L. Somerville, 2008
2008/453.4

Georges de La Tour
Saint Anne with the Infant Jesus
c. 1645–1650
oil on canvas
66 × 55 cm
Art Gallery of Ontario
Anonymous bequest, 1991
91/415

Andrea Mantegna
The Battle of the Sea Gods
(left portion of frieze)
before 1481
engraving on paper
28.7 × 39.5 cm
Art Gallery of Ontario
Gift of Dr. and Mrs. Gilbert Bagnani,
1988
88/232

Hendrick ter Brugghen
Melancholy
c. 1627
oil on canvas
67 × 46.5 cm
On loan to the Art Gallery of Ontario
from a private collection
18793

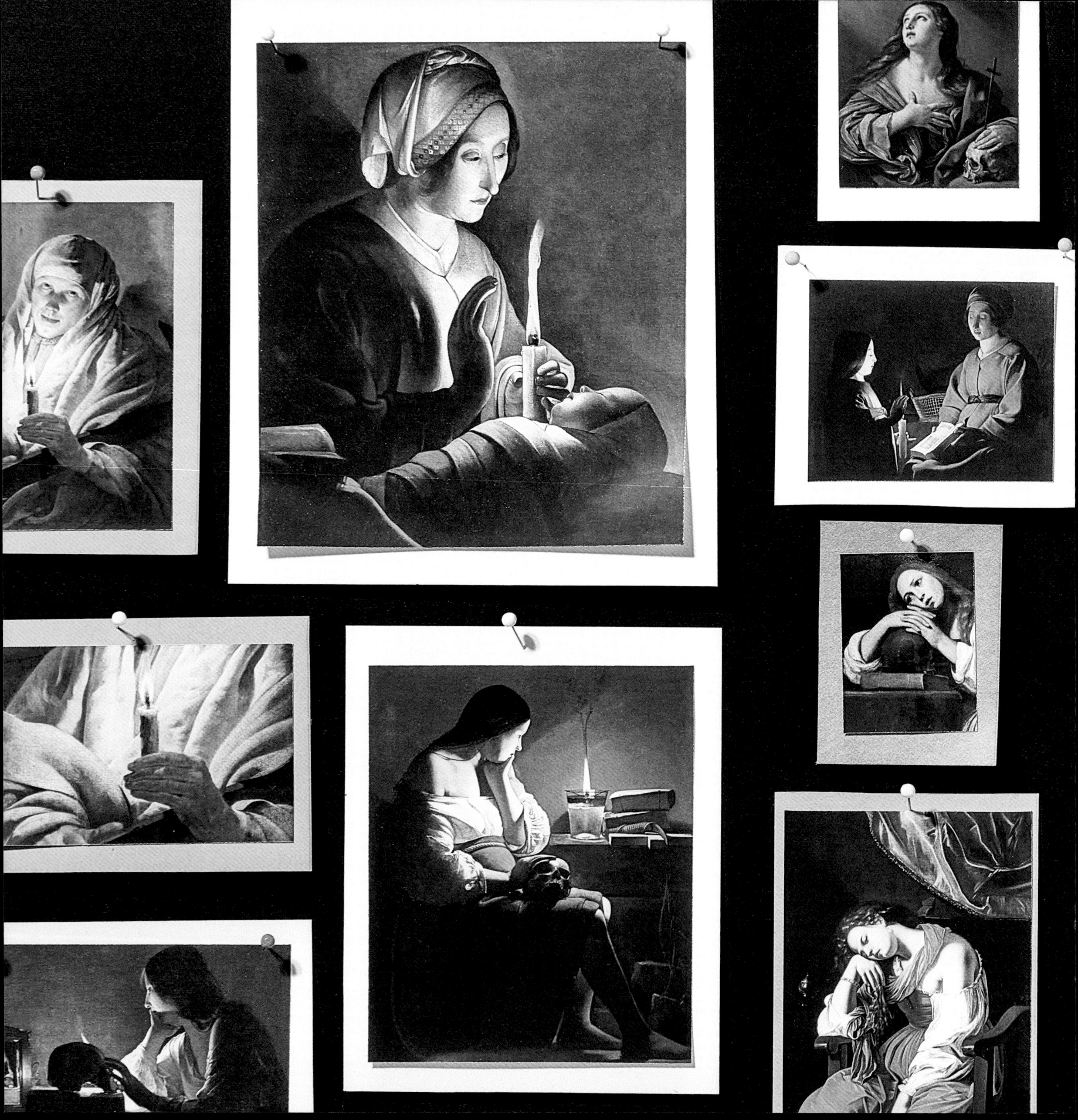

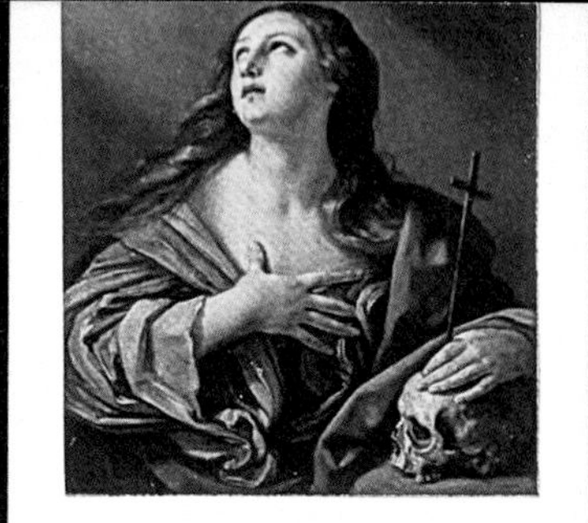
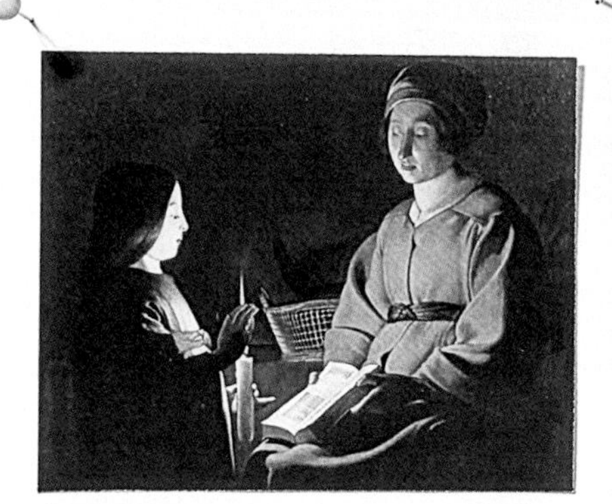
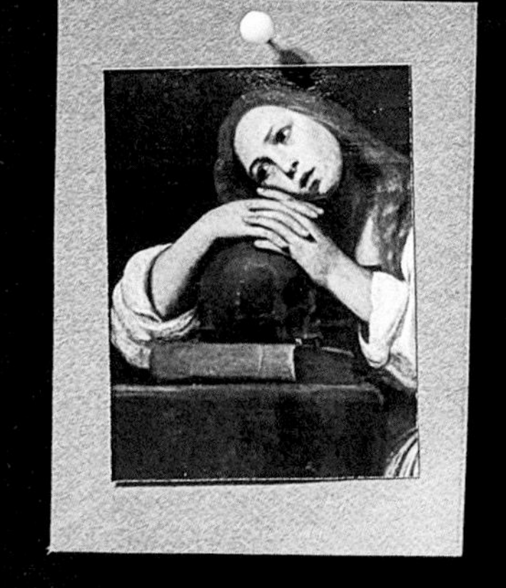
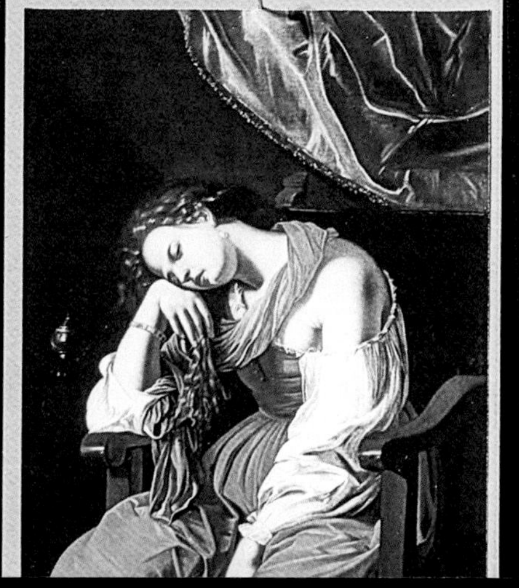

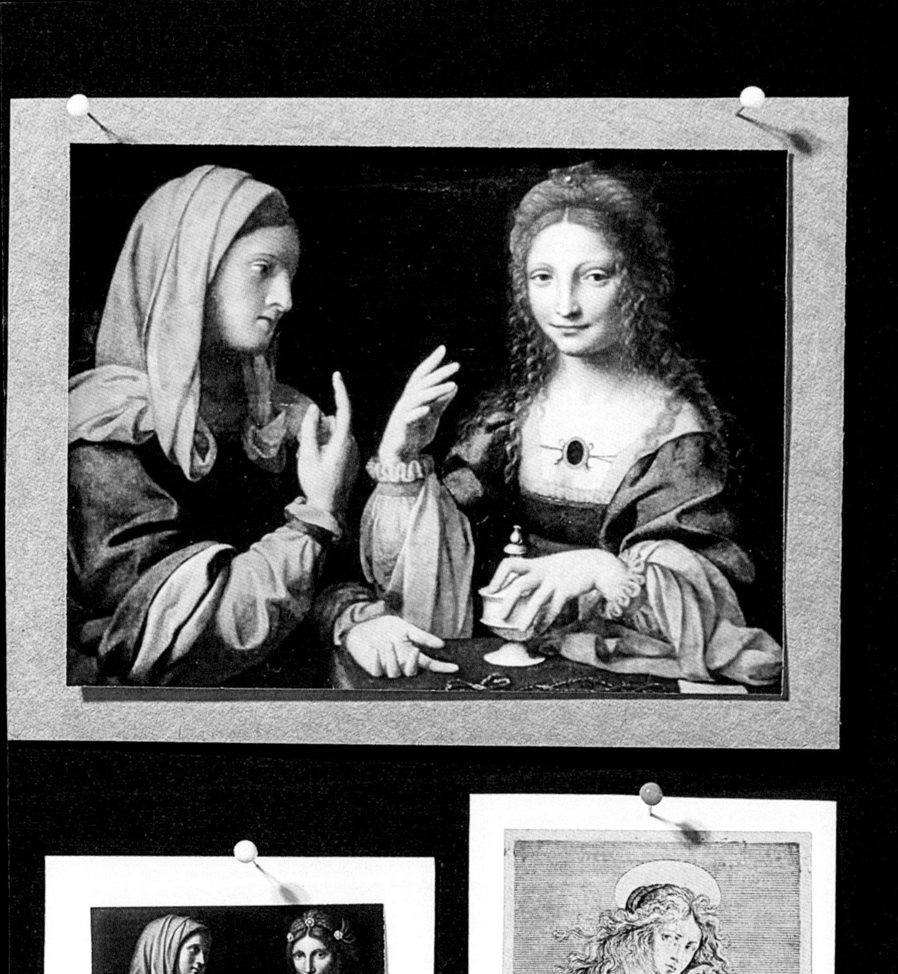
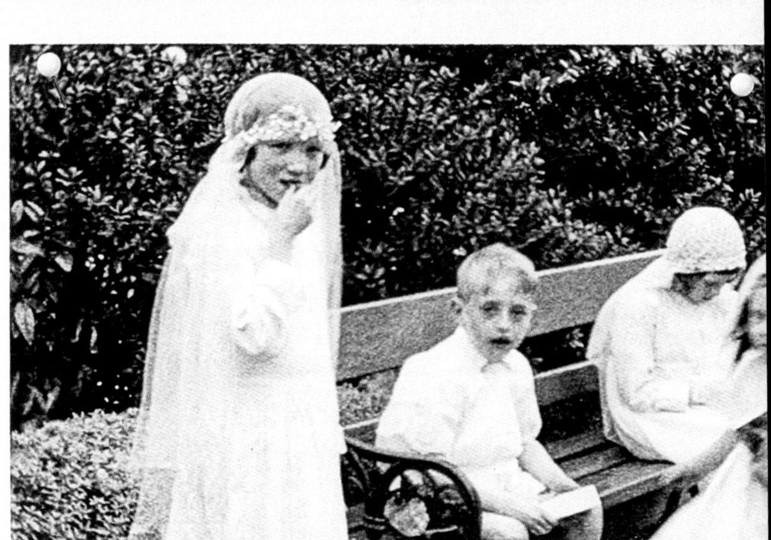
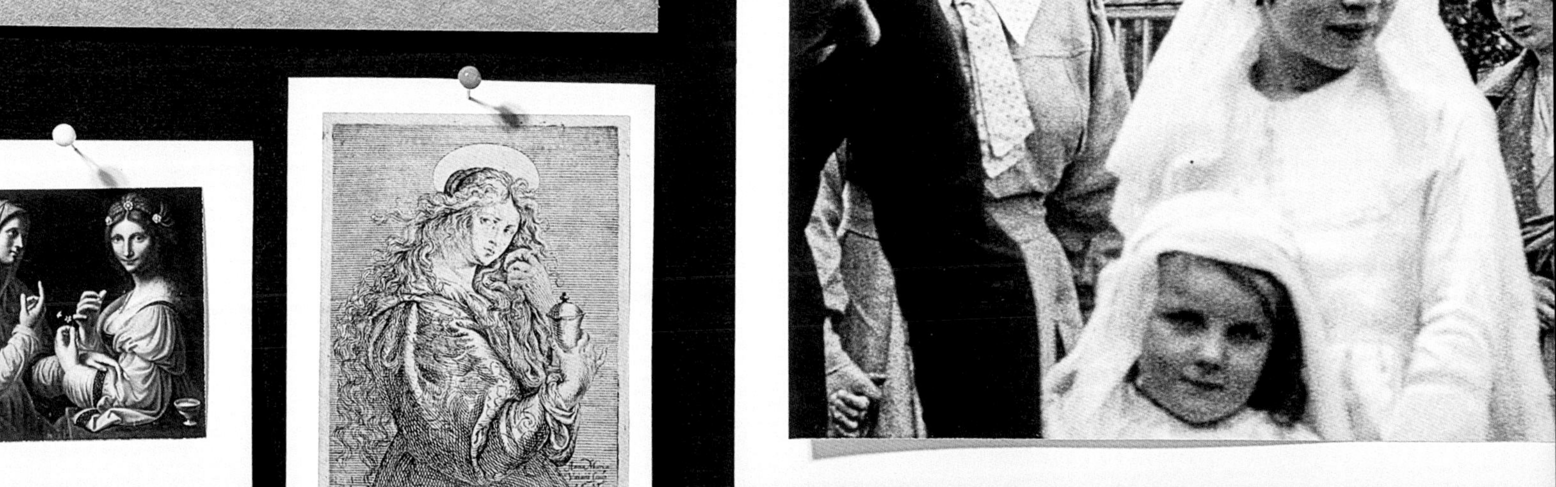
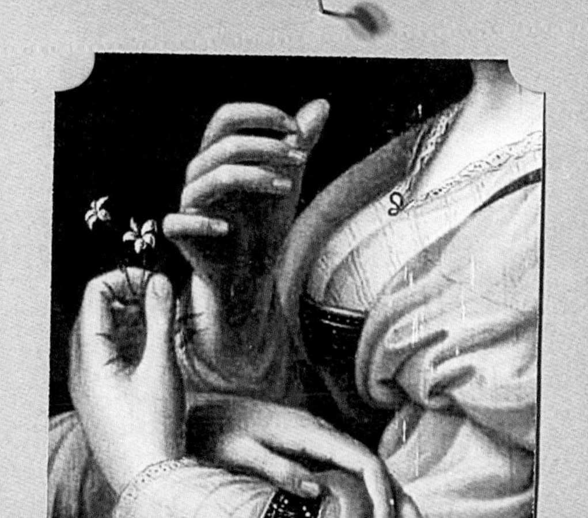
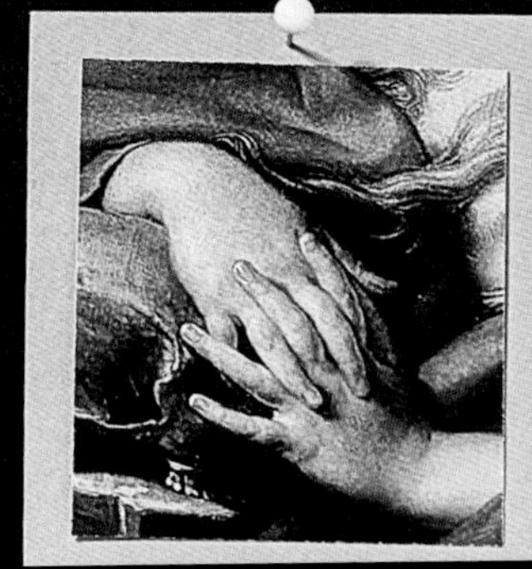
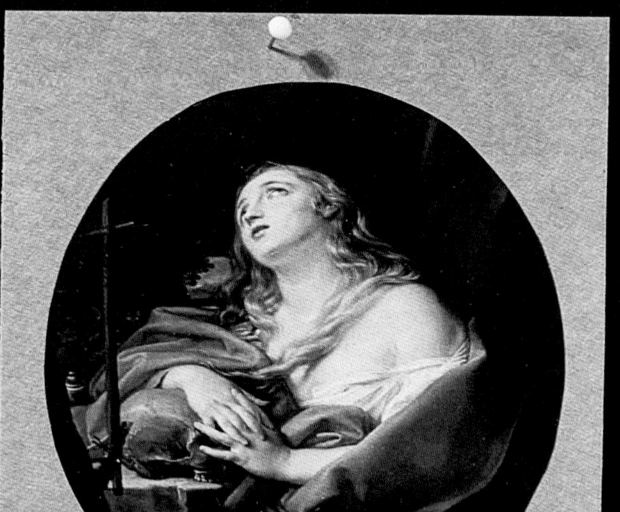

Credits

Endpapers and pages 24–25, 46–47, 94–95, 100–101

Cherubino Alberti (after Polidoro da Caravaggio), *The Rape of the Sabine Women and The Triumph of Two Emperors*, c. 1600. Five engravings printed on separate pieces of yellow silk satin backed with heavy paper, 21.6 × 223.5 cm. National Gallery of Art, Washington, Patrons' Permanent Fund (2004.114.2).

Andrea Andreani (after Giambologna), *Rape of a Sabine Woman*, 1584. Chiaroscuro woodcut from three blocks in grey-brown, 43.7 × 20.2 cm. The Metropolitan Museum of Art, New York, Rogers Fund, 1922 (22.73.3-70).

Christoph Angermair (attributed to), *Judith with the Head of Holofernes*, c. 1630. Ivory, 18.5 × 14.5 cm. The Thomson Collection at the Art Gallery of Ontario (29177). Photo: Michael Cullen.

Hans Baldung Grien, *Adam and Eve*, 1511. Woodcut; line block, 37.6 × 25.8 cm. The Metropolitan Museum of Art, New York, Harris Brisbane Dick Fund, 1933 (33.54.1).

Hans Baldung Grien, *Harmony (The Three Graces?)*, 1541–1544. Oil on panel, 151 × 61 cm. Museo Nacional del Prado, Madrid (P002219). Image copyright © Museo Nacional del Prado.

Hans Baldung Grien, *The Ages of Woman and Death*, 1541–1544. Oil on panel, 151 × 61 cm. Museo Nacional del Prado, Madrid (P002220). Image copyright © Museo Nacional del Prado.

Baccio Bandinelli, *Apollo and Daphne*, 1518. Engraving, 23.3 × 17.5 cm. Wellcome Collection, London (11237i). Image © The Wellcome Trust.

Pompeo Batoni, *Santa Maria Maddalena*, c. 1745. Oil on canvas, 97.5 × 75.8 cm. Private collection.

Sebald Beham (after Barthel Beham), *Adam and Eve*, 1543. Engraving on paper, 8 × 5.4 cm. The Metropolitan Museum of Art, New York, Bequest of Grace M. Pugh, 1985 (1986.1180.15).

Gian Lorenzo Bernini, *Apollo and Daphne*, 1622–1625. Carrara marble, 243 cm. Galleria Borghese, Rome, Purchased by Italian state, 1902. Photo: © Ministero dei Beni e delle Attività Culturali e del Turismo / Galleria Borghese.

Gian Lorenzo Bernini, *The Ecstasy of Saint Teresa*, c. 1645–1652. Marble, 350 cm. Church of Santa Maria della Vittoria, Rome.

Francis van Bossuit, *The Judgement of Solomon*, c. 1670–1680. Ivory, 12.7 × 21.6 × 2.5 cm. The Thomson Collection at the Art Gallery of Ontario (29187). Photo: Carlo Catenazzi.

Francis van Bossuit, *The Judgement of Solomon*, c. 1670–1680. Ivory, 16.5 × 24.1 × 3.8 cm. The Thomson Collection at the Art Gallery of Ontario (29188). Photo: Carlo Catenazzi.

Magdalena Bouchard (after Cesare Ubertini), Mandrake (Mandragora Fructu Rotundo), from Giorgio Bonelli's *Hortus Romanus*, vol. 1, 1772. Hand-coloured engraving on paper, 36.8 × 22.9 cm (plate); 54.6 × 39.4 cm (sheet). Philadelphia Museum of Art: Gift of Frank and Alice Osborn, 1966 (1966-68-74).

Valentin de Boulogne, *Le Jugement de Salomon*, 1627/1629. Oil on canvas, 176 × 210 cm. Musée du Louvre, Département des Peintures (INV 8246). Image © 2015 GrandPalaisRmn (musée du Louvre) / Franck Raux.

Giacinto Calandrucci, *The Ecstasy of St. Theresa*, date unknown. Pen and brown ink with traces of white over black chalk on paper, 24.1 × 18 cm. Art Gallery of Ontario, Gift from the Estate of R. Fraser Elliott, 2005 (2005/200). Photo: AGO.

Caravaggio, *Judith Beheading Holofernes*, c. 1599. Oil on canvas, 145 × 195 cm. Palazzo Barberini, Italy (inv. no. 2533).

Timothée Chalamet in Saint-Tropez for *Document* (Fall/Winter 2020). Photo: Hedi Slimane.

Jacob Cornelisz van Oostsanen, *Saul and the Witch of Endor*, 1526. Oil on panel, 87 × 121.6 cm. Rijksmuseum, Amsterdam (SK-A-668).

Guillaume Coustou the Elder, *Chevaux de Marly*, 1743–1745. Carrara marble, 340 × 284 × 127 cm. Château de Versailles.

Guillaume Coustou the Elder, *Chevaux de Marly*, 1739–1745. Carrara marble, 340 × 284 × 127 cm. Musée du Louvre, Département des Sculptures, Richelieu (MR 1803). Photo © Marie-Lan Nguyen / Wikimedia Commons.

Guillaume Coustou the Elder, *Study for one of the "Chevaux de Marly,"* c. 1740. Black chalk on paper, 43 × 35 cm. The Metropolitan Museum of Art, New York, Harry G. Sperling Fund, 2006 (2006.137).

Lucas Cranach the Elder, *Adam and Eve*, 1533–1537. Oil on panel, 107.5 × 36.5 cm (left panel, *Adam*); 107.6 × 36.4 cm (right panel, *Eve*). Art Institute of Chicago, Charles H. and Mary F.S. Worcester Collection (1935.294 & 1935.295).

Lucas Cranach the Elder, *Adam and Eve in Paradise (The Fall)*, 1533. Oil on beech wood, 350 × 504 cm. Gemäldegalerie, Berlin (inv. no. 567). Image: Google Arts & Culture; photo: © b p k – Photo Agency / Gemäldegalerie, Staatliche Museen zu Berlin / Jörg P. Anders.

Jacques-Louis David, *Napoleon Crossing the Alps*, 1800. Oil on canvas, 259 × 221 cm. Château de Malmaison (M.M.49.7.1).

Father Jack Delany, *Magdalene Laundry*, 1940s. Film (10 min., black and white, silent). Irish Film Institute, Father Jack Delany Collection: Communion Processions (AC287). Image courtesy of the IFI Irish Film Archive.

Albrecht Dürer, *Nemesis*, c. 1502. Engraving on paper, 33.3 × 22.9 cm. Art Gallery of Ontario, Gift of Dr. and Mrs. R. Ian Hector, 1989 (89/398). Photo: AGO.

Albrecht Dürer, *The Four Witches* [*Die vier nackten Frauen*], 1491. Engraving on paper. The Warburg Institute, University of London.

Billie Eilish, 2021. Photo: Kelia Anne Maccluskey / Interscope Records.

Ignaz Elhafen (ivory); Octavian Cocssel (silver), *Tankard: The Abduction of the Sabine Women, and Samson and the Lion*, 1697. Ivory, gilded silver, 30.5 × 22.9 × 16.5 cm. The Thomson Collection at the Art Gallery of Ontario (29189). Photo: Michael Cullen.

Ignaz Elhafen, *The Abduction of the Sabine Women,* early eighteenth century. Ivory, 10.8 × 17.5 × 2.4 cm. The Thomson Collection at the Art Gallery of Ontario (29179). Photo: Larry Ostrom.

Louis Ferdinand Elle the Younger, *Portrait of an Unknown Woman as Iris, formerly identified as Madame de Montespan*, c. 1651–1700. Oil on panel, 36.5 × 28.5 cm. Château de Versailles, Musée de l'Histoire de France, Domaine de Trianon (MV 3542). Image: © Château de Versailles, Dist. GrandPalaisRmn / Christophe Fouin.

Eucalyptus, tree leaves, Anglers Rest, Victoria, Australia. Photo: John O'Neill.

Eucalyptus tree, Australian Botanic Garden Mount Annan. Photo: Mayumi Kataoka.

Giovanni Battista Foggini, *The Rape of Orithyia by Boreas*, before 1702. Bronze, height: 54.5 cm. Art Gallery of Ontario, Purchased from the collection of Margaret and Ian Ross with assistance from the Volunteer Committee Fund, 1982 (82/71). Photo: AGO.

Giovanni Battista Foggini, *The Rape of Proserpine by Pluto*, before 1702. Bronze, height: 54.5 cm. Art Gallery of Ontario, Purchased from the collection of Margaret and Ian Ross with assistance from the Volunteer Committee Fund, 1982 (82/70). Photo: AGO.

Giovanni Antonio Galli, *Saint Mary Magdalene*, c. 1625–1635. Oil on canvas, 133 × 98.7 cm. The Walters Art Museum, Baltimore, Maryland, Acquired by Henry Walters with the Massarenti Collection, 1902 (37.651).

Artemisia Gentileschi, *Mary Magdalene as Melancholy*, 1622–1625. Oil on canvas, 136 × 100.5 cm. Museo Soumaya, Fundación Carlos Slim, Mexico City. Image: Google Arts & Culture.

Artemisia Gentileschi, *Mary Magdalene in Ecstasy*, c. 1620–1625. Oil on canvas, 81 × 105 cm. Private European collection at The National Gallery, London. Image: Google Arts & Culture; photographed by Dominique Provost.

Giambologna, *Rape of the Sabine Women*, 1583. Marble, 410 cm. Loggia dei Lanzi, Florence, Italy.

Luca Giordano, *The Abduction of the Sabine Women*, c. 1675. Oil on canvas, 260 × 295 cm. Art Institute of Chicago, Major Acquisitions Centennial Endowment; Charles H. and Mary F.S. Worcester Collection (1991.295).

Luca Giordano, *The Judgement of Solomon*, c. 1670–1685. Oil on canvas, 185 × 240 cm. Musée cantonal des Beaux-Arts de Lausanne, Gift of Georges Mörikofer, 1922 (inv. no. 1223). Image © Musée cantonal des Beaux-Arts de Lausanne.

Francois Girardon, *Rape of Proserpina by Pluto*, 1699. Marble, 270 cm. Château de Versailles.

Guercino (Giovanni Francesco Barberi), *A Witch, Two Bats, and a Demon in Flight*, c. 1610–1666. Pen and brown ink, brown wash on paper, 11.7 × 25.7 cm. Art Gallery of Ontario, Purchased as a gift of the Trier-Fodor Foundation, 1986 (86/194). Photo: AGO.

Domenico Guidi, *Andromeda and the Sea Monster*, 1694. Marble, 163.5 × 117.8 × 87.9 cm. The Metropolitan Museum of Art, New York, Purchase, Josephine Bay Paul and C. Michael Paul Foundation Inc. Gift and Charles Ulrick and Josephine Bay Foundation Inc. Gift, 1967 (67.34).

Peter Heinrich Hencke, *The Rape of the Sabines*, 1743. Ivory, 32.7 × 48 cm. Victoria and Albert Museum, London, Given by Alfred Spero, London, in 1949 (A.7-1949). Image © Victoria and Albert Museum, London.

René-Antoine Houasse, *Apollon et Daphné*, 1677. Oil on canvas, 158 × 120 cm. Musée du Louvre, Département des Peintures. On long-term loan to Château — Domaine national de Versailles, Versailles (INV 8598). Image © 2007 GrandPalaisRmn (musée du Louvre) / Gérard Blot.

Jean-Auguste-Dominique Ingres, *Jean-Pierre Cortot*, 1815. Oil on wood, 41 × 33 cm. Musée du Louvre, Département des Peintures (DL 1970 10). Image © 1988 GrandPalaisRmn (musée du Louvre) / Blot/Jean.

Italian, sixteenth century, *Apollo Pursuing Daphne*, 1500s. Pen and brown ink, green wash and gouache on green prepared paper, 27 × 21.6 cm. Art Gallery of Ontario, Gift of Sidney and Gladye Bregman, 1999 (99/883). Photo: AGO.

Abraham Jamnitzer, *Statuette of Daphne*, late sixteenth century. Silver, chased, cast, punched, etched, gilded; coral, 64.6 cm. Staatliche Kunstsammlungen Dresden (SKD), Green Vault, Dresden State Art Museums, Germany (IV 260). Image: Google Arts & Culture; photo: Jürgen Karpinski.

Carl Wilhelm Kolbe the Elder (after Salomon Gessner), *Apollo and Daphne*, 1805–1811. Etching on paper, 61.8 × 46.3 cm. Art Gallery of Ontario, Gift of Philip R.L. Somerville, 2008 (2008/453.4). Photo: AGO.

Ludwig Krug, *Two nude women*, c. 1515–1530. Engraving, 12.7 × 8.3 cm. The Metropolitan Museum of Art, New York, Bequest of Gertrude Jelinek, 2024 (2024.418.2).

Georges de La Tour, *Saint Anne with the Infant Jesus*, c. 1645–1650. Oil on canvas, 66 × 55 cm. Art Gallery of Ontario, Anonymous bequest, 1991 (91/415). Photo: Carlo Catenazzi.

Georges de La Tour (studio of), *The Education of the Virgin*, c. 1650. Oil on canvas, 83.8 × 100.3 cm. The Frick Collection, Purchased by The Frick Collection, 1948 (1948.1.155).

Georges de La Tour, *The Magdalen with the Smoking Flame*, c. 1635–1637. Oil on canvas, 117 × 91.8 cm. Los Angeles County Museum of Art, Gift of The Ahmanson Foundation (M.77.73).

Georges de La Tour, *The Repentant Magdalen*, c. 1635–1640. Oil on canvas, 113 × 92.7 cm. National Gallery of Art, Washington, Ailsa Mellon Bruce Fund (1974.52.1).

Bernardino Luini (after Leonardo da Vinci), *Martha and Mary (The Conversion of the Magdalen)*, c. 1520. Oil on canvas, 68.6 × 78.1 cm. Rothschild collection (inv. no. 91).

Bernardino Luini (after Leonardo da Vinci), *Martha and Mary (The Conversion of the Magdalen)*, c. 1520. Oil on panel, 64.8 × 82.6 cm. San Diego Museum of Art: Gift of Anne R. and Amy Putnam in memory of their sister, Irene (1936.23).

Mandrake (Mandragora officinarum). Image: Floridaseeds.

Andrea Mantegna, *The Battle of the Sea Gods* (left portion of frieze), before 1481. Engraving on paper, 28.7 × 39.5 cm. Art Gallery of Ontario, Gift of Dr. and Mrs. Gilbert Bagnani, 1988 (88/232). Photo: AGO.

Peeter F. Martenasie (after Peter Paul Rubens), *Rape of the Sabines*, eighteenth century. Etching print on paper. Victoria and Albert Museum, London, Bequeathed by Rev. Alexander Dyce (DYCE.2393). Image © Victoria and Albert Museum, London.

Giovanni Maria Mosca, *Lucretia*, c. 1550. Marble with lapis lazuli, 34.5 × 24 cm. The Walters Art Museum, Baltimore, Maryland, Acquired by Henry Walters, 1928 (27.252).

Mugwort (Artemisia vulgaris), flowers. Photo: Chris Jeffree, 2023.

Mugwort (Artemisia vulgaris), leaves and stem. Photo: Chris Jeffree, 2023.

Jan Muller (after Adriaen de Vries), *The Abduction of a Sabine Women (view from behind)*, c. 1598. Engraving on paper, 39.6 × 28 cm. The Metropolitan Museum of Art, New York, Purchase, Anne and Carl Stern Gift, 1959 (59.642.21).

Myrrh tree. Photo: Paradise Found Nursery.

Edward James Physick, *Pluto and Proserpine*, 1849. Cast plaster relief, 124 × 107 × 23 cm. Victoria and Albert Museum, London, Presented by Belinda Physick in memory of her father, David Physick (A.1-2005). Image © Victoria and Albert Museum, London.

Nicolas Poussin, *The Abduction of the Sabine Women*, probably 1633–1634. Oil on canvas, 154.6 × 209.9 cm. The Metropolitan Museum of Art, New York, Harris Brisbane Dick Fund, 1946 (46.160).

Raphael, *The Judgement of Solomon*, 1509–1511. Fresco, 120 × 105 cm. Stanza della Segnatura, Palazzi Pontifici, Vatican City.

Guido Reni, *The Penitent Magdalene*, c. 1635. Oil on canvas, 90.8 × 74.3 cm. The Walters Art Museum, Baltimore, Maryland, Museum purchase with funds provided by the W. Alton Jones Foundation Acquisition Fund and the Sales & Accessions Purchase Fund, 1987 (37.2631).

Sebastiano Ricci, *The Battle of the Romans and Sabines*, c. 1700. Oil on canvas, 197 × 303 cm. Liechtenstein, The Princely Collections, Vaduz–Vienna (inv. no. GE 243).

Sebastiano Ricci, *The Rape of the Sabine Women*, c. 1700. Oil on canvas, 197 × 304 cm. Liechtenstein, The Princely Collections, Vaduz–Vienna (inv. no. GE 245).

Rihanna, 2011. Photo: AP.

After Peter Paul Rubens, *The Judgement of Solomon*, c. 1640. Oil on canvas, 155 × 210 cm. Liechtenstein, The Princely Collections, Vaduz–Vienna (inv. no. GE 92).

Peter Paul Rubens (attributed to), *The Judgement of Solomon*, 1615–1618. Oil on canvas, 234 × 303 cm. Statens Museum for Kunst (inv. no. KMSsp185). Image: Google Arts & Culture.

Peter Paul Rubens, *The Massacre of the Innocents*, c. 1610. Oil on panel, 142 × 183 × 1.9 cm. The Thomson Collection at the Art Gallery of Ontario (2014/1581). Photo: Sean Weaver.

Peter Paul Rubens with Jan Wildens, *The Rape of the Daughters of Leucippus*, c. 1618. Oil on canvas, 224 × 210.5 cm. Alte Pinakothek, Munich, Bavarian State Painting Collections (inv. no. 321).

Peter Paul Rubens (after Polidoro da Caravaggio), *The Rape of the Sabines*, date unknown. Pen and brown ink and wash over black chalk, heightened with white and oil paint on brown paper, 27.7 × 39.7 cm. Art Gallery of Ontario, Purchase, 1983 (83/8). Photo: AGO.

Hunter Schafer as Jules Vaughn in *Euphoria* for *Vogue International* (September 2019). Photo: HBO, Eddy Chen.

Hunter Schafer for *AnOther Magazine* (Autumn/Winter 2023). Photography by Viviane Sassen, Styling by Katie Shillingford.

Massimiliano Soldani, *Apollo and Daphne*, c. 1700. Terracotta, 55.5 × 34.2 × 21.9 cm. The Cleveland Museum of Art, The Severance and Greta Millikin Purchase Fund (1992.230).

Matthias Stom, *The Judgement of Solomon*, c. 1640. Oil on canvas, 157 × 222 cm. Currier Museum of Art, Henry Melville Fuller Fund (2017.13).

Tilda Swinton, c. 2008.

Godfrey Sykes (after Raphael), *The Judgement of Solomon*, pre 1867. Oil on canvas, 45.7 × 36.8 cm. Victoria and Albert Museum, London, Purchased, 1867 (45-1867). Image © Victoria and Albert Museum, London.

Hendrick ter Brugghen, *Allegory of Faith*, c. 1626. Oil on canvas, 72.3 × 56.3 cm. The Leiden Collection (HBr-100).

Otto Wilhelm Thomé and Walter Migula, *Hogweed (Heracleum sphondylium)*, plate 451 in *Prof. dr. Thomé's Flora von Deutschland, Österreich und der Schweiz, in wort und bild, für schule und haus... mit...* vol. 3, 1905. Biodiversity Heritage Library. Image: NCSU Libraries.

Bertel Thorvaldsen, *Nessus Abducting Dejanira*, modelled 1814–1815, carved 1821–1823 or 1826. Marble, 100.3 × 125.7 × 14.6 cm. The Metropolitan Museum of Art, New York, European Sculpture and Decorative Arts Fund, 2004 (2004.174).

Giovanni Battista Tiepolo, *Apollo Pursuing Daphne*, c. 1755/1760. Oil on canvas, 68.5 × 87 cm. National Gallery of Art, Washington, Samuel H. Kress Collection (1952.5.78).

Giovanni Battista Tiepolo, *Apollon et Daphné*, 1741. Oil on canvas, 96 × 79 cm. Musée du Louvre, Département des Peintures (RF 2107). Image © 2009 GrandPalaisRmn (musée du Louvre) / Franck Raux.

Nicolas Tournier, *The Judgement of Solomon*, c. 1625. Oil on canvas, 156 × 209 cm. On loan to the Art Gallery of Ontario from a private collection (18797). Photo: AGO.

Unknown maker, *Apollo and Daphne* (from Christine de Pizan's *La Cité des Dames*), 1410–1411. Ink and colour on vellum. British Library, London, UK, shelfmark: Harley 4431, f.134v (BL3247648). © From the British Library archive / Bridgeman Images.

Unknown maker, *Métamorphose de Daphné en laurier* (from *L'Ovide moralisé*). Bibliothèque Nationale de France, Bibliothèque de l'Arsenal (MS 5069, fol. 4r.).

Unknown maker, *Métamorphose de Daphné* (from Christine de Pizan's Épître *d'Othéa*), c. 1400–1410. Bibliothèque Nationale de France, département des manuscrits (MS fr. 606, fol. 40v.).

Unknown maker (Central Italian, 17th century), *The Rape of the Sabines*, seventeenth century. Red chalk on paper, 19.1 × 28 cm. Private Collection, Toronto (127149). Photo: Craig Boyko.

Anna Maria Vaiani, *Saint Mary Magdalene, Half-Length*, 1627. Etching and engraving with plate tone on paper, 18.5 × 14.1 cm (plate); 19.9 × 15.5 cm (sheet). Philadelphia Museum of Art: The Muriel and Philip Berman Gift, acquired from the John S. Phillips bequest of 1876 to the Pennsylvania Academy of the Fine Arts, with funds contributed by Muriel and Philip Berman, gifts (by exchange) of Lisa Norris Elkins, Bryant W. Langston, Samuel S. White 3rd and Vera White, with additional funds contributed by John Howard McFadden, Jr., Thomas Skelton Harrison, and the Philip H. and A.S.W. Rosenbach Foundation, 1985 (1985-52-14659).

Jesse Mockrin in conversation with Adam Harris Levine
Pages 26–45

FIG. 1 Jesse Mockrin, *A stranger came last night*, 2019. Oil on cotton, 33 × 48.3 cm. Collection of Laurie Ziegler. © Jesse Mockrin 2025. Image courtesy of the artist, James Cohan, New York, and Night Gallery, Los Angeles. Photo: Marten Elder.

FIG. 2 René-Antoine Houasse, *Apollon et Daphné*, 1677. Oil on canvas, 158 × 120 cm. Musée du Louvre, Département des Peintures. On long-term loan to Château — Domaine national de Versailles, Versailles (INV 8598). Image © 2007 GrandPalaisRmn (musée du Louvre)/Gérard Blot.

FIG. 3 Baccio Bandinelli, *Apollo and Daphne*, 1518. Engraving, 23.3 × 17.5 cm. Wellcome Collection, London (11237i). Image © The Wellcome Trust.

FIG. 4 Gian Lorenzo Bernini, *Apollo and Daphne*, 1622–1625. Carrara marble, 243 cm. Galleria Borghese, Rome, Purchased by Italian state, 1902. Photo: © Ministero dei Beni e delle Attività Culturali e del Turismo/Galleria Borghese.

FIG. 5 Georges de La Tour, *Saint Anne with the Infant Jesus*, c. 1645–1650. Oil on canvas, 66 × 55 cm. Art Gallery of Ontario, Anonymous bequest, 1991 (91/415). Photo: Carlo Catenazzi.

FIG. 6 Nicolas Tournier, *The Judgement of Solomon*, c. 1625. Oil on canvas, 156 × 209 cm. On loan to the Art Gallery of Ontario from a private collection (18797). Photo: AGO.

FIG. 7 Studio reference photo of the artist's arm for *A story told this many times becomes the forest*.

FIG. 8 Studio reference photo of Mariquita Davis.

FIG. 9 Jesse Mockrin, *A story told this many times becomes the forest* (detail), 2025. Oil on linen, three panels, 124.5 × 83.8 cm (each); 124.5 × 251.5 cm (overall). Collection of Mark and Louise Nelson, Sydney, Australia. © Jesse Mockrin 2025. Image courtesy of the artist, James Cohan, New York, and Night Gallery, Los Angeles. Photo: Izzy Leung.

FIG. 10 Ignaz Elhafen, *Pan and Syrinx*, 1690–1695. Ivory, gilded silver, 26.7 × 19.1 × 3.8 cm. The Thomson Collection at the Art Gallery of Ontario (29190). Photo: Larry Ostrom.

FIG. 11 Jesse Mockrin, *Syrinx* (detail), 2018. Oil on linen, two panels, 172.7 × 119.4 cm (each); 172.7 × 238.8 cm (overall). Collection of Ellen and Jamie Copaken, Kansas City. © Jesse Mockrin 2025. Image courtesy of the artist, Night Gallery, Los Angeles, and James Cohan, New York. Photo: Marten Elder.

FIG. 12 Ignaz Elhafen (ivory); Octavian Cocssel (silver), *Tankard: The Abduction of the Sabine Women, and Samson and the Lion*, 1697. Ivory, gilded silver, 30.5 × 22.9 × 16.5 cm. The Thomson Collection at the Art Gallery of Ontario (29189). Photo: Michael Cullen.

FIG. 13 Luca Giordano, *Bathsheba Bathing*, c. 1663. Oil on canvas, 196 × 247 cm. Art Gallery of Ontario, Gift from the family of Max Tanenbaum in his memory, 1991 (91/88). Photo: AGO.

FIG. 14 Book cover of *The Power of Women* by Susan L. Smith.

FIG. 15 Jan Massys, *Judith with the Head of Holofernes*, 1543. Oil on panel, 102.2 × 75.6 cm. Museum of Fine Arts, Boston, Abbott Lawrence Fund and Picture Fund (12.1048). Photograph © 2025 Museum of Fine Arts, Boston.

FIG. 16 Francesco Furini, *The Birth of Benjamin and the Death of Rachel*, first half of the seventeenth century. Oil on canvas, 189 × 232 cm. Alte Pinakothek, Munich, Bavarian State Painting Collections — State Gallery in the New Palace Schleissheim (inv. no. 9884).

FIG. 17 Book cover of *Eve's Herbs* by John M. Riddle.

FIG. 18 Book cover of *Caliban and the Witch* by Silvia Federici.

FIG. 19 Detail of an illuminated manuscript featuring a female healer (Trota), holding urine flask, fourteenth century. Pen and ink wash. Wellcome Library at the Wellcome Collection, London (MS 544). Image © The Wellcome Trust.

FIG. 20 Fennel (Foeniculum vulgare) in *Köhler's Medizinal-Pflanzen*, vol. 2, 1890, p. 515, pl. 88.

FIG. 21 Mugwort (Artemisia vulgaris), leaves and stem. Photo: Chris Jeffree, 2023.

FIG. 22 Dittany (Cunila origanoides), flowers. Photo: Fritz Flohr Reynolds.

FIG. 23 Magdalena Bouchard (after Cesare Ubertini), Mandrake (Mandragora Fructu Rotundo), from Giorgio Bonelli's *Hortus Romanus*, vol. 1, 1772. Hand-coloured engraving on paper, 36.8 × 22.9 cm (plate); 54.6 × 39.4 cm (sheet). Philadelphia Museum of Art: Gift of Frank and Alice Osborn, 1966 (1966-68-74).

FIG. 24 Italian (Venice or Padua), *The Betrayal and Arrest of Christ, and The Entombment*, late fourteenth century. Ivory, traces of gilding, 20.2 × 10.7 × 0.8 cm. The Thomson Collection at the Art Gallery of Ontario (29115). Photo: AGO.

FIG. 25 Antonio del Pollaiuolo, *Mary Magdalene communicated by Angels*, c. 1460. Tempera and oil on panel, 209.5 × 166.2 cm. Museo Pala del Pollaiolo, Staggia Senese, Italy.

FIG. 26 Father Jack Delany, *Magdalene Laundry*, 1940s. Film (10 min., black and white, silent). Irish Film Institute, Father Jack Delany Collection: Communion Processions (AC287). Image courtesy of the IFI Irish Film Archive.

FIG. 27 Francisco de Zurbarán, *Saint Agatha* [*Sainte Agathe*], c. 1635–1640. Oil on canvas, 127 × 60 cm. Musée Fabre, Montpellier, France (inv. no. 852.1.3).

FIG. 28 Ludovico Carracci, *Saint Sebastian Thrown into the Cloaca Maxima*, 1612. Oil on canvas, 163.5 × 232.4 cm. The J. Paul Getty Museum, Los Angeles (72.PA.14).

FIG. 29 Jesse Mockrin, *Outcast*, 2021–2022. Oil on cotton, 254 × 177.8 cm. Collection of Sally Taylor and Ralph Tawil. © Jesse Mockrin 2025. Image courtesy of the artist, James Cohan, New York, and Night Gallery, Los Angeles. Photo: Marten Elder.

FIG. 30 Lucas Cranach the Elder, *Adam and Eve*, 1533–1537. Oil on panel, 107.5 × 36.5 cm (left panel, *Adam*); 107.6 × 36.4 cm (right panel, *Eve*). Art Institute of Chicago, Charles H. and Mary F.S. Worcester Collection (1935.294 & 1935.295).

FIG. 31 Lucas Cranach the Elder, *Portraits of Martin Luther and His Wife, Katharina von Bora*, 1472–1553. Oil on panel, 19.5 × 31.5 cm (unframed); 33.7 × 45.7 cm (framed); 10.3 cm (left portrait); 10.1 cm (right portrait). The Morgan Library & Museum, Purchased by Pierpont Morgan, 1909 (AZ038). Photo: The Morgan Library & Museum, New York.

FIG. 32 Artemisia Gentileschi, *Susanna and the Elders*, 1610. Oil on canvas, 170 × 119 cm. Schönborn Collection, Pommersfelden.

Jesse Mockrin gratefully thanks the Art Gallery of Ontario, Adam Harris Levine, Stephan Jost, Jacoba Urist, Carmen Maria Machado, Sascha Feldman, David Norr, James Cohan, Jane Cohan, Caterina Prestia, Davida Nemeroff, William Hathaway, Brian Faucette, Rachel Jennings, Marco Cheuk, Evelina Petrauskas, Melissa Ramage, Wendy Hebditch, Alina Skyson, Kieran Grant, Kathryn Yuen, Jim Shedden, Paul Weeks, Jonathan Rider, Robert Simon, Tania Qurashi, Akira Gordon, Jennifer Archie, Nikki Delhomme, Mariquita Davis, Sarah Townsend, Stephen Marks, and the patrons who made this exhibition possible.

Land Acknowledgement

The Art Gallery of Ontario operates on land that is the territory of the Anishinaabe (Mississauga) nation and is also the territory of the Wendat and Haudenosaunee. The Dish with One Spoon Wampum Belt Covenant is an agreement between the Haudenosaunee Confederacy and the Anishinaabe Three Fires Confederacy to peaceably share and care for the resources around the Great Lakes. Toronto is also governed by a treaty between the federal government of Canada and the Mississaugas of the New Credit (Anishinaabe nation). Toronto has always been a trading centre for First Nations.

Thank You

Presenting Partner

MaxMara

Generous Support

Robert & Cecily Bradshaw

David Cottingham &
Kathryn Wyatt Cottingham

Gennaro and Rosalia Family
Charitable Foundation

The Art Gallery of Ontario is partially funded by the Ontario Ministry of Culture. Additional operating support is received from the City of Toronto, the Department of Canadian Heritage, and the Canada Council for the Arts.

Contemporary programming at
the Art Gallery of Ontario is supported by

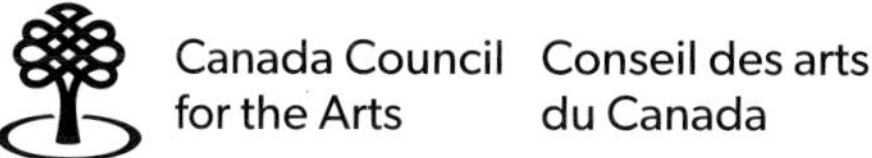

The AGO wishes to recognize
the support of James Cohan, New York.

PUBLICATION

Editor: Adam Harris Levine

Publishing Director: Jim Shedden

Publishing Coordinator: Kathryn Yuen

Production and Content Editor:
Kieran Grant

Proofreader: Judy Phillips

Book Designers:
Alina Skyson with Ryan Crouchman (LG2)

Photographers:
Craig Boyko, Dan Bradica,
Phoebe D'Heurle, Marten Elder,
Izzy Leung, Nik Massey,
Karl Puchlik, Paul Weeks

Pre-Press: Paul Jerinkitsch

Printing: Type A Print Inc.

EXHIBITION

Deputy Director & Chief Curator:
Julian Cox

Curator: Adam Harris Levine

Curatorial Coordinator,
European Art and Prints & Drawings:
Wendy Hebditch

Project Manager: Melissa Ramage

Interpretive Planner: Nadia Abraham

Editor: Kieran Grant

Production: Evelyn Quinn

Exhibition Designer: Marco Cheuk

Graphic Designer: Evelina Petrauskas

Exhibitions, Collections, and Conservation

Chief, Exhibitions, Collections & Conservation:
Jessica Bright

Director, Exhibitions: Laura Comerford

Registration:
Donna Austria, Alison Beckett, Jerry Drozdowsky,
Joel Herman, Alison Lindsay, Dale Mahar,
Doug Moore, Sabine Schaefer

Collection Information:
Alexander Arslanyan, Alexandra Cousins,
Tracy Mallon-Jensen, Liana Radvak, Olga Zotova

Conservation:
Julia Campbell-Such, Lisa Ellis, Christina McLean,
Meaghan Monaghan, Brent Roe, Rachel Stark,
Maria Sullivan, Tessa Thomas, John Williams

Logistics and Art Services

Director, Logistics and Art Services: Iain Hoadley

Manager, Art Services: Craig Whiteside

Curtis Amisich, Paul Ayers, Gregory Baszun,
Michael Beynon, Scott Cameron, Colin Campbell,
Corinne Carlson, Brian Davis, Alex DiGiacomo,
Christian Echeverri, Andre Ethier, Randal Fedje,
Tina Giovinazzo, Ruth Jones, David Kinsman,
Nanthini Kirupakaran, Paul Mathiesen, Phil Scott,
Damian Seguin, Sasi Sivapalan, Stephanie Vittas,
Phil Woollam, Darla Yorston, Tanya Zhilinsky

EDUCATION AND PROGRAMMING

Richard & Elizabeth Currie Chief,
Education & Programming:
Robert Durocher

Charlotte Big Canoe, Maureen DaSilva,
Nathan Huisman, Jesse King, Natalie Lam,
Zavette Quadros-Evangelista,
Tiana Roebuck, Annie Roper, Bojana Stancic,
Joey Suriano, Ida Zongo

MEDIA PRODUCTION

Chief, Brand & Business Officer:
Ros Lawler

Director, Brand, Marketing: Kimber Slater

Associate Director, Brand and Marketing:
Suman Chahal

Senior Manager, Creative Studio:
Malene Hjørngaard

Manager, Digital Projects:
Catherine Thomson

Media: Fraser Wrighte

Photographers:
Craig Boyko, Steve Jacobs, Ian Lefebvre,
Leah Maghanoy, Tracey Owusu, Dean Tomlinson,
Sean Weaver

DEVELOPMENT

Chief Development Officer: Kate Halpenny

Senior Director, Major Gifts and Campaign:
Andrea Orr

Director, Corporate Partnerships
& Development Special Events:
Taryn Sarkozi

Philanthropy: Anastasia Hare, Erin Thadani

Donor Relations:
Michelle Greenspoon, Matt Semansky

This book was published on the occasion of *Jesse Mockrin: Echo* organized by the Art Gallery of Ontario, exhibited September 13, 2025, to March 8, 2026.

Published in 2025 by the Art Gallery of Ontario and DelMonico Books • D.A.P.

Unless otherwise noted, all photography courtesy of the artist, James Cohan, New York, and Night Gallery, Los Angeles.

Every effort has been made to trace ownership of visual and written material used in this catalogue. Errors or omissions will be corrected in subsequent printings provided notification is sent to the publishers.

Cover Image
Jesse Mockrin, *Fracture* (detail), 2024. Oil on linen, 91.4 × 142.2 cm. Art Gallery of Ontario, Purchase, with funds from the F.P. Wood Fund, 2025 (2024/390). © Jesse Mockrin 2025. Image courtesy of the artist, James Cohan, New York, and Night Gallery, Los Angeles. Photo: Phoebe D'Heurle.

Pages 114–116
Photo: Sascha Feldman.

Printed and bound in Belgium.
Printed on Magno Volume 150gsm.
Cover in Brillianta Cloth (4003).

Set in Sabon Next and Diatype.

ISBN: 978-1-63681-187-1

10 9 8 7 6 5 4 3 2 1

Library and Archives Canada Cataloguing in Publication

Title: Jesse Mockrin : echo / edited by Adam Harris Levine.
Other titles: Echo

Names: Levine, Adam Harris, editor. | Container of (work): Mockrin, Jesse, 1981– Paintings. Selections. | Art Gallery of Ontario, host institution, publisher.
Description: Exhibition catalogue for *Jesse Mockrin: Echo* held at the Art Gallery of Ontario from September 13, 2025 to March 8, 2026. | Includes bibliographical references and index.
Identifiers: Canadiana 20250194678 | ISBN 9781636811871 (hardcover)
Subjects: LCSH: Mockrin, Jesse, 1981-—Exhibitions. |
LCGFT: Exhibition catalogs.
Classification: LCC ND237.M63 A4 2025 | DDC 759.13—dc23

Art Gallery of Ontario
317 Dundas Street West
Toronto, Ontario
M5T 1G4
Canada
ago.ca

DelMonico Books
available through ARTBOOK | D.A.P.
75 Broad Street, Suite 630
New York, NY 10004
artbook.com
delmonicobooks.com

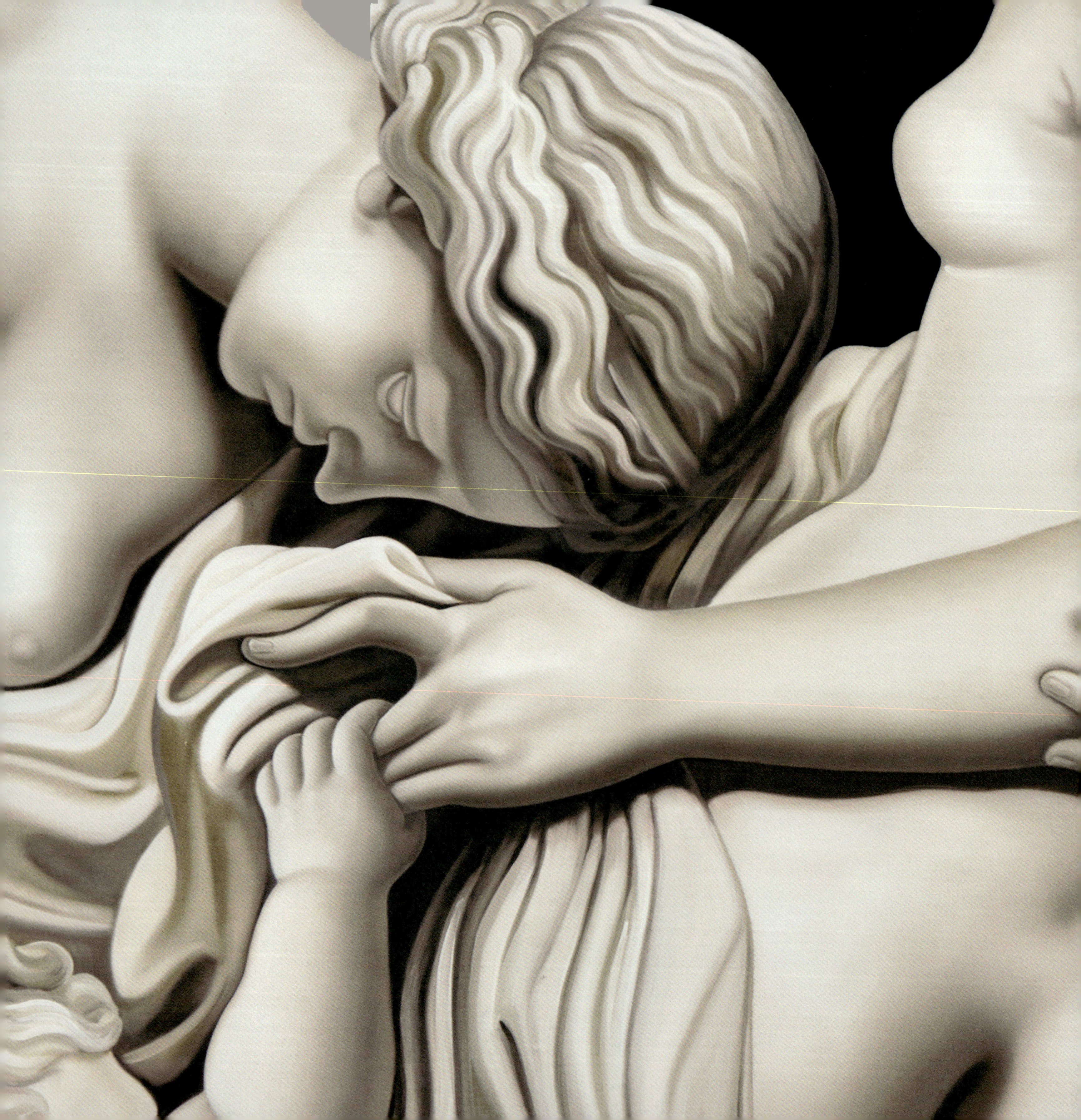

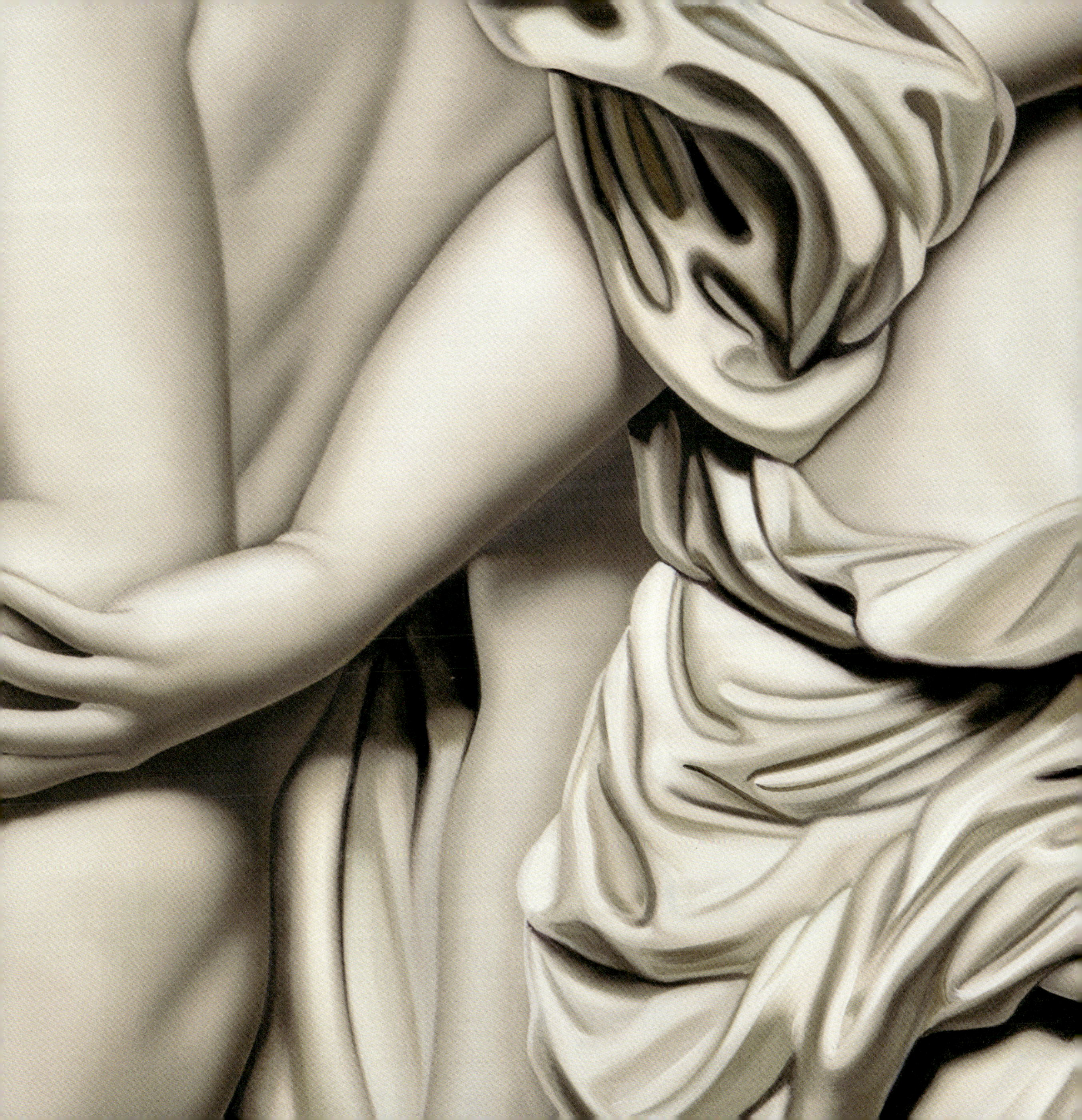

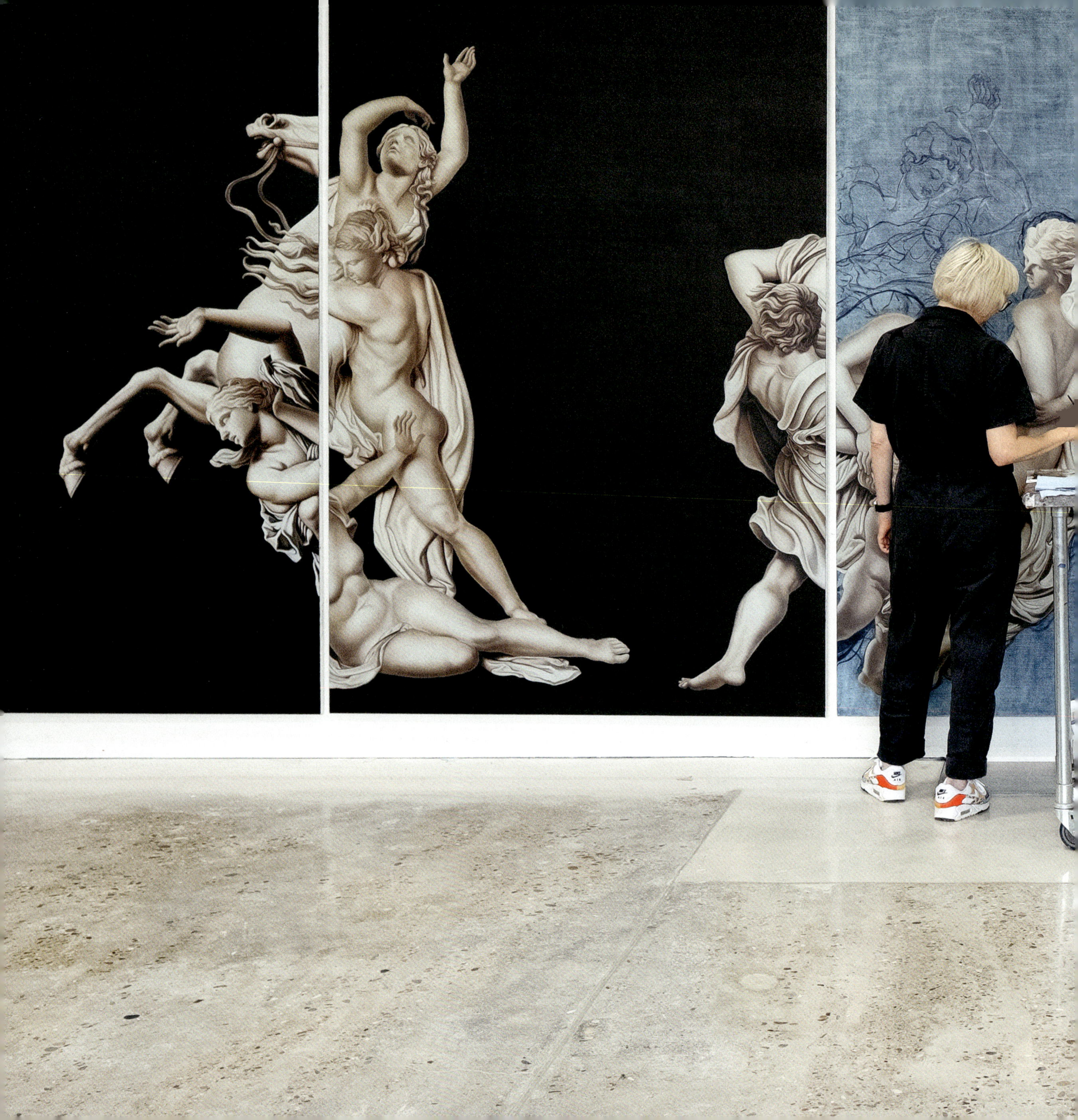

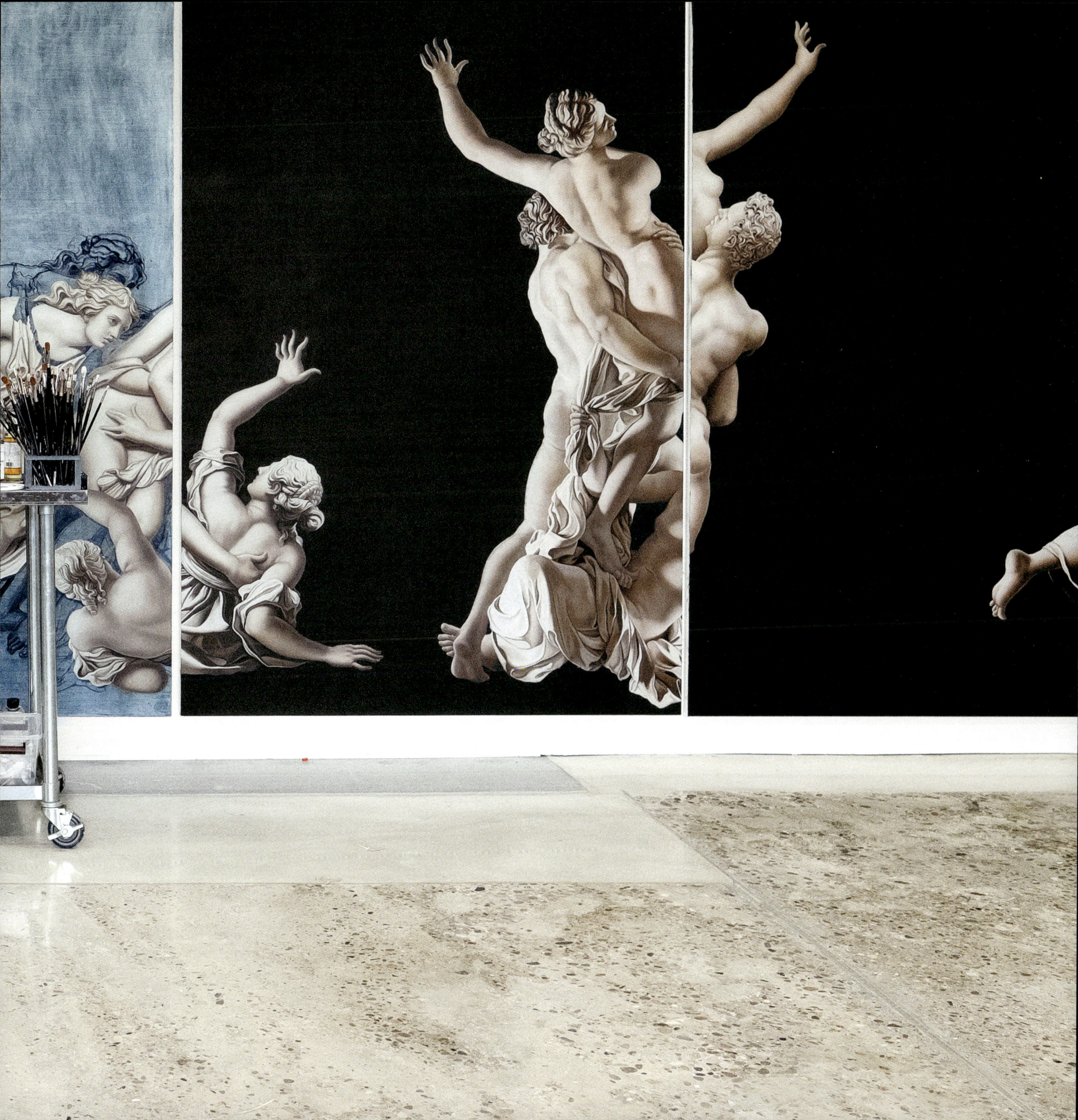

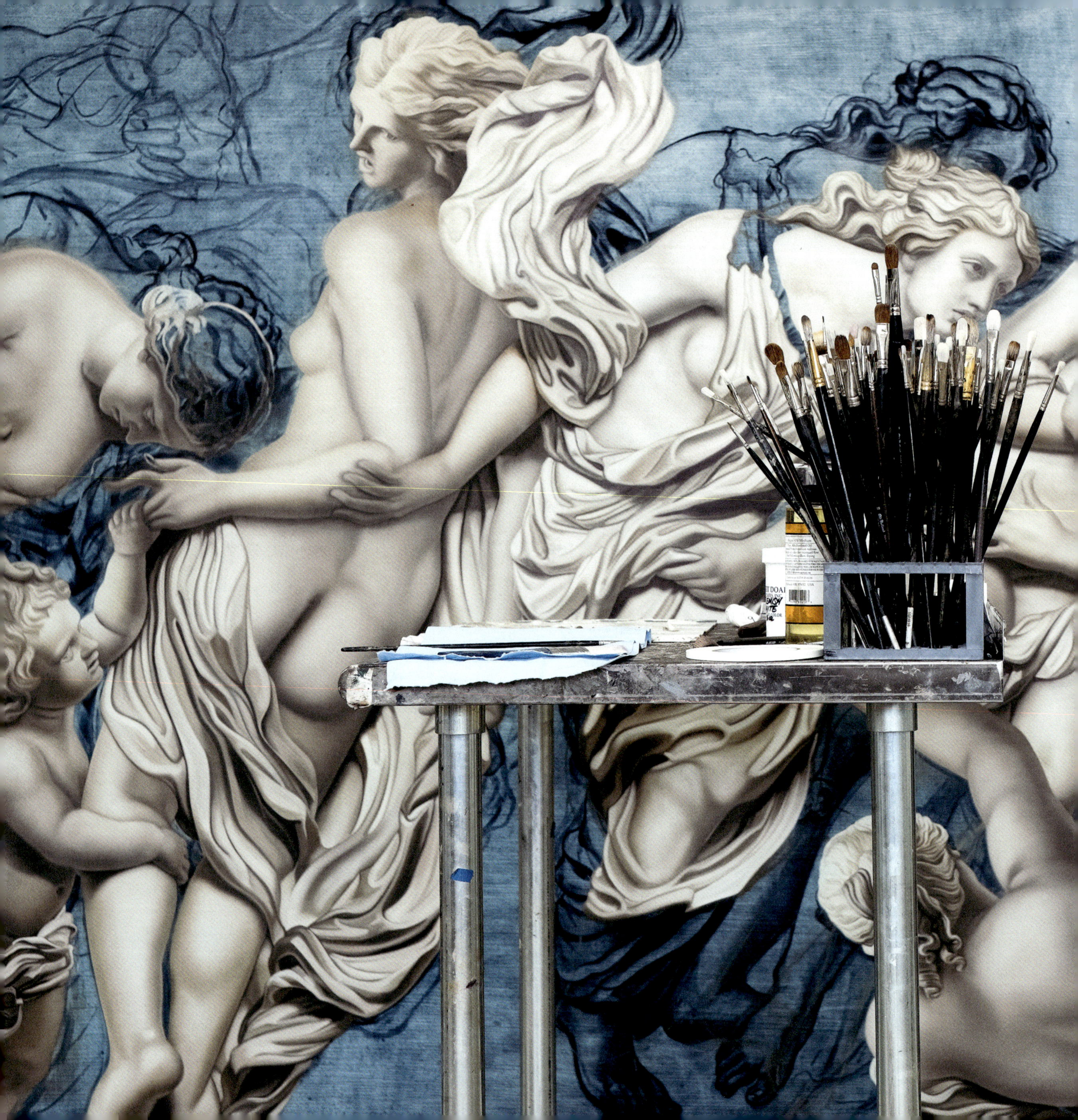

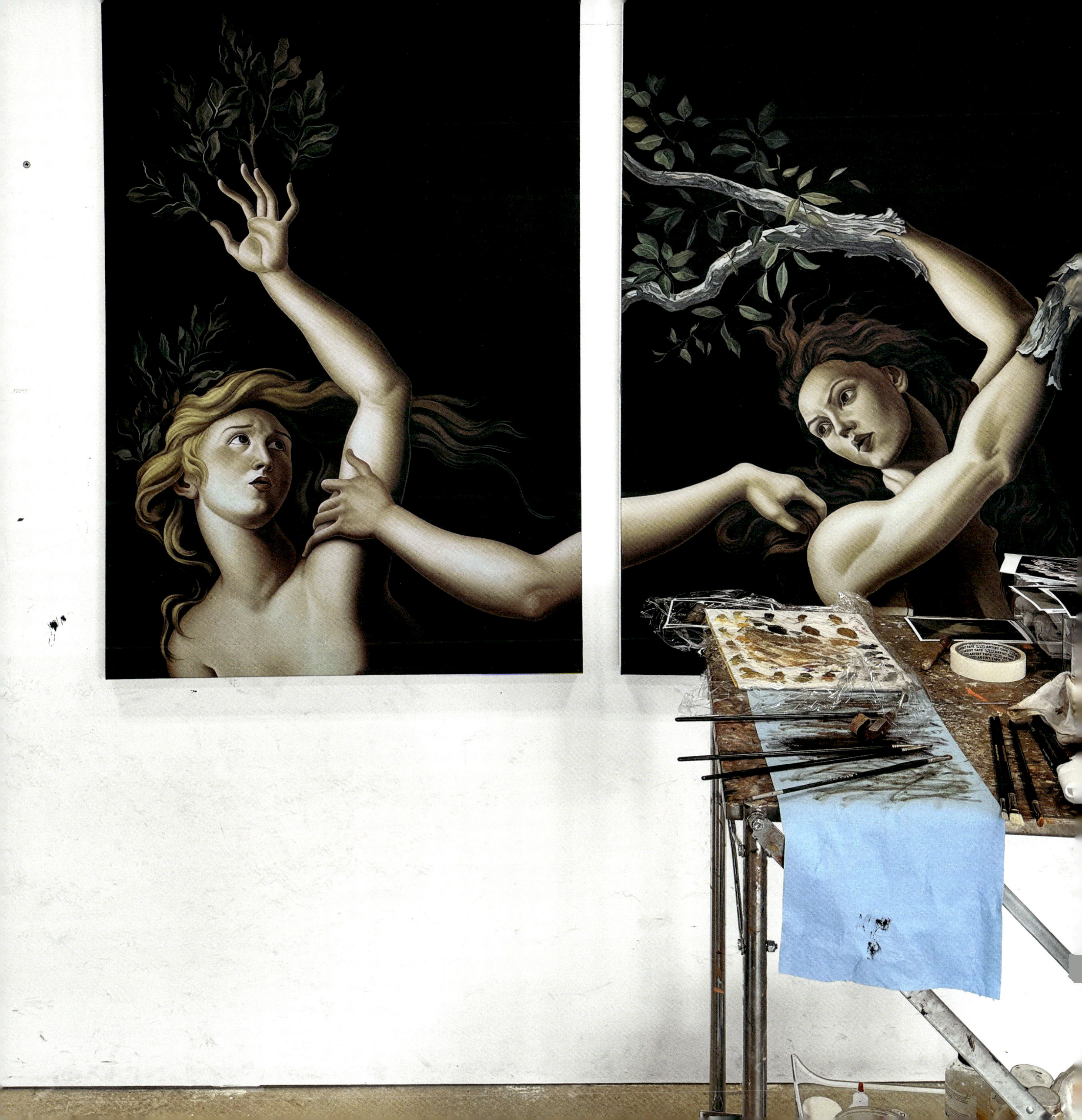

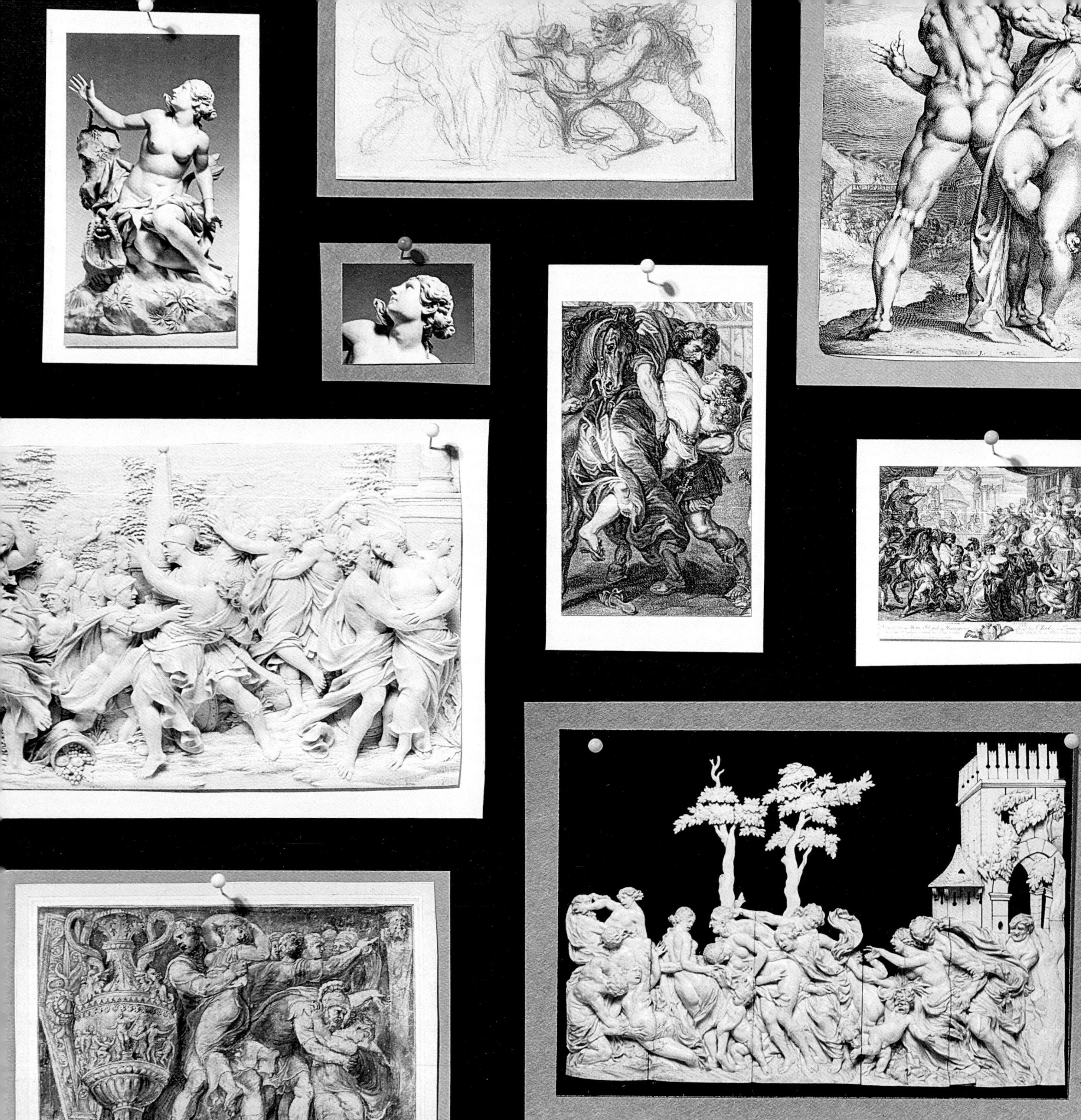